THE DEALER

THE DEALER

Drug Smuggling on the Costa del Crime

Maurice O'Connor

Milo Books Ltd

Published in November 2012 by Milo Books

ISBN 978-1-908479-20-4

Typeset by Jayne Walsh

Printed and bound by
CPI Group (UK) Ltd, Croydon, CR0 4YY

MILO BOOKS LTD
www.milobooks.com

This book is dedicated to Ana Galvez-Pastor, my wife, and Lisa Mernock, my penpal. With special thanks also to Gemma and Andy, without whose generous extension of credit this effort may well have never got cobbled together.

'The art of good business is being a good middleman.'

Eddie Temple, *Layer Cake*

'At the risk of appearing pretentious, I feel it is the duty of those who endured the conflict to relate their experiences for those who follow.'

Jo Nesbo, *The Redbreast*

(I know he was talking of a totally different conflict, but still.)

CONTENTS

Contrary to all you may have read in the popular press, most major drug busts are rarely the result of diligent police work or sophisticated undercover operations. More often than not they are the result of incompetence, stupidity, carelessness or plain, old-fashioned bad luck. Or good luck on the part of the forces of law and order.

It has to be remembered though, that whilst the would-be drug trafficker has to remain lucky all the time, the Old Bill has only got to get lucky once. I speak as someone with a degree of experience in these matters.

I'm forced to admit that my chronology may be a little suspect in places – one of the problems that come with age. Chronology aside, all the people, places and events described herein are completely genuine. Obviously, many of the names have been changed to protect the guilty.

Maurice O'Connor
Figueres Prison
Gerona
Spain

PART ONE

MARBELLA 1983-85

Costa del Crime

Marbella is a great town but I do have a couple of bits of advice for anyone planning a visit. If your idea of the perfect holiday destination is somewhere you can walk inconspicuously along the seafront in a kiss-me-quick hat and Union Jack shorts, Marbella is probably not the place for you. And if you're hoping to find one of those friendly neighbourhood bars with a welcoming sign advertising two or three drinks for the price of one, happy hour and karaoke, then you might be better restricting your search to the likes of Torremolinos or Benidorm.

In any case, people at the budget end of the holiday market would be struggling to find accommodation. When I arrived in Marbella in 1983, there were only three hotels to speak of in the whole town. There was the five-star Don Pepe at one end of town, the four-star El Fuerte at the other, and the Hotel Skol bang in the middle. The Skol was about as much of a concession to the package tour trade as Marbella made, but even so it wouldn't be cheap. The fact that George Best made it his second home for most of the Seventies bears that out. Mind you, the availability of young Swedish blondes might have had more to do with his choice than price.

Another thing hard to find there, amazingly enough, was Spaniards, at least local ones. In all my time in Marbella I don't think I ever met a genuine native. All the workers seemed to come from Seville, Granada and Cordoba and the ones with money seemed to come from Madrid and Barcelona. Makes you wonder who lived there before the tourist boom.

One thing that wasn't in short supply was celebrities. The first Marbella resident that always springs to mind is Sean Connery who, with his wife Micheline, owned a villa on the Benahavis road. Fellow actor Donald Pleasence and his wife Linda lived just down the road in Calahonda. Omar Sharif, a mad gambler, used to pop over on a fairly regular basis to play in bridge and backgammon tournaments at the Marbella Club. Stewart Granger was also around for a while until he got embroiled in some timeshare swindle. TV personalities were ten a penny. Cilla Black, Bruce Forsyth, Ronnie Corbett and Kenny Lynch were all spotted regularly around town. Jimmy Tarbuck was involved in a restaurant with the Italian tenor Tony Dalli.

From the world of music, the star of the show was Rod Stewart, who had a place in San Pedro, as did Shirley Bassey. Bill Curbishley, the manager of The Who, had an apartment in town and Roger Daltry was a regular visitor. Madeline Bell – remember her? Blue Mink? 'Melting Pot'? – had a live music bar called Bourbon Street in Estepona port. Lee Hazlewood ('These Boots Were Made for Walking' with Nancy Sinatra) lived in Fuengirola. Tony Christie lived in Almeria. Phil Coulter, the Irish singer/songwriter, had a place on the Costa del Sol, as did his compatriot Dickie Rock. Dickie never had huge international acclaim but in Ireland he'd be as big as, say, Tom Jones in Wales or Cliff Richard in England, having had, to date, thirteen Irish number ones.

The weather and facilities made the coast a sportsman's paradise. A golfer with a half-decent drive could probably play his way from the airport to Gibraltar without leaving a fairway. James Hunt, the ex-world motor racing champion, retired from Formula One and opened a discotheque in town. England soccer captain Kevin Keegan had an apartment on Los Monteros golf course. Lew Hoad, fifty per cent of Hoad and Rosewall, the Australian pairing who won multiple tennis doubles titles, including Wimbledon, had a tennis village on the Mijas road, while Manolo Santana had another in the Puente Romano complex. There were golfers, boxers, jockeys and football players everywhere you looked.

There was also a fair sprinkling of lower echelon Northern European royalty. I can't remember the last time Germany had a king – I do seem to recall the Kaiser and King George being cousins, so obviously a bit of blue blood there – but even so, there seemed to be an extraordinary amount of Germans walking about calling themselves Count, Baron, Prince and Princess. Eat your heart out poor old Monte Carlo, with only three princesses and a couple of princes to rub together.

With the fierce row going on in the Lebanon in the Seventies, Beirut was no longer the Middle Eastern playground for wealthy Arabs that it had been, so they were also looking for new venues to get up to all the things that they couldn't be seen to be getting up to back home. Marbella appeared to fit the bill perfectly. I had known an Arab student in Manchester, Amir Al-Madani, who, besides becoming a captain of industry, went on to become a director at Manchester United. Amir's father is generally credited with setting the ball of Arab investment in motion when he bought into the Marbella Club and the luxury Puente Romano complex. The Saudi royal family had a spectacular mansion opposite Puente Romano and the mosque was built next door. Adnan Khashoggi, the Saudi arms dealer and spectacular party-thrower, moored his yacht in Puerto Banus. Arab nightclubs and restaurants started to spring up and before long the Arab banks were opening in town, notably Aresbank and (excuse me while I spit, but we'll come to that later) the Bank of Credit and Commerce International.

So, all very upmarket and glamorous. Why, then, was it christened the Costa del Crime?

Britain and Spain had been at loggerheads for years over the sovereignty of Gibraltar, which, admittedly, is perfectly obviously a part of the Spanish mainland but has been a British colony since the 1700s. Spain, by the way, was itself apparently able to overlook the fact that the Spanish enclaves of Melilla and Ceuta are just as obviously part of the Moroccan mainland. Be that as it may, it all came to a head in 1978.

The Spanish Government closed the border crossing at La Linea, thereby isolating The Rock and its 40,000 inhabitants. Even more bizarrely, they revoked the Anglo-Spanish extradition treaty. What pressure they thought this would bring to bear on Britain remains a mystery, but it meant anyone wishing to avoid British legal jurisdiction simply had to make their way to Spain and sit in the sun with impunity. No small number did just that.

A few fairly spectacular robberies went off in Britain in 1983, most notably the £25 million-worth of gold that went missing from the Brink's-Mat depository at Heathrow and the £6 million in readies that disappeared from the Security Express depot in Shoreditch, east London. It was the notoriety of two of the alleged participants in the bit of work at Shoreditch, Ronnie Knight and Freddie Foreman, that would more than anything else give rise to the coining of the phrase 'Costa del Crime'. Ronnie was the ex-husband of Carry On film star Barbara Windsor and had recently been acquitted of the murder of the man thought to be responsible for killing Ron's brother. Freddie Foreman had been a high-ranking member of the Kray organisation and had not long finished a ten-year sentence for disposing of the body of one of the Krays' victims. All this made for terrific copy for the popular press. Who actually came up with the phrase Costa del Crime – not that it took an awful lot of coming up with – is shrouded in the mist of time but my personal nomination would be Nigel

Bowden, local correspondent of the *Sun*, aided and abetted by Roger Cook of *The Cook Report*.

Whilst the robberies were massive by any standards, there had been another little bit of business going on in London for a few years that made them pale into virtual insignificance. It was commonly known as 'the Great VAT Swindle' or simply 'the Gold' and the scam was basically the buying and selling of gold and the pocketing of the Value Added Tax. Very little about it ever made the papers and very few people were ever charged over it.

One of the few who were arrested was the Great Train Robber Charlie Wilson. Charlie had moved to Spain shortly after his release from prison, as had his fellow train robber Gordon Goody, who owned a beach bar in Mojacar. On a trip home, Charlie was arrested, charged with VAT fraud and held on remand. Eventually a deal was struck whereby he agreed to forfeit the hundred and sixty grand that had been confiscated from him in return for the charges being dropped. Ironically enough, that was about ten grand more than Charlie's share from the train robbery, if you believe the figures from the book by Piers Paul Reed. Tragically, Charlie would be murdered at his villa in San Pedro in 1989.

The VAT swindle, having started in a very small way, soon mushroomed, with dozens of people, mainly Londoners, all tucking away their two or three million for a rainy day. When the rainy day arrived, most of them headed for Spain, and it wasn't just because of the extradition situation. Actually the penalties for VAT fraud weren't that severe, since, when the legislation was drawn up, nobody envisioned anyone evading millions of pounds. Years later another friend of mine, Stevie Rich, was arrested over his part in the scam. Having little choice, he pleaded guilty, but when sentencing him to two years the judge remarked how frustrated he felt that this was the maximum. He added that if he had his way, Stevie would be doing ten. With remission and time spent on remand he was home in less than twelve months.

The other big incentive to move to Spain was the Spanish banks' broad-minded attitude to cash. If you walked into a Spanish bank with a suitcase full of readies and a passport, you had already answered all the questions you were ever likely to be asked. Obviously, this held a certain appeal for anyone who might have struggled to show provenance for their bit of dough.

The advantages didn't stop there. If you were prepared to take a chance on the exchange rate fluctuations and convert your money into pesetas, you would draw eighteen per cent a year tax-free interest. A relatively small nest-egg of a hundred grand would give you eighteen grand a year before you got out of bed on January 1. Now eighteen grand a year in Marbella wouldn't get you your villa with a pool and a Porsche to run about in, but it would rent you a nice seafront apartment and a tidy hire car, keep you fed and clothed and still leave enough to get drunk most nights.

So my first problem, on arriving in Marbella, was where to find the other ninety-eight grand, to go with the two grand I'd scraped together before I left Manchester, to make the hundred grand I needed to give me my eighteen grand a year income. Sounded straightforward enough.

My own criminal career had been spectacularly unspectacular, consisting entirely of relatively small, unsophisticated fraud. On three occasions I had fallen foul of the Old Bill and had had to suffer the consequences, serving sentences of eighteen months, three years and six years. All part of the life I had chosen to lead and no-one to blame but myself.

I was born in 1950 in Dublin, barely. I think I was six or eight weeks old when we moved to Liverpool. My father was attending the police training centre in Warrington, having enrolled in Liverpool Police. Ironically enough, twenty-two years later I was sentenced to eighteen months and sent to Appleton Thorn open prison, where I was detailed to work on the outside gardens party. I spent the next six months hoeing the flower-beds at my dad's old alma mater. Dad didn't last long in the police, just a couple of years. He went into office work and was employed by the Lyons Maid ice cream company. In 1959 he was promoted to depot manager and transferred to Manchester, so we moved again.

Pupils at the school I attended were about fifty per cent Irish or of Irish immigrant descent. We were educated by Irish nuns and the biggest day of the year was Saint Patrick's Day. We all had to get up and sing stuff like 'The Merry Plough Boy'. I suppose this background is what gave rise to my Republican leanings. It's often the case that expats and second and third generations have stronger patriotic feeling than their kin who never left home, looking back as they do through rose-tinted glasses.

I couldn't wait to leave school and left at fifteen with zero in the way of qualifications, but quickly got a job in a salesroom. Salesrooms were a variation on the old mock-auction scam, but unlike the mock auctions you did actually get what you paid for, even if the quality was a bit questionable. I worked in several over the next couple of years, followed by a few other dead-end jobs.

In 1970, I moved to London and got a job with a bookmaking chain, who enrolled me at the London School of Turf Accountancy. London is an expensive town and the wages weren't great but I was able to supplement my income by sticking the odd bet through the till on very short-priced favourites. They never get beat, do they? Well, sometimes. All went fine for twelve months or so, then one day I invested £350, which I didn't have, on a two-to-seven chance that looked past the post. It got beat. Still, not to worry, there's a one-to-five chance in an hour's time. Two grand will win me back the three-and-a-half I'm behind plus the fifty I was stuck for in the first place. Everything will be fine.

When the second one got beat it was approaching the time when even the likes of myself had to begin to worry. Because of the size of the bet, I'd had to ring it through to head office and they had a very strict policy as to how much cash could remain on the premises. A security man was sent around to pick up the surplus cash, little realising his trip would be futile. I gave him a fanny about how I had taken the bet over the phone, although I knew it was against company rules, but it was a very close personal friend and no doubt he'd be around any minute with the readies.

I made a cup of tea and the security man, who was a fifty-odd-year-old ex-copper, waited patiently. After about ten minutes his patience ran out.

'I am of the opinion that your story is total bollocks,' he told me. 'And you're sacked.'

Fair enough, lucky not to be nicked I suppose.

I returned to Manchester looking for some sort of move. There used to be a twenty-four-hour snooker hall called St James's in town and it was a bit of a thieves' kitchen. One pal of mine always referred to it as the 'waiting room for Strangeways'. I headed there to renew a few acquaintanceships and see if anything was afoot.

Credit cards were just coming into common usage. When Access and Barclaycard were first launched, they were sent out, unsolicited, to anyone who had even a half-decent account. They were accompanied by a letter saying that if you didn't want to make use of the service, simply cut the card in half and dispose of it. Very few were ever cut in half and any amount of cards could be bought in places like St James's for about fifty quid apiece. I had a very good year or so before luck ran out, hence my stay at Appleton Thorn.

When I came home, I went into the car business – sort of. There is a vast difference between buying a car on hire purchase and buying one on credit sale. A car on HP remains the property of the finance company until the final payment is made. A car on credit sale is owned by the purchaser from the moment he signs the contract and he's entitled to dispose of it any time he wants, but still owes the money. Credit sale cars are worth much more money on the black market than HP cars, likewise with TVs, washing machines or any other goods. That seemed to be the route for me. Of course, nobody was going to sell me a car or anything else on credit if I told them the truth, and telling lies to get credit makes the whole thing out-and-out fraud. I did make money but the net result of it all was a three-year stay at Kirkham Prison.

Back on the streets, I made an attempt at going straight. I tried a bit of cab-driving and poker-dealing, but it wasn't really for me. One morning I made a conscious decision to have one more go at getting a lump of dough together. I was determined to put all my admittedly limited talents into one orchestrated campaign of fraud and deception. Credit cards, cars, furniture, the odd caravan and a boat or two were all grist to the mill. I earned a lot of money but never seemed able to hold onto it. I think it was Mr Micawber, or maybe Mr Pickwick – certainly someone from Dickens – who spoke of the problems when expenditure expands to exceed income. That has always been my problem and the result this time was six years in Featherstone Prison.

I hadn't been in prison long when I was taken back to court

over a previous incident in Sid Otty's gambling joint. There was an inveterate gambler called Cockney Bernie who used the place who was a grumpy old bastard without much in the way of pals. He'd probably been a bit of a chap in his time, with a broken nose and a cauliflower ear, but by this time he'd have been well into his sixties. Although quite wealthy, he was so mean he would get up every morning and walk three miles to the Jewish Commercial Club to steal the newspaper. Knowing his own weakness for gambling, he had put all his assets into a trust fund in an effort to avoid devastating his life's savings, and received a dividend cheque every three months. When the cheque arrived, he would appear at Sid's and play cards for two or three days at a stretch until the money ran out, at which point he would disappear until the next cheque arrived. His name was good and if he ran out of cash during the night, as he frequently did, he would be allowed to play to a cheque until the banks opened.

One morning I was lounging about in Sid's when Bernie asked if there was anyone who would go to the bank for him. I volunteered. Bernie gave me a cheque for £1,500 and went to the phone.

'I'm sending someone with a cheque for fifteen hundred pounds. A nice, honest-looking boy. Please make sure it's honoured,' he instructed the bank manager, who obviously said he would. Off I went to his bank in Spring Gardens to cash the cheque.

At the time I had a girlfriend living in Didsbury in south Manchester. To get from the bank in Spring Gardens to Didsbury meant driving back along Princess Street, where the club was. As I turned onto Princess Street, I spotted Bernie hovering on the steps of Sid's. He gave me a wave. The wave turned to a howl as I drove straight past him and away. Dodging through three lanes of rush-hour traffic, he began to chase me, screaming abuse. The lights at Portland Street were on red so I took a right into Faulkner Street. My last sight of Bernie, through the rear-view mirror, was him stumbling halfway down Faulkner Street and lying in the road punching and kicking the tarmac.

I heard later that Bernie picked himself up, returned to Sid's and went straight to the phone.

'Have you cashed that cheque?' he asked the bank manager.

Obviously getting a reply in the affirmative, he screamed 'You CUNT!'

Fifteen hundred quid was a significant bit of dough back then but not a life-changing amount, and the next day, by which time I was installed in the Regent Palace Hotel in London, I was having second thoughts. I phoned Sid's and Bernie was put on the phone.

'How do you feel about settling for a grand and calling it a draw?' I asked him.

'Oh, come on. I know you're a good boy really and you're only kidding,' was the misguided reply.

I phoned again the next day and before I could speak, Bernie said, 'Alright. I'll take the grand. Where can I pick it up?'

Unfortunately, the previous night I'd met with a bit of an accident falling over a roulette table. Oh, and a dice table. So I wasn't really in a position to give him a grand.

'How do you feel about seven and a half?' I asked him. 'Best I can do.'

'You've got to be fucking…' was as far as he got before I hung up.

A few days later I phoned again, a monkey being the figure I had in mind, but by that point negotiations had irreparably broken down.

By the time the Old Bill caught up with me I was on remand on the fraud charges, so Bernie and his £1,500 were the least of my worries. I gave the police a fanny about having won the money off him in a card game, he gave me the cheque and I cashed it. End of story. They asked if there were any witnesses to this card game. In gambling circles it's rare to know anyone's full name, any more than I'd known Bernie's name was Bernard Gold until I'd seen it written on the cheque. I gave them the nicknames of several mythical witnesses to the mythical card game, bade them farewell and wished them the best of luck.

I had been surprised when the police came to visit me in the first place. I was therefore amazed when they charged me and totally astonished when the Director of Public Prosecutions allowed it to go to trial. The whole performance lasted something under four minutes. The prosecutor was just getting into his opening ramble when the judge stopped him.

'Look,' said the judge, who had obviously taken the trouble to skim through the depositions, 'Mr Gold claims the money was stolen and the defendant maintains that he had title to it. The whole case comes down to a matter of credibility, and from what I've seen of the people involved I wouldn't believe any of them if they told me the time of day.'

The charge was dismissed. This would prove to be the only time in my life I would ever be found not guilty of anything. That is if you can count being described as someone who wouldn't be believed about the time of day as exoneration.

Years later I bumped into Bernie, appropriately enough in Sid's. By coincidence a pal of mine, Bob Driver, walked in immediately behind me. It turned out that Bob had had Bernie over in some scam involving cup final tickets, in which they would both have earned a fortune if Bernie had pulled up the readies. Instead the readies got ate.

Spotting us both, Bernie jumped to his feet and shouted, 'Fuck me! I don't believe it. I've got the fucking Tote Double up.'

He pulled me to one side and whispered, 'Look son, I know you get your hands on the odd decent parcel. Give me first refusal and let me try and get my dough back.'

Apparently Bernie did a bit of fencing on the side, but where he got the idea I came across parcels of stolen jewellery I don't know. And I've never seen him from that day to this.

I came home from prison in 1981 just in time for a major property boom, into which I dived head-first. Given the conspicuous gaps in my CV, I had to be a little creative with my status details when applying for mortgages, but then again who isn't creative with mortgage applications? Come the days of self-assessment mortgages, you were actively encouraged to be creative. Of course, the Fraud Squad took a different view. When they got wind of my burgeoning property portfolio, they came up with an omnibus charge of 'obtaining or attempting to obtain a hundred thousand pounds' worth of valuable securities by deception'. Given my previous form and the repetitive nature of the offences, I was probably looking at a fairly lengthy sentence. I felt this was unjustified. After all, I wasn't going anywhere with the bricks and mortar and with a little patience everyone would have got paid.

Having managed to get bail, I decided to take advantage of the extradition situation in Spain, and packed my bags.

Puerto Banus and the Boat

If you accept that Marbella is the crown of the Costa del Sol, then Puerto Banus is unquestionably the jewel in the crown. This was where the rich and famous rubbed shoulders with the rich and dubious. When I arrived it was still quite tiny but very exclusive. It was kept exclusive by the simple expedient of charging an arm and a leg for everything. Poor people need not apply. So, I hear you ask, what was I doing there? Well, if you have any hope of making money you have to be where the money is, and this certainly seemed the place.

I have always been a firm believer in the old maxim that while it's not a crime to be skint, it is a crime to look skint. If you're reasonably well presented and conspicuously make the odd flamboyant gesture – one of those I'll-get-those-and-make-them-large-ones type of things – it's easy to give the impression that money isn't important because you've got lots and lots of it.

I was able to sustain this devil-may-care façade thanks mainly to a steady supply of hooky credit cards a pal sent over from England. Spanish banking procedures in general, and credit card security in particular, were still in the Stone Age at that time. Most credit card outlets didn't even have a telephone and relied on stop lists to check a card's validity, if they bothered at all. These lists were usually months out of date and I often had a more recent one myself.

I had another little asset that added to the masquerade of apparent wealth. Two pals of mine, Vinny and Steve, had been living on a boat in the port for about six months, and being a boat owner's friend carried a certain amount of prestige. I should also point out that being a boat owner's friend is much more financially viable than being a boat owner while still carrying most of the advantages.

Boats fell into two main categories in Banus. Boats that occasionally moved in and out of the port, generally little boats, and boats that never turned a screw from one year's end to another, generally big boats. Vinny's fell firmly into the latter group. The really, really big stuff was all on the first line, with the *Shaf*, £12 million-worth of floating Arab real estate, being the star of the show. The only thing bigger was Adnan Khashoggi's yacht, which was too big to fit in a berth and was moored along the sea wall, with his visitors having to be flown back and forth by one of the several helicopters that came with it. Vinny's was about the biggest on the second line, at nearly seventy foot. It was a lovely old thing, built in the 1930s and full of mahogany, with brass portholes and clocks. There was a very pleasant shaded dining area, and during the six months they had been in the port, it had become a kind of floating clubhouse.

Communications were a major problem: you couldn't get a phone installed at home for love or money. Phone numbers for the entire province of Malaga carried only six digits and flats and villas often changed hands at a premium if they had a phone. The boat, however, did have the facility to receive calls via the harbour control tower. This meant that half the UK had the phone number of the boat and every afternoon any amount of people would be sitting about waiting for a call. Although Vinny was a teetotal keep-fit fanatic, there was always plenty of beer and wine in the fridge and usually someone would send out for a couple of roast chickens and a bit of salad. Before long a game of cards or backgammon would break out. All in all, a very pleasant way to while away an expatriate afternoon.

I knew Vinny from the clubs in Manchester, where he was a regular visitor, and had also bought a few cars from his dealership over the years. He and Steve had run into their own problems back home. They had, allegedly, been involved in what in other circumstances would have been a fairly minor insurance fraud. Unfortunately they had been caught in the crossfire of the Stalker Inquiry and, since the alleged fraud had taken place in Northern Ireland, the charges had been inflated out of all proportion. John Stalker, the Deputy Chief Constable of Greater Manchester, had been tasked with conducting an inquiry into a suspected shoot-to-kill policy by the security forces in Ulster. It would have far-reaching repercussions, of which I will explain more later; suffice to say that Vinny and Steve found themselves embroiled inadvertently. Their problems would resolve themselves in the fullness of time but it was a safe bet that they wouldn't be going anywhere near British jurisdiction in the near future.

When I told Vinny the saga of my own run-in with the very, very Serious Fraud Squad, his best advice was to go home and try fighting it, as he had found very little success at making a living in the time he had been in Spain. Without totally ignoring his advice, and being of a less ambitious nature than him, I thought I'd give it a go. It didn't seem such a bad place to me.

After the day lazing on the boat, the serious business of where to go for a drink and where to dine had to be considered. For reasons that I was never able to fathom, we always had our first drink in Sinatra's Bar at the gates of the port. This place rates some sort of mention in *The Guinness Book of Records* under the category 'bars that take the most money in relation to their square footage'. Inside it was about the size of two telephone boxes, with a small terrace outside. People would stand six-deep at the bar and overflow into the street, fighting to pay three quid for a twenty pence bottle of beer which was slung at you as the barman made an effort to cram as much dough in the till, or his pocket, as possible in the shortest time. The bar next door, Salduba, was bigger, more comfortable and marginally cheaper but most nights you could fire a cannon across their terrace and not hit anyone. I suppose you'd just have to put it down to the herding instinct. When it came to dining, the choice was almost limitless: sea-food, of course, steakhouses, Italian, French, Chinese, Indian. Pretty much spoiled for choice. My only criteria were that they accepted major credit cards and, ideally, didn't have a telephone. Not a lot to ask.

So, aperitif'd, wined and dined, where to go to continue the festivities was the next executive decision. Although I keep moaning about the prices I must admit the entertainment in the bars was a million miles in front of the run-of-the-mill pub singer stuff you would expect in a resort location. There were three piano bars that we used regularly: Duke's, Old Joys and the Play Bach. Duke's was owned by Bill 'the Duke' Meeks, a six-foot-four 'Texan' (from Oklahoma) and his wife Jocelyn, a Canadian (from Canada). Bill was ex-US military, something to do with underwater salvage, I think. I remember him getting called up from the reserves the time the Yanks lost a couple of atomic bombs off the coast of Almeria. He tried, however, to give the impression that his military career was of a more clandestine nature and would drop remarks into conversations like, 'And when I was at Langley ... oops, shouldn't have told you that.' Only barely failing to add, 'Now I'll have to kill you.' They would bring over Country and Western-type bands from the States and there was a resident pianist. Bill would usually get up and do a few numbers to get the ball rolling, but to be honest if they shot him for being a singer they'd be shooting an innocent man. His repertoire consisted almost solely of Kris Kristofferson's 'Me and Bobby McGee' and Willie Nelson's 'On the Road Again'. Still, the place had character, which is something money can't buy, and it was my personal favourite watering hole. In fact I liked it so much I came close to cobbling together a deal to buy the place. Probably just as well my would-be financial backer got cold feet. The place is now a tee-shirt shop, and I can't imagine how many tee-shirts I'd have to sell to get out of trouble.

Old Joys was owned by a big Spanish concern and the music was provided mostly by Mel Williams. Mel had been around the music scene all his life. He'd been in Hamburg in the Sixties when the Beatles made it, London in the Seventies, he'd worked in the Caribbean and the United States and was always just a step away from the big time. He wasn't just an excellent singer – he didn't sound unlike his big idol Joe Cocker, with the sort of voice that only comes after years of too many Marlboros and too much Jack Daniel's – he was also a more than competent songwriter. I have to this day a CD of his with a dozen tracks he wrote himself. It must be very frustrating to know you've got the talent and never quite make the big time, given the crap that makes big money these days. Is it any wonder that so many of these rap singers end up getting shot? If I had my way there'd be a season for it, like grouse shooting. Every August 12 we could all go out and shoot a brace or two of rap singers. Soon put a stop to all that nonsense. Still, that's the music business and at least Mel has made a good living all his life doing something he enjoys.

The Play Bach was owned by a Frenchman called Claude and his brother. The resident singer, Gilly Burns, was another of those victims to the vagaries of the music game. She had just finished playing Nancy in the stage show *Oliver!* with Roy Hudd in the West End and was, not unreasonably, expecting big things to happen at any moment, the likes of Andrew Lloyd Webber knocking on her door with a lucrative contract. She was very attractive with that slightly understated horniness we all find so attractive in a nightclub singer. Or is that just me? Her father, Ray Burns, did make it big and was at one time reputed to be Britain's highest-paid entertainer. Shortly after that was quoted in the trade papers, Ray was appearing on the south coast and Max Bygraves was spotted in the audience. The spotlight was put on him and he was greeted with a round of applause. He shouted to Ray that he'd only come to see who it was that had topped him up as Britain's highest earner. Most of his wealth went on gambling and booze and the rest he squandered but one thing he never lost was his voice, and he could be talked into getting up and doing a few numbers when he was over. Still as great as ever.

Later Gilly would open her own place in partnership with ex-boxing champion Eddie Avoth and called it Pinky's In The Port. Rod Stewart came to the opening night with his girlfriend, to whom someone had presented an enormous bouquet. When they left, the flowers were forgotten and so a waiter snaffled them for his girlfriend, who worked next door as a barmaid. The following night, Rod returned looking for the bouquet and of course the waiter denied all knowledge, but sidled off next door to tell his girlfriend to remove them from display in case that was Rod's next port of call.

Another night, Gilly brought in Engelbert Humperdinck. I'd known Engelbert slightly back in Manchester in the Sixties when he was still Gerry Dorsey and still had an English accent, but a friend of mine, Freddie Brennan, had been his close pal. Freddie was a burglar by trade; when asked what he did for a living, he would reply, 'I'm a burglar but a damned good one.' This wasn't in fact the case, he was a fairly indifferent burglar and therefore spent a large part of his life in the nick. I asked if Engelbert remembered Freddie and he said sure, how was he, was he in the nick? I had to tell him that sadly Freddie was now in the big exercise yard in the sky.

For a late night drink there was the Navy Bar, owned by the same crowd that owned Joys. Mel did the music there as well, but it was a show more aimed at dancing. Not being a dancer, it was not really my cup of tea. The booze was alright though, if a bit pricey.

Sunday night the port was like a ghost town, mainly because everyone got drunk Sunday afternoon at Mel's Beach Bar. This was one of those venues that evolved purely by fluke. There had been a sort of unofficial gathering of bar owners looking for acts, and acts looking for work, at a beach bar at El Cortijo Blanco just outside San Pedro. Mel moved the meet to a bigger bar next door and before long a couple of thousand people were turning up on a Sunday afternoon. Some of the more adventurous seafarers would make the long voyage of about two hundred yards from the port and moor off the beach. Bikini-clad girls would whizz back and forth between the bar and the boats. The music was great, the food was passable and the booze was as cheap as booze got in that neighbourhood. If you need a better excuse to get drunk I'm afraid I'm stumped.

So, there you have it. Go home and go to prison or stay here? Stay here or go home to prison? Hmmm. Bit of a no-brainer really. Just a matter of waiting for something to turn up.

It's amazing that, in a place with wall-to-wall restaurants, one should stand head and shoulders above the rest. It wasn't that the food in Silks was any better or worse than anywhere else – anyone who can grill a steak or roast a leg of lamb will do for me – it was that intangible ingredient, atmosphere. The decor had a horseracing theme, with the walls covered in racing prints and horsey memorabilia and all the waiters dressed in racing silks. One big fat fellow made a very unconvincing jockey.

The place was run by Eddie Avoth, a Welshman from Porthcawl. Eddie was the ex-British and Commonwealth Light-Heavyweight champion and, as you might expect from a former light-heavy who loved his food and drink, he had the appearance of a huge, amiable, Havana-smoking teddy bear. He knew everybody. His connections attracted fellow sports personalities and I spotted the likes of Henry Cooper, Lloyd Honeyghan and Frank Bruno dining there. All the resident and visiting celebs ate there and all their photos were on the wall to prove it. Unlike many celeb eateries, most of the photos were pretty recent and all of them genuinely taken in the restaurant.

Not long after I arrived, they started shooting the film *Marbella*, with all of the outside scenes filmed in and around the port. The two stars, Rod Taylor and Britt Ekland, ate in Silks most nights and one unusually quiet night, Eddie introduced us to them. I kept calling Rod 'Boysie' after his role in the Sixties thriller *The Liquidator*, not realising at the time how diverse his career had been. Amongst others he'd played Captain Nemo, Sean O'Casey and an army commander in *The Mercenaries*. Britt Ekland, on the other hand, is mostly famous for being famous and having famous boyfriends like Peter Sellers and Rod Stewart. Eddie got a small part in the film playing a nightclub heavy running a few girls but I don't recall it becoming any sort of blockbuster. We finished up having a drink or two with them a few times over the following couple of weeks.

Another night, Kevin Keegan came in. Vinny had had a message from Lou Macari, whom Vinny knew well from Lou's playing days at Old Trafford, to say that if he spotted Keegan, would he try and get his address, as Lou wanted him to play in a charity soccer match. We got Eddie to introduce us. We had finished our meal and, since Keegan was on his own, he joined us for a drink. We got to talking and I slipped a credit card to the waiter. I must have become distracted – to use the footballing parlance, took my eye off the ball – because the next minute the waiter appeared.

'American Express would like to speak to Mr Evans,' he shouted.

'Eddie, do something,' I said, realising that was the name on the card I had given him.

'Mr Evans has paid cash and left,' Eddie told AmEx, thereby solving the problem.

Shortly afterwards I did both, I suppose leaving behind a slightly bemused Keegan, wondering what he had said to offend us. These were the type of impromptu booze-ups that Silks was famous for.

I'm normally up and bustling about most days by the crack of noon but one particular day, after an extra-hectic night before, it was close to two when I was roused from my slumbers by someone jack-booting around on the deck above. I never could understand why everyone ignored the sign asking them to remove their shoes on board. It was the only bit of nautical etiquette that Vinny tried to enforce. I had spent the night on the boat rather than risk the drive back to Marbella; in those days you didn't get nicked much for drink-driving, you just got killed. I went upstairs – or aloft, I suppose the correct term is – to find out what all the noise was about.

As it happened it was Eddie with a few of his previous night's diners. This was a fairly common occurrence. I always found it amusing how even the rich and famous had the sole ambition of getting their arses down on a boat when they came to the port. Today's visitors included jazzman Kenny Lynch, the

English character actor Ronald Fraser and a society hairdresser from London. I know he was a society hairdresser because, two weeks later, he was all over the *News of the World*, or News of the Screws as we referred to it, for, allegedly, having it with Peter Stringfellow's estranged wife.

Vinny isn't much of a film buff but he immediately recognised Ronnie from his part in *The Wild Geese*.

'Must of got a few quid for that, hey Ron, *The Wild Geese*?' said Vin.

'Got a few quid? My dear chap, do you realise that I was working with Richard Burton, Richard Harris and Roger Moore? By the time they were paid, there was fuck-all left for me.'

In an effort to change the subject, Vinny suggested a drink.

'Can't drink any more, old chap. The old liver's gone,' said Ron. 'But I do enjoy the occasional herbal Woodbine.' Of course he meant hashish, marijuana or simply a bit of puff. A rose by any other name and all that. I translated for Vinny's benefit.

There was a fella on a boat a few berths down that was fairly obviously in the puff game: the Ferrari, gold Rolex and trophy girlfriend shopped it a bit. He was a Londoner of Greek extraction and everyone, including himself, referred to him as The Bubble, as in bubble-and-squeak, Greek. I wandered down to see if he might have a small piece of puff to oblige our guests. When I asked him he said, 'Yeah, sure, just a minute.' I was expecting something about the size of an Oxo cube, so I was surprised when he threw me a bar about four by two by one inches. This, I was soon to learn, was known in the trade as either a soap-bar, because of its shape, or a nine-bar because of its weight: 250 grams, or nearly nine ounces.

'How much do I owe you?' I asked him.

'You're alright,' he said. 'I get these samples all the time.'

At that time, in Manchester, an ounce of puff, if you knew where to buy and didn't have to go through too many middlemen, would cost you about £120. That made The Bubble's sample worth around a grand back home. Any business that gave away £1,000 samples 'all the time' was a business I wanted to know more about. The Bubble didn't know it yet, but he was about to become my new best, best friend.

I took the bar back to the boat and was greeted with a chorus of surprised delight. They had only ever seen the stuff in Oxo-cube-sized portions as well. The only dissenting note came from Vinny, who was totally anti-drugs. He must have decided that it was time for a frank exchange of views.

'I want that to be the last time I see any of that shit on the boat,' was his view.

'Aye, aye, Cap'n,' was as much of a reply as I could think of, since Vinny's opinion was the only one that carried any clout and I didn't have a leg to stand on.

I didn't realise it at the time but this one small step for me was to become a giant leap into the world of puff smuggling.

The Only Game in Town

Over the next couple of weeks I spent a fair amount of time with my new best friend, The Bubble. This was no great hardship because I enjoyed his company. He was a big, amiable man but I would soon discover he lost a lot of his amiability when business entered the picture. He obviously had plenty of money and knew how to enjoy it. He liked good food and booze, drove a fifty-grand sports car and I couldn't begin to guess what the boat was worth. As for his clothes, I wouldn't have wanted to keep up with his laundry bill, let alone his tailor's bill. We would sit on the boat, sipping wine and playing backgammon, while I pumped him for as much information as he'd part with on the ins and outs of the puff smuggling job.

Gradually I began to get a fair idea of how the game went. Basically, buy a bit of puff, get it home, sell it and live happily ever after. The only stumbling block appeared to be my lack of funds.

Puff smoking has been around since time immemorial. In the Middle Ages, there was a band of Arab hired killers known as Hashishins, or hashish-eaters. Apparently they munched a bit of hash before going out on a night's graft, hence the word 'assassin'. North Africa has been awash with the stuff ever since. The main producers are the Berbers, who live in an autonomous region of Morocco and seemingly have some sort of historic concession to grow it. There's certainly nothing clandestine about the operation, I've been there and seen hundreds, maybe thousands, of acres. Quite what they're supposed to do with it after they grow it is a mystery.

When King Hassan died and his son Mohamed VI came to the Moroccan throne, things changed a bit. Mohamed VI was pro-European and there was even some talk about Morocco joining the European Union. In an effort to curry favour with his Euro neighbours, he agreed to take steps to curtail puff production. There was TV coverage of farms being set ablaze by the military and he also got some financial assistance from the Yanks, who are never shy at sticking their noses in.

I've been told, quite reliably, that the farm-burning was little more than propaganda and that for every farm burned, twenty were left to conduct business as usual.

The boom years for the UK drug market started with the hippy movement in the early Sixties. The Beatles spent a bit of time in Morocco in their flower-power period and the Crosby, Stills and Nash hit 'Marrakesh Express' made that a popular destination. Droves of hippies would travel along the coast heading for Algeciras and the ferry to Tangiers. More than a few brought a bar or two of puff back and a fair amount of them finished up languishing in the dungeons of Puerto Santa Maria prison.

Soon people realised the potential for an earn and began to get more organised but it was still on a small scale, five or ten kilos in the tank of a camper, that sort of thing. But things would escalate. The Brits were the first and biggest to get into mass transportation from Morocco to Spain, probably because Britain was the biggest single market for the stuff. The Moroccans seemed happy to sell their gear at home, leaving the onward transportation up to whoever was buying. Despite all this going on in their own backyard, the Spanish didn't play any large part, except for the police, many of whom had their hand out. I had arrived at the tail-end of the hippy and amateur era and the beginning of the more organised teams, with the likes of The Bubble already established.

The Only Game in Town

Puff, at least most of the puff smoked in Europe, originates in the Rif mountains of Morocco in an area around the small town of Ketama. The closer to Ketama you buy your puff, the cheaper it gets, while the closer you get to the streets of, say, Manchester the dearer it gets. This means the most profitable course of action would be to buy your puff on Ketama high street and sell it on a street corner in Moss Side. This system has its flaws.

Buying the puff in Ketama at something under £100 a kilo presents no problem in itself, assuming you've got the money, and is apparently quite legal. It's the transporting it out of the area that's illegal, and more than a little serious. And expensive. The people who drive the puff down the mountain have to be paid whatever people get paid for driving wagon loads of puff down mountains. To get down the mountain to the beach they have to pass through several police and army checkpoints, the staffs of which also need to be paid. On the beach, there's more military looking for their bit of readies, as are the workers who have to load it onto barges and the people who sail the barges out to the waiting transport vessel. And, of course, the crew of the Customs patrol boat want their few quid. All in all, not a project to be taken on without considerable help from the local community, and nerves of steel.

There is, however, another way and it was apparently the system used by The Bubble. The gear can be bought 'on the water' – that is, you only take on the responsibility when it is delivered to your transport vessel. This leaves all the drama and expense of getting it there in the hands of your Moroccan supplier. Of course the value has appreciated at this point and you would now have to pay close to £300 a kilo.

Even this system has its pitfalls. The Moroccan supplier will never be short of an excuse why a parcel couldn't be loaded on any given night: too much moon, not enough moon, sea too rough, wrong beach patrol working, wrong captain on the patrol boat working and a host of others. It wasn't unusual for the transport to go over three or four times before getting loaded. These delays had to be accepted philosophically. The philosophical acceptance wasn't reciprocal. If, for any reason, no matter how genuine, the transport vessel failed to turn up, that was always the night when everything was perfect and everyone was paid off and please could he have another ten grand to pay them all again.

Once the gear finally gets loaded, getting it to Spain is a piece of cake. That is, barring mutinies, hijacking, tidal waves and the long arm of the Spanish Customs. Assuming it gets safely to Spain, it's now worth, top wholesale price, £700 a kilo, but of course the people who brought it over weren't working for nothing. The going rate for this transport was thirty per cent of the parcel. So, say we're talking a ton, you now have seven hundred key (kilos) at £700 a unit, worth £490,000. Since the parcel would stand in at close to £300,000, this didn't sound like the licence to print money that I'd been led to believe.

But, of course, The Bubble had no intention of selling the gear in Spain, or certainly not all of it. His ambition was to get it back home, where it would be worth two grand a key. Allowing a few quid for expenses, that would leave a nice round £1 million profit. A respectable enough figure for sure, but bearing in mind the number of times the gear could have been lost and the number of people who could go to prison, it still didn't strike me as the El Dorado I'd anticipated.

I had fallen into the trap of paying attention to what I'd read in the press. I had seen articles where HM Customs and Excise had seized a hundred key with a street value of a million quid. The Bubble said he'd love to know what street they sold their gear on because he couldn't make a shilling more than two grand a key. The inflated values were presumably published to give Customs and the police an exaggerated success profile. And give the judge a bit more leeway to err on the side of severity when it came to sentencing.

So that was the business in a nutshell. Even if I wasn't too impressed with the risk-to-gain ratio, it was still the only game in town. My best hope was that The Bubble could find a little niche in his empire for a trier like me. Eventually my perseverance paid off.

One afternoon, The Bubble asked me if I had any plans for Saturday night. I said I hadn't anything important on. He had a boat due to arrive and could use an extra pair of willing hands on the beach if I was interested. This wasn't quite the role I'd cast myself in, but I suppose everyone has to start somewhere. My enthusiasm increased slightly when he told me there was two-and-a-half grand wages in it. Besides, it would have appeared churlish to refuse after all the ear-bashing I had been giving him. I said it would suit me fine, only lying slightly.

The Bubble had a sort of major-domo called Gordo. He was one of those expats that had gone native and did all his socialising in Spanish bars, probably paying a fraction of what we were paying. I had assumed his real name was Gordon but it turns out he was nicknamed Gordo, which is Spanish for 'Fatty', by a barman at one of his locals. The arrangements were for me to meet Gordo on the car park of the Artola Hotel, halfway to Fuengirola, and from there he drove us down to the beach. There two more lads were waiting with two four-wheel drives, probably nicked for the occasion judging by the way the seats had been ripped out.

The whole performance had a very relaxed air about it. We opened a few cans of beer and sat around rabbiting. Communications were still very primitive and Gordo would walk down to the water's edge every five minutes and flash a torch.

After about half an hour, a massive black Zodiac inflatable, carrying what looked like a giant haystack of puff, nudged up onto the beach and the game was on.

There was a ton of gear in forty bales of twenty-five key, so ten bales each. Gordo had some theory of physics that carrying two bales was easier than carrying one, since two kept you balanced. You can take it from me that this theory is absolute bollocks. Carrying two twenty-five key bales of puff fifty yards uphill over a sandy beach is exactly twice as difficult as carrying one. Paradoxically, carrying two isn't even any quicker since carrying one you spend miles less time falling flat on your face and quivering like a blancmange. After the first trip, I carried one. Making my ninth trip for my tenth bale I met Gordo coming the other way carrying three of the things. He said I was okay, that was the lot. Fucking pity there wasn't a fourth one, just to keep him balanced.

Still, the whole thing was done and dusted in less than fifteen minutes. The bales were slung into the jeeps and Gordo threw a couple of blankets over the gear so it wouldn't look like two jeeps full of puff. More like two jeeps full of puff with blankets thrown over it. Hopefully they didn't have far to go.

Gordo had arranged to meet The Bubble in a very discreet little brothel up in Nueva Andalucia which, besides the traditional amenities, had the advantage of a bar that served twenty-four hours a day. The Bubble slipped me an envelope containing half a million pesetas, which sounded like a fortune until I did a little arithmetic. Try as I might, I couldn't get it to come to any more than £2,242.46. I queried this with Gordo and he told me that they always called a million pesetas five grand.

I was to learn that a bit of dexterity with exchange rates was a fundamental part of the puff business.

The Only Game in Town

The Bubble's beach parties were only ever, at best, once a month. So, having done my month's work in something under forty-five minutes, I felt I had earned a lie-in, and it was mid-afternoon the next day when I arrived on the boat. I was confronted by the usual suspects drinking, playing cards, talking about things of little importance and awaiting phone calls.

During a lull in the conversation, someone mentioned that Manchester United were playing in Algeciras, a port a hundred kilometres down the coast, the following day. This struck me at the time as being a particularly improbable venue for United to be playing, but with the host of European tournaments, who knows? It was agreed pretty unanimously that we would all go.

'Why don't we go on the boat?' suggested someone, obviously someone of limited intelligence. I can only assume his thought process went something like: Port? Water. Boat! For some bizarre reason this suggestion was greeted with a chorus of approval. Did these people not know that, while the boat was perfect for sitting on and having a beer, it hadn't turned a screw in living memory? Yet even Vinny, normally the most sensible of people, didn't totally dismiss the notion. He got out his AA road map to check the logistics. A road map? He even said he'd ring Bill Whitaker, an American yacht skipper, to see if he was available to do the driving. He was, the bastard. In no time provisions were being ordered – food, booze, cigarettes – and arrangements made with the fuelling dock to fill the tanks. We would leave bright and early the next morning.

It was just before we were to set sail that we realised we had made a small mistake. The match wasn't taking place in Algeciras, sixty miles west, but in Algeria, four or five hundred miles south east. A different proposition altogether. What a shame, we'd have to cancel. But wait a minute, we had a boatload of fuel, stacks of booze and enough sandwiches to make a significant dent in

Third World famine. We'd have to go somewhere.

Someone, and I'd bet money it was the same moron, suggested Gibraltar. I thought I was as surprised as a human being can get that the notion of taking the boat out at all was accepted so enthusiastically. But I was wrong. I found that my surprise capacity had been multiplied when this idea wasn't greeted with the contempt and ridicule it deserved. Bearing in mind our passenger list included Ronnie Knight, Fred Foreman and a few of their cohorts, half a dozen major players from the VAT swindle, Vinny, Steve and myself, even Algeria seemed a preferable destination. There were three barmaids from a nightclub in Manchester who, to the best of my knowledge, had no skeletons in the cupboard but that was about it as far as straight-goers were concerned.

It may sound slightly implausible that a small-time fraudster from Manchester was all of a sudden consorting with some of the most high-profile fugitives in Europe but that's just how things were back then. The expats, straight and otherwise, pretty much drank in the same bars and ate in the same restaurants. Steve was a transplanted Cockney who had lived in Manchester for years and Vinny knew a lot of Londoners from his boxing and football jaunts. Besides the convenience of the phone, the boat provided a little more privacy than sitting in a bar so it wasn't long before anyone with nothing on their hands but time made a beeline for it. Hence our high-profile fugitive pals.

'Can anyone explain to me what the difference is, looking at the prospect from a purely legal jurisdiction viewpoint, between sailing into Gib and sailing into, say, Birkenhead?' I asked.

I asked this because … well, quite frankly, I was fucked if I could see a difference. No-one really had a definitive answer but Captain Bill, may his children walk backwards, threw his two cents' worth in.

The Only Game in Town

'With the border crossing at La Linea closed, the only way into Gib is by boat and there are so many day-trippers sailing in and out that they scarcely get a look at.'

It was on the tip of my tongue to ask him to quantify scarcely but I could see I was pissing against the wind. The genie was out of the bottle and there was no putting it back. We were off to Gib.

Ropes were being untied; I think it's actually called casting off but I could be wrong, I often am. All this nautical jargon was like trying to learn a foreign language but I was doing my best. When they park – sorry, 'moor' – a boat, that thing they do with the ropes is definitely called tying-up, so when they leave why isn't it called tying down? Or simply untying, like I said in the first place. No, these nautical bastards have to have a special word for it. Perhaps I was just getting a little petulant. I poured myself a drink and went to lie down on the floor at the pointy bit up the front.

The sun was shining, the water was flat as a pancake, the engines were making a reassuring purring noise and there was certainly nothing wrong with the whiskey and coke. Maybe I'd been worrying over nothing. Then we got out of the harbour mouth and it was a different story.

The boat was sort of going up and down and left to right at the same time. I feel sure the boatie people have a name for that motion but I was at a loss to bring it to mind. The purring noise of the engines had become clearly less rhythmic and the faint puffs of white smoke from the exhaust had become grey clouds. Speaking of grey clouds, the sky had become a bit overcast, too.

Captain Bill, and bad luck to the captain that brought him over, said there was no need to worry. The engines had been turned over regularly to charge the batteries and were fine but some silt had built up on the bottom of the tanks and the yawing motion – I knew they had a name for it – had caused the silt to mix with the fuel. It would soon blow itself clear.

An hour later, we were just off the port of Soto Grande, and far from blowing themselves clear the engines were rougher than ever. Then one of them gave up the job completely. Surely now we'd have to call it a day and pull in? Captain Bill, may he be roasting in hell before St Peter knows he's dead, said there was no cause for alarm and we could manage perfectly well on one engine. That being the case, I wondered why God in his wisdom had seen fit to give us two. By now I wasn't the only one who thought Soto Grande harbour was looking very inviting. Someone, almost certainly our resident cretin, shouted, 'For fuck sake, it can't be far, you can see Gib over there.' Since you could see Gib from the comfort and safety of the berth back in Banus, this didn't give me any reassurance but, as is usually the case, the voice of reason was ignored.

We got as far as the entrance to Gib harbour before the second engine gave up the ghost. There probably aren't many worse stretches of water on the planet to find yourself without power than the entrance to Gib harbour. This is where the Atlantic and the Med meet, with all the undertows, tides and currents. Not to mention all the barely submerged jagged rocks. Even Captain Bill had lost some of his self-assurance.

The more perceptive reader may have noticed a certain animosity when I mention the Captain's name. This is only partly because I blamed our current plight on his availability in the first place and his constant optimism in the second. The other, and more important reason, is that he would subsequently turn out to be a grass. This has become quite a common trait amongst Yanks of late. I hold the American judicial system to blame, where the first one to hold up his hands and put all his pals in it gets the best deal. That's what always happens on *Law and Order* anyway. Even the staunch old Mafia types, with their codes of silence and omerta, seem to go over these days when the shit hits the fan. Just ask John 'Teflon Don' Gotti how he feels about Sammy 'The Bull' Gravano if you don't believe me. Actually, you can't because he's dead, but if he were alive I'm sure he wouldn't have anything very complimentary to say about old Sammy. Howard Marks, in his book *Mr Nice*, gives a very graphic description of the pitfalls that can be encountered doing business in that part of the world. He got forty years over a bit of puff. Anyway, more about the Captain later. In the meantime, back to Gib.

'There's a police launch approaching,' announced the Captain. 'Anyone who doesn't want to be seen had best get below decks.'

When I looked into the salon I was reminded of the scene from the *Marie Celeste*: half-drunk beers, half-smoked cigarettes, half-played hands of cards and not a soul in sight.

The police constable, who today would probably be chief constable of Gibraltar had he realised who had so nearly fallen into his grasp, arranged for a tug boat to come out and tow us in. This was no straightforward matter, since none of us were too familiar with the rules of salvage and that sort of thing. Eventually we agreed to give the tug captain a couple of hundred quid. I'd have gladly given him one of my kidneys.

Our 'innocent day-tripper' status was rapidly evaporating but at least we were safe on dry land. Neil Robertson, one of the lads from the VAT swindle, suddenly realised that it was his birthday and that that was a good excuse to go for a drink. I thought being alive was excuse enough already.

There's not a lot to say about Gib. It's a bit like a small Aldershot in the sun, but fortunately with plenty of pubs. We set off exploring. The first job was to find accommodation, since it was a sure thing we wouldn't be going anywhere that day and there wasn't room for everyone to sleep on the boat.

This didn't concern me, as I would be sleeping on the boat, so I cut to the chase and went for a drink.

The lucky ones got rooms in the Rock Hotel, which is quite nice. The less fortunate got rooms in the Montariq, which isn't. Neil, the birthday boy, and his pal Micky were two of those in the Montariq. There's a quirk in the design of this hotel: you enter the lift on one side and exit it on the other. By the time Neil was ready to retire for the night, he was in no condition to cope with this complication. He got in the lift, pressed the button for the third floor and spent a couple of minutes pushing on the wall before returning to the foyer to complain.

'Can't get out of the lift, my old mate,' he said

The night clerk, an Indian gentleman, had probably had to put up with this rigmarole most nights for whatever number of years he'd worked there.

'Please turn around, sir,' said the Indian, twirling his finger.

Neil thought this was some sort of Hindu ritual – he knew Sikhs normally had beards and turbans and this chap hadn't, but he was munching a bag of pork scratchings, so he probably wasn't Muslim. Neil may have been drunk but he wasn't stupid, so not wanting to be rude, he turned 360 degrees and repeated that he couldn't get out of the lift. The night clerk sighed, took Neil by the hand, put him in the lift and pressed the button for his floor. He turned Neil 180 degrees and gave him a gentle push, saying, 'Please to go to bed, sir.'

In the meantime, Micky was in bed. It was quite a chilly night and, not knowing when or even if Neil would return, he had decided to make use of Neil's eiderdown. Neil undressed and got in under his one thin sheet, mumbling about it being a bit parky. Then he noticed that Micky had an eiderdown, not noticing Micky in fact had two eiderdowns.

He rang down to his pal the night porter.

'Couldn't rustle up an eiderdown for me, could you, Gunga?' he asked.

'I'd a what, sir?'

'Eiderdown. Ei-der-down. Oh, for fuck sake. A FUCKING EIDERDOWN. Micky's got one and I'm freezing my bollocks off.'

'I am very sorry, sir. I am not understanding you. Please go to sleep,' said the Indian, and with that he disconnected the phone.

Neil re-dressed in every stitch he had, including baseball cap, and did his best to get a night's sleep.

My night's sleep wasn't much better. They had given us a windswept berth alongside the airport runway, and with no shore power, there was no heating. At about five in the morning, RAF jets started taking off right outside my porthole, probably off to bomb Iraq or wherever Britain had fallen out with at the time. On top of all this, Vinny had been working all night on the engines. One of our passengers, Norman Gallagher, was by trade a marine engineer and he and Vinny had been doing whatever marine engineers do to engines that don't work. I know it entailed a lot of banging and blowing through pipes. By eleven o'clock, I gave up trying to sleep and went in search of breakfast.

All the waifs and strays began to arrive back on the boat by midday and there was an air of optimism, with the engines sounding sweet as a nut. Norman pointed out that the true test wouldn't come until we got back out on the open seas. Since the only other way off Gib was to take the morning ferry to Tangiers, which we'd already missed, and the evening ferry back to Algeciras, we were going to have to give the boat a go. Nobody fancied another night on The Rock.

We were no sooner out of the harbour entrance than the coughing and spluttering began. We managed to limp as far as La Duquesa before we knew we would have to pull in.

One good thing came out of the whole escapade. There were loads of food products that you couldn't get for love nor money in Spain at the time that were available in Gib: Bird's Custard Powder, Oxo cubes, Bisto gravy, tea-bags, bacon. When the wives of the passengers heard we were in Gib, shopping lists were prepared, so when we docked everyone was carrying two or three shopping bags. I was completely amazed that there wasn't sight, sound or smell of any sort of Customs official or inspection.

Sixteen people walking off a boat carrying thirty-odd shopping bags of groceries couldn't look any different to several people carrying several shopping bags of puff. I filed away this little piece of intelligence and it was to prove very useful in the future.

Learning the Puff Job

My next 'beach party' with The Bubble went much the same way as the first, with no real problems, but I was rapidly coming to the conclusion that this was not where my future lay. It wasn't the risk element; there didn't seem to be much of a risk element. And it certainly wasn't the money, as half a million pesetas seemed ample reward for the work. No, it was the physical humping of the gear that was getting to me. I made up my mind to see if The Bubble might be able to find some role more in keeping for a presentable chap like myself, perhaps something in the sales department.

One day I asked him if, hypothetically speaking, a very close personal friend of mine happened to be on the lookout for a small parcel, would he be prepared to serve him and, if so, how much would he have to pay? He said if he had some about him that he wanted to be out of, he'd let me have it for seven hundred quid a key. This was as cheap a price as I'd heard mentioned. Seven fifty was about par for the course. That might not sound a massive margin but on fifty key I'd earn as much as I was getting for doing the beach work. A much better proposition altogether. All I had to do was find someone looking for fifty key that wanted to be my very close person friend.

This wasn't the mammoth task that the uninitiated might assume it to be. It's impossible to over-emphasise how much the puff job was the only game in town. There was the odd burglar still getting a crust, despite all the iron bars and steel grilles everywhere, but with four police forces – national, local, secret and Guardia Civil – to contend with, armed robbery was a non-starter. On top of that there was an army, in fact several armies, of private security guards all armed to the teeth. The language problem complicated any sort of bank fraud, so what was left? The only hope your average ducker and diver had of getting off the floor was to put himself in the middle of some deal involving the buying, selling or transporting of a bit of puff. For this reason the word 'puff' was on everyone's lips.

On a Tuesday afternoon there was 'friendly' football kickabout in Fuengirola, UK v Spain. I restricted my own participation to spectating and the after-match light ale but Vinny wouldn't have missed it for the world. The Spaniards had been having things pretty much their own way of late but things were about to change. We had dozens of pro footballers visit us on the boat and this particular week we had most of the Manchester United team on board. When they heard about the match, a few said they would come along.

Our starting line-up included Sammy McIlroy, Bryan Robson, Scott McGarvey and Frank Worthington. There was a bit more ammunition on the bench. The Spaniards, most of them semi-pros themselves, took a bit of a dim view of all this, looking on it as unsporting. The tackles were getting rougher and rougher and, as the game was played on a shale pitch, it was starting to look like someone could get hurt. United had just paid £1.5 million for Bryan Robson, the British transfer record at the time, and I had visions of him having to go home and explain a broken leg to Ron Atkinson, his manager at the time.

At half-time we were winning thirty-seven or thirty-eight to nil. There was some dispute as to whether Sammy Mac was in an offside position – whatever an offside position is – when Bryan Robson scored his eleventh, or twelfth, as the case may be. We decided to declare.

This meant that the after-match light ale session started forty-five minutes early, which suited me fine. The habitual venue for this drink was the Cepa Bar in the church square. There used to be a bar like the Cepa in most resort towns, a place where expats could meet in a sort of mutual co-operation society. There was a noticeboard where customers could advertise services like baby-sitting, flat cleaning, bike and cot hire and articles for sale. I don't recall an advert specifically for drugs bought and sold but, like most bars, a fair amount of such business was discussed. Or maybe it was just the bars I used.

The lads were all in a celebratory mood after their victory and the booze was flowing. I got into conversation with a couple of lads from Glasgow and it turned out that they knew a few of the Scottish lads that I knew from Manchester, a tough little firm who had moved to England after some problems north of the border. In fact the brother of one of them had been in Strangeways with me in '72. I don't know if this somewhat tenuous connection would put them in the category of very close personal friends in the eyes of The Bubble, but it did transpire that they were over to buy a small parcel. Twenty-five key was the figure they had in mind.

'I could certainly organise that,' I said, secretly hoping that I could.

'Fine,' one said, 'and when can we see a sample?'

Sample? The thought hadn't even crossed my mind. And what sort of sample were they thinking of? One of those soap bars would cost me nearly a two-er, so they certainly wouldn't be getting one of them. I thought of going out and buying ten or twenty quid's worth around the corner and giving them that but decided that the best course of action would be to go and speak to Gordo.

concocted a fanny as to why it would take me an hour or two and set off for Marbella in search of Gordo. I found him at the third attempt and took him out of the bar for a chat, bringing him up to date on developments.

'What about a sample?' I asked.

'Sample? Course they can't have a sample. What does a sample prove? For all they know you could have just gone out and bought ten or twenty quid's worth around the corner.'

Great minds think alike.

He then went on to explain, in agonising detail, exactly how the deal would be conducted, if it was to be conducted at all. I suppose I'd been a bit naive to imagine I'd just take one of those bales I was so familiar with to a pre-arranged, discreet bar, the Jocks would bring a bag of readies and we'd have a swop over.

'Apart from everyone getting nicked, there were only really three things that could go wrong at the point of exchange,' said Gordo. 'The buyers could try to steal the sellers' puff, the sellers could try to steal the buyers' money, or the gear was crap. My system eliminates the first two and puts the onus for the third squarely on the toes of the buyers.'

He went on, 'Go and book a room at the Artola Hotel. The Jocks must arrive in a small, inconspicuous motor. A little hired Fiesta or Panda will suit perfectly. They are to leave the car on the car-park and bring the money to your room, where you will count it and put it in the safe. In the meantime I will take the car away, put the gear in the boot and return it to the car-park. With the counted money in the safe, one of the Jocks can take the car away and examine the puff to his heart's content while the other one can wait with you and the dough until his pal confirms that the material is everything it should be. No samples required and very limited opportunities for any skulduggery.'

To add insult to insult, Gordo added, 'It would be as well to learn the right way to do the job in case a worthwhile deal comes up.' Where I come from, any deal that involves someone parting with eighteen and three-quarter grand would definitely come under the heading of worthwhile.

I went back to Fuengirola and the Jocks and told them how things had to be done, expecting all sorts of counter proposals. Amazingly enough, everything seemed to suit them fine and we arranged the meet at lunchtime the following day.

And that's just how my first deal went down. No snags, money right to the penny, gear bang on, everyone happy. And I'd earned £1,250. This was the end of the business to be in. I went off to see The Bubble and thank him for his help.

It didn't take him long to piss on my parade.

'What the fuck is that?' he growled, pointing to the money heaped up on his lounge table.

'Looks like the seventeen and a half grand you told me to return,' I said, somewhat puzzled.

'You're almost right. What it actually is is seventeen and a half grand of fucking Scottish sterling and what the fuck am I supposed to do with it?'

'Well, change it into pesetas.'

'Have you ever tried to change Scottish money?' he asked.

I admitted that I hadn't.

'Hmm, then I suggest you try. In fact I more than suggest.'

Taking out the newspaper to check, he told me, 'The current rate of exchange is two hundred and twenty pesetas to the pound. I want you to take away the Scottish shit and return with either three million, eight hundred and fifty thousand pesetas or seventeen and a half grand of English sterling. I don't really care which or how you manage it.'

It was on the tip of my tongue to ask, 'What happened to

always calling a million pesetas five grand,' but I could see he wasn't in the mood for nitpicking.

I had noticed when counting the money that it was a bit cumbersome but it never occurred to me there would be a problem changing it. There are five or six Scottish banks who all issue their own banknotes, all different shapes, sizes and colours. I had been undecided whether to compile it by denomination or issuing bank and in the end had done both, so it was pretty neat and tidy. There was one bundle of five hundred that was a bit messy, consisting of all the orphans that didn't belong in any of the other bundles. It even included fifty quid in one-pound notes, which I thought had ceased to exist years before, and two £100 notes that I never knew existed at all.

I set off in search of bureaux de change. I tried five grand in the first one and he laughed at me. After a couple more blanks, I found one that would change five hundred, and so it went on. At nine o'clock they were all closing, so I called it a day and went for a drink.

Next morning, bright and early, I set off for Fuengirola and met with fairly limited success. Benalmadena wasn't any better and two o'clock found me in Torremolinos just as they were closing for siesta. I was beginning to think that I had fewer problems when I was dealing in forged money and stolen travellers' cheques.

On the main street of Torremolinos there's a little place that's a cross between a bar and fishmongers. They stock every type of prawn known to man, which they sell by weight and grill in front of you. I ordered a kilo of the biggest ones and a bottle of the only wine they sell, which arrives in a bottle with no label. It's not bad though.

By four thirty, after two bottles, I was feeling a bit mellower and went back to work. I found a couple of victims on the

Calle San Miguel and, after a few blanks, another in a side street. Crossing a small plaza, I then spotted a travel agent with a hand-written sign in the window saying, 'We change sterling.' I went in.

The place was owned by a Pakistani who spoke perfect English. I threw him the tidiest bundle of a grand.

'Ah, Scottish,' he said. 'I can only give you two sixteen to the pound for this.'

Obligingly enough, he went on to explain why. 'I earn a very small commission on money changing but I also earn money changing pesetas back to sterling for people travelling to countries where sterling is more acceptable than pesetas. That is to say, almost everywhere. However, people buying sterling wouldn't want a bag of Scottish fivers and tenners, so I'm stuck with just the small commission.'

I had a quick count up and asked could he do any better if I changed the fourteen grand I had left.

'I can't. In fact, to change that much I'd be tempted to offer you less, but having said two sixteen I'll stick to it. And for me to change that much you'd have to wait an hour or two.'

Four pesetas to the pound on fourteen grand would cost me fifty-six thousand pesetas, a bit over a two-er. The way things were going I could spend that much in shoe leather before I got it all changed. And I would still earn a grand on the deal. He put on the kettle while we waited for a pal of his to rustle up the necessary.

All in all it had been a fairly satisfactory twenty-four hours. I learnt how to conduct a puff deal, found someone who would change Scottish money – the charge for which would be passed on in any future deals – and earned a grand. I went and paid The Bubble and told him it had been a pleasure doing business with him. Almost meaning it.

Vinny's partner, Jack Trickett, came over every few weeks for a couple of days. Jack was a Manchester hotelier and car dealer by trade but his main interest was boxing promotion and management. He was quite unusual in the boxing world in that he was in it more for the love of the game than the money. Being a shrewd businessman, he wouldn't turn his nose up at a few quid but it wasn't his real motivation.

Jack had a few problems of his own at home, but only tax problems. I'm allowed to say 'only' because it has been my life's ambition to have tax problems, as opposed to problems with the bailiffs and liquidators. And the very, very serious fraud squad. Jack took matters more to heart.

His first interview with the tax Gestapo went less than satisfactorily. The Gruppenführer started by complimenting Jack on his business acumen. He said he was aware of this because their last record of Jack was thirty-odd years earlier, when he had been delivering coal for thirty shillings a week. He now owned a hotel conservatively valued at a couple of million. The Gruppenführer said he would appreciate it if Jack could fill in a few of the gaps. Apparently the gap-filling wasn't as comprehensive as the Gruppenführer would have liked and the files had gone up to a higher authority. With all this going on, it was no wonder that all Jack wanted to do on his couple of days' break was to have a drink and relax.

One afternoon, Jack and I were having a glass of lunch in the Red Pepper when we were joined by Jack's pal Tommy McCarthy and his friend Patsy Boggs. Tommy was a London publican and at the time owned the Stag pub on Ascot racecourse. We ordered some prawns, the house speciality, and a couple of bottles of Viña Sol and settled back to enjoy a leisurely afternoon. Then Vinny arrived.

Vinny is very much a let's-do-things type of person and a bit of a workaholic. The boat was always spotless and the decks were washed down every morning to stop them drying up and cracking. God knows who did it before Vinny took up residence. When people were coming over, they'd phone to see if we needed anything. My list was restricted to tea-bags, bacon and sausages. Vinny's would contain things like varnish and paint brushes. Mind you, Vinny looked on the boat as a bit of stock and when the right offer came along it would be sold. The only way that was going to happen was if it was kept looking as good as could be.

Jack started to get a lecture from Vinny about what a wasted opportunity it was to spend all day sitting in a bar when there was so much to see and do in Spain. It wasn't so much that Vin frowned on us having a drink, it was more that, in his role as genial host, he felt it his duty to make sure his guests got as much as possible from their breaks.

'What you got in mind, Vin?' asked Jack.

After a bit of thought, Vinny said, 'Well, we could take a trip to Granada and see the Alhambra Palace.'

I should point out that the Alhambra Palace is some sort of historic building, not a nightclub. Jack asked how long it would take and Vinny guessed at a little over an hour. Before I could delay matters by ordering another bottle of wine, the decision was made and we were off to Granada.

In those days there were few motorways in Spain and the Malaga bypass hadn't been built. On a good day you could do the Port to Malaga in about forty minutes. This hadn't been a particularly good day; getting through Malaga city centre was in the lap of the gods. We had been driving for an hour and a half when we finally made it to the Granada road, and signposts kept coming up telling us the distance to Granada. Vinny did his best to distract Jack's attention but since they came up every kilometre it was only a matter of time before Jack spotted one. Granada 113 km.

'HOW FUCKING FAR!' screamed Jack.

'Calm down,' said Vinny. 'We're over the worst now and there's a lovely restaurant, part of a trout farm, not far ahead. We'll stop there and have a bite to eat.'

Sure enough, twenty minutes later we were pulling into the Rio Frio Trout Farm and Restaurant. We all baled out and had a stretch. In the foyer of the restaurant was a glass display cabinet and the centrepiece, for some obscure reason, was a suckling pig.

'That'll do me, I love a bit of suckling pig,' said Jack, who is very fond of his food.

The rest of us ordered trout, which arrived quite promptly, but the suckling pig took a while longer. If fact we had almost finished by the time Jack got served.

'How's the suckling pig, Jack?' I asked.

'Fucking long time since it did any suckling. Tastes like it's been on remand for a month or two,' was the reply.

His description of the pig gradually deteriorated the more he wrestled with it, until he eventually gave up the struggle. I called for the bill.

'What tip shall I leave?'

'Tell him to fucking close,' was Jack's suggestion.

Tommy, ably abetted by Patsy, began to wind up Jack, going into raptures about how good the trout had been, how the subtle blend of herbs had enhanced the flavour and so on. Personally I had no strong feeling one way or the other about the trout but I've always had a compulsion, when spotting a bandwagon, to jump on. I threw in my two bob's worth about how the roasted almonds had been a very pleasant touch. Jack said the pig was crap. Tommy pointed out that in the unlikely event that he visited a pig farm he wouldn't order trout, implying that that was more or less what Jack had done in reverse.

Vinny put a stop to the banter by announcing that we

were approaching the outskirts of Granada and would be at the Alhambra Palace in a few minutes. Jack said how much he was looking forward to it. I remember his exact words: 'Can't fucking wait.'

After only two or three wrong turns and after going around the town centre roundabout only twice, we found the road to the Alhambra and pulled into the car park at two minutes to five. The exact time is quite relevant, which is probably why I remember it.

'Lo siento, señores. Cerramos a las cinco. Pueden volver mañana.'

I was the only one of us that had even a smattering of Spanish so it was left to me to translate what the car-park attendant was saying. The gist of it was that he was sorry, they closed at five and he suggested that we come back the next day.

Fortunately Jack was torn between opening the door and winding down the window to get his hands on the man's throat, giving Vinny the chance to slip into reverse and back out of the entrance, a manoeuvre that undoubtedly saved the attendant's life.

Next to the car-park was a small parade of shops, one of which was an ice-cream parlour. Vinny pulled up next to it and we all baled out again. Beside the ice-cream parlour was a souvenir shop, and while they were ordering ice-creams I wandered in. I found a very nice pictorial guide to the Palace and bought it for Jack so he could at least see pictures of the sights he'd missed.

'Well, thanks very much but in case you don't know they sell those fucking things in Puerto Banus,' was as much gratitude as I got.

It was a very subdued drive back to the port. We didn't stop again at the Rio Frio.

Dipping My Toe in the Export Market

The Jocks had been back over twice in pretty rapid fashion and had built their order up to forty kilos a time. I had also made contact with a little firm from Manchester that was planning a fairly sophisticated piece of work and would be looking for fifty key any minute. I thought it was about time I chanced a small investment myself, but was riddled with indecision as to which mob to go with. The Jocks had a proven track record but they didn't seem to be doing anything any more elaborate with their transport than stuffing the gear behind the panels in the boot and crossing their fingers.

The Manchester people were going about the work in a much more professional manner. They had brought over a welder and he had fabricated a metal box that was welded under a Volkswagen pop-top. The brake, clutch and accelerator cables had been cut and re-routed through a conduit running over the box and the whole job had been under-sealed. The van was then driven over some dusty back roads to get the bottom suitably camouflaged. Of course I now know that it's very hard to think of a more conspicuous vehicle than a Volkswagen pop-top, as it's got hippy dope-smoker written all over it. Still, I didn't realise that at the time. The decision as to where to put my few quid was made for me. Forty key was every gram that would fit in the Jocks' car and, unsurprisingly, they wanted it all for themselves. So it was the Manchester crew.

Looking on the two deals as one week's work, I was in a healthy position. The commission on the ninety key came to

£4,500. The five key I was having on for myself cost me £3,500. If it got home safely and the lads sold it for me, I'd earn a total of eleven grand and if it didn't I'd still earn a grand. This sounded more like the profit margin I had assumed was in the game.

The Jocks were home, gear sold and back before the Manchester mob had even left. When their transport did leave, looking perfect and driven by two young women with two screaming kids to distract the Customs, it was captured before it even got to the ferry at Calais. I once read somewhere that when Napoleon was thinking of promoting a junior officer, he would gather all his generals about him and they'd mull over the candidate's qualifications. Did he come from a good family? Was he honest? Was he brave? Did he have a good wife? A good mistress? If all the ticks were in the right boxes, he would then ask the most important question: is he lucky? I decided this would probably be a good policy to adopt when selecting someone to take a bit of puff home.

Pop-tops aside, things had been going pretty well. In fact, my biggest problem was finding gear for the number of clients I was now attracting. Gordo didn't always have something he wanted to sell, and the only thing I had in my favour was the advantageous price I was paying him. I was a bit stumped. Then I met a bloke from Liverpool, Jack, who knew a Spanish gypsy in La Linea, José, who could always put his hands on a bit of gear. He took me down to meet him.

La Linea, being only nine miles across the Straits from Morocco, was awash with gear and the price was appreciably cheaper, as it was entitled to be given the inherent risks buying it there. Unfortunately La Linea's other cottage industry was smuggling cigarettes from Gibraltar, which meant that the police activity around the town was horrendous. On top of that, you had to run the gauntlet of the most dangerous hundred kilometres in Spain back to Fuengirola.

Watching the cigarette smugglers work was quite amusing. There could be fifteen or twenty Guardia Civil four-tracks parked shoulder to shoulder along the seafront for up to two days at a time. When they got fed up, or when they had earned enough in overtime and pulled away, the cigarette boats would arrive. I was never sure if they were called cigarette boats because of their cargo or because of the shape. In any case, they would pull up to the shore and start hurling cases of cigarettes to a gang of waiting teenagers, who'd grab as many as they could carry and scuttle back to the apartment blocks across the street. I never once saw anyone getting nicked.

Still, as I say, all this made the puff traffickers' job that much more difficult. Some people wouldn't take delivery in La Linea if the gear was free. Others took the view that they'd come to Spain fully intending to run the gauntlet back to the UK, so what difference did another sixty miles make? Another problem was that there was no comfy hotel room to sit and count the money and no taking the puff away to inspect at your leisure. They had to give me the dough, back their car up to a lock-up garage, open the boot, clump-clump, and see you later. Not the way you'd want to do a deal of any significant nature.

For bits and pieces it was fine and even on small parcels the profit wasn't bad. The price in La Linea was 135,000 pesetas a key, which, going back to the old 'a million is five grand' formula sounds like £675. In fact at the true rate of about two twenty pesetas to the pound it was less than £600. Retailing it at the normal £750 – and on little bits the customers wouldn't get it cheaper anywhere, if they could get it at all – meant a parcel as small as ten earned £1,500 so was worth the trip for me.

I had stopped worrying about the professionalism as regards how my clients were getting their purchases home. I didn't really care if it was just three or four people sticking three or four key each in their underpants and jumping on a plane, I tried to get something small on with everyone. A fair proportion of it got home and a fair proportion of those that got it home came back and weighed-in with my little corner.

Despite all the pitfalls, I really can't remember a major disaster occurring working down there. The quality was always fine, no rip-offs on either side and no-one was getting nicked. That is, except poor old José. The last time I went down there, his wife told me that the Old Bill had crashed into the garage one morning and nicked José and a couple of his pals. If not for that, I'd probably still be running down there regularly.

My spasmodic working hours and the influx of cash allowed me plenty of time to enjoy the port's constant social whirl. There was very rarely a quiet night.

Joe Parkinson had been in the bookmaking business in quite a big way back in Manchester, having a fair-sized chain of shops. I dare say I made no small contribution to his empire over the years. In his sixties he had retired, gone to live in Spain and got bored. For reasons best known to himself, he decided to open a snooker hall in Fuengirola. Spaniards don't play snooker at all, though they do play a bit of pool. Trying to get the Brits to come off the beach to play snooker when they can play to their hearts' content the other fifty weeks of the year at home was always going to be an uphill struggle.

The place was done out to a very high standard with little expense spared: ten full-sized tables and a few pool tables, a nice lounge bar, satellite TV, and a decent bit of grub. What more could you want? Customers, I suppose. They were doing absolutely no good. They had been open a few months when Joe decided to have a 'grand opening night' to try to put the place on the map. For the occasion he invited over the twice world champion, Alex Higgins.

Whether you like Alex or loathe him, and there are plenty in both camps, there's no denying the contribution he made to snooker and the influence he had on the money that is now in the game. When he won the world championships in 1972, the prize money was £400. When he won it again in 1982, the prize money was £40,000. The two big reasons for the increase were Higgins' charisma and the arrival of colour TV.

The first snooker programme ever was called *Pot Black*, which started when colour TV sets were still a rarity. One time the commentator made one of those bloomers that get replayed over and over again, something along the lines of, 'For the benefit of people watching in black and white, the brown ball is the one behind the green.' Nice to get that cleared up. Still, snooker was the perfect sport for colour TV: there were no worries about having to cancel for bad weather and the bonus was that the whole thing could be presented for the price of a bowl of soup.

Higgins arrived on the scene at the perfect time. His style of play earned him the name 'Hurricane' and his showmanship got the sport the publicity it needed. Joe hoped he could do the same for his little enterprise. We got a phone call from Joe saying Higgins was coming over. He asked if he could stay on the boat and if we would make sure he turned up on the night. This last request was repeated on a daily basis for the week he was with us.

As I recall, Alex only went out twice that week: once for three days and once for four. He started in Sinatra's and gradually worked his way around the port getting himself barred from places. He could be a terrible nuisance in drink.

On the opening night, Vinny dragged him out of bed at six in the evening and he pulled on a pair of jeans, knee-high cowboy boots and a V-necked sweater. Vinny asked him where his dinner-suit was, knowing a lot of people would want photos with him, but he replied that he had been paid already so they'd just have to take him as he was. There was plenty of local press in attendance and Higgins played about a dozen exhibition frames. I played him myself. Then he did a routine of trick shots and that was about it. The publicity did give the place a shot in the arm for a while, though.

Joe then came up with another idea. Spain had never had an official champion, so Joe sponsored a tournament and called it the Spanish Open. It was won by his barman, Pepe, who thereby qualified for the world championships the following year at Sheffield. This wasn't the start of an illustrious career. The last time I saw Pepe he was driving a taxi in Fuengirola. The snooker hall is now a car-park.

Having a snooker world champ, numerous football players, a few stars of the silver screen and several celebrity bank robbers on the boat gave us a certain social standing, but our next guests put us on a new level altogether. There had been an after-hours drinker in the Whalley Range area of Manchester that was officially called the Show Biz Hotel, but was known to everyone as 'Phyllis's'. I dare say in the days of the cabaret clubs and theatre clubs, there was probably a place on the lines of Phyllis's in most provincial towns, though I doubt there was any as good. It was a place that travelling entertainers – singers, dancers, comedians and actors – could call home from home. Phyllis's always reminded me of my grandmother's parlour. It had leather settees with antimacassars, bowls of fruit and flowers on crocheted doilies and old framed photos on the walls. I'm not sure there was a potted aspidistra but there might well have been. The bar opened at one thirty in the morning, as the club turns were finishing work and wanting a drink. Most of the clientele were people who worked unsocial hours in clubs and casinos, and a few cab drivers. The rest were mostly night people.

Phyllis's son was Phil Lynott of Thin Lizzy fame, probably rivalled only by U2 as Ireland's greatest ever rock band. Much of the inspiration for Phil's songs came from nights in the bar. There had been a bank robbery in Ilkeston, Derbyshire, and when the unjustly accused defendants – or lucky bastards, depending on your point of view – were acquitted, they held the post-trial celebrations in Phyllis's. The result was 'The Boys Are Back in Town'.

Another Thin Lizzy track, 'Johnny the Fox Meets Jimmy the Weed', refers to a friend of mine Jimmy 'The Weed' Donnelly, a very well-known character in Manchester. 'Waiting for an Alibi' was inspired by Joe Leach, who had an amazing ability to fabricate an excuse for a delinquent husband to give to his irate wife to explain his thirty-six hour absence. This ability probably sprang from the years of experience Joe had with excuses to his own wife, Pam, who wasn't the sort of girl you'd want to go home to with less than a watertight alibi. You'll now have an idea of who made up the balance of the customers.

Phil Lynott came to stay with us on the boat for a month, bringing with him his pal David Coverdale from the band Whitesnake. Rock music wasn't really my thing – I'm more a Motown fan – but apparently rock bands don't get a lot bigger than Whitesnake. Their arrival caused quite a stir in the port. Phil had taken to wearing a full-length black cape which gave him a bit of a look of Count Dracula. Not what I'd have chosen myself for September in southern Spain, but what's the point of being an international rock star if you can't be a little extrovert?

I took full advantage of our enhanced social status. My enthusiasm for any particular watering hole was in direct proportion to the likelihood of the proprietor showing his appreciation in a practical way. One publican that fell firmly into the right category was Peter Tilleni. Peter had owned night clubs in London's West End for years, the best known being probably the Latin Quarter, and had recently opened the Ra-Ra Club across the road from the port on the ground floor of the Andalucia Plaza Hotel. There was not much in the way of discos back then around the port, live music was still the thing, but the Ra-Ra was the place to be late at night. I took the lads there. It was packed, and Peter, the ever genial host, made sure the booze was flowing. I left the lads in the company of four stunning black girls.

The next day when I walked towards the boat, there was a larger crowd of rubber-neckers than usual and I soon saw why. Phil and Dave and the four girls from the previous night were all having a drink on the sun deck. Phil was wearing his black cape and the girls were wearing a smile.

It turned out that the girls were Wonderlove, Stevie Wonder's backing group, and would be playing the Marbella football stadium on the Saturday night. Naturally, we all had to go. The girls got us the best seats and Phil and Dave got invites to the after-show party at the Marbella Club. I tried to bluff my way in but so did twenty thousand or so others, so I had no success.

Phil was quite genuinely thrilled the next day when he came to the boat.

'I actually got to meet Stevie Wonder,' he gushed.

'On the other hand, Stevie Wonder got to meet you,' I told him.

As any fans of rock music know, Phil would be dead the following Christmas, another victim of the rock-and-roll culture. His death was a very sad loss for Irish music and a tragedy for Phyllis.

The End of the Party

Earlier on I mentioned the Stalker Inquiry and it deserves a bit more explanation, as another pal of ours, Kevin Taylor, got himself caught up in the crossfire and was ruined as a result. It's also where Captain Bill comes back into the story.

John Stalker was the Deputy Chief Constable of Greater Manchester Police and was appointed to head an inquiry into allegations that the Royal Ulster Constabulary had deliberately shot dead suspected Republican terrorists – or freedom fighters, depending on your point of view – and then covered up their actions. The expectation was that Stalker would pop over, find that everything was hunky-dory, rubber stamp the reports and come home. Unfortunately he was a bit too straight for his own good and found several incidents where the explanations appeared to be at odds with the known facts. He dug his heels in.

One incident in particular got his back up. Two young men entered a barn where illicit arms were being stored and were shot by the security forces; one died and the other was wounded. Stalker had his doubts about the reported chain of events and learned that the barn was under MI5 surveillance and an audio tape of the shooting was in existence. He demanded to hear it. He was refused. Stalker insisted but got no further.

At about the same time, a strange thing happened. An unreliable petty criminal and part-time snitch starting making claims to his police handlers in Manchester that Stalker was 'bent' and had been consorting with known villains. What a coincidence! A secret inquiry was launched into Stalker by his own force, sanctioned at the highest Government level. Stalker at first knew nothing of this and carried on with his work.

This is where Kevin Taylor entered the picture. Kevin was a Manchester businessman and chairman of the Manchester Conservative Association and his daughter went to the same school as Stalker's daughter. Stalker and Kevin came into contact through events like parent–teacher meetings and school activities. Having made a few quid, Kevin bought a yacht, the *Diogenes*, and Stalker and his wife spent a few days on board during a trip to Florida. Kevin also bought and refurbished an old mill-house in Summerseat near Bury and held a lavish house-warming party. The guest list included local politicians, several of the cast of *Coronation Street*, business associates and John Stalker.

In earlier times, one of Kevin's business interests was a secondhand car dealership called Vanland on Great Ancoats Street, an area of Manchester with wall-to-wall car dealerships. While I wouldn't go as far as to say most secondhand car dealers are retired armed robbers, I would say that a lot of successful retired armed robbers are car dealers. The rest are usually publicans or scrap metal merchants. Kevin invited some of these business neighbours to the same house party, one of whom was Jimmy the Weed. I should add that there was a pretty widespread rumour at the time that a firm of Manchester villains had a senior police officer on the payroll.

This rather tenuous connection of Stalker via Kevin to the party guests was enough to lead to Stalker's suspension and his removal from the Northern Ireland inquiry, pending investigation into the possibility that he had committed the disciplinary charge of 'discreditable conduct' for consorting with known criminals. To substantiate the suspicions against

Stalker – and in truth they were little more than suspicions, subsequently rejected – a thorough investigation of Kevin was instigated. This ultimately led to Kevin being charged with having defrauded the Co-op Bank by over-valuing assets used as security for loans. The bank's corporate business manager was asked to testify against Kevin but refused. He said as far as the bank was concerned, Kevin had always honoured his commitments and was in fact a valued client. The manager was then arrested and charged as a co-conspirator.

When you're in the midst of lengthy criminal proceedings, your bank accounts have been frozen and your reputation in the local business community is in tatters, probably the last thing you need is a hundred grand's worth of ocean-going yacht sitting in Puerto Banus, costing you five or six hundred quid a month in maintenance and mooring fees. Actually no, that's probably the second last thing you need. The very last thing you need is that same boat sailing up the Manchester Ship Canal carrying a couple of tons of puff.

Captain Bill had approached Kevin knowing that the *Diogenes* was very much for sale. He told Kevin that he had a client who was keen to buy it and wanted to take it on sea trials. Bill said this was standard procedure in the purchase of a boat and that he would personally skipper it for the trials. What he didn't tell Kevin was that the first port of call on these trials would be Larache on Morocco's Atlantic coast, where they would take on ballast in the form of the two tons of puff.

By the time the boat and its illicit cargo were halfway across the Bay of Biscay, Kevin, still in Manchester and having heard nothing from Bill, assumed the boat-buying deal had come to nothing. Perhaps the boat didn't suit the buyer's requirements and was safely back in its berth in Banus. Having other things to worry about, he put the matter out of his mind.

In the end the yacht never did sail up the Manchester Ship

Canal. The cargo, worth upwards of four million quid, was successfully unloaded onto the Cornish coast and nobody needed to be any the wiser. Except for one additional development.

A few months later, a friend sent me a video of a very thinly disguised Captain Bill being interviewed by Trevor McDonald on Granada TV and telling the whole story from start to finish. The reason for these disclosures is a mystery to me to this day. Bearing in mind that this was the period between Kevin's arrest and his trial, conspiracy theorists might be inclined to think that these disclosures were another attempt to blacken Kevin's name and thereby Stalker's. The fact that, despite his admissions, Bill was never charged with anything gives some weight to such a theory.

Kevin's trial got off to a bit of a rocky start for the prosecution. The first witness, a police officer, testified that Kevin had never been a suspected drug dealer. The defence found that strange because the warrants to examine his bank accounts were obtained on the basis that he was a suspected drug dealer. Also, he was arrested and charged by the Drugs Intelligence Unit, a new unit that in its eighteen months of existence had arrested no-one but Kevin. Someone was obviously telling porkies.

Another witness was called to testify as to the value of one of the assets alleged to be overvalued. The asset was a gravel pit in Cheshire and the expert witness gave the cubic capacity of the pit, the amount of gravel that could be removed and the current market value of gravel. The resultant figure was much less than Kevin had borrowed against it. So, QED? Well, not quite.

The defence asked the witness what would be left after the gravel was removed. He had a bit of a think and replied, 'A big hole in the ground.' He was asked what a big hole in the ground would be worth if planning permission had been obtained for a refuse landfill site. He admitted that pricing holes in the ground wasn't really his area of expertise – I would have thought that was precisely his area of expertise – but that he would imagine an awful lot of money. The relevant permissions were put into evidence, proving the site was worth three or four times the amount secured.

The trial went on in much the same vein until eventually the ref had to step in to stop further punishment. The jury was directed to return a verdict of not guilty on all counts.

Kevin would eventually take action against James Anderton, the Chief Constable of Greater Manchester, and against Manchester Police Authority for malicious prosecution. The case was heard a few years later at Liverpool Crown Court. Kevin was awarded two or three quid short of £1 million in compensation. Despite the award, which Kevin always claimed was only a fraction of the amount he was on the verge of making before his troubles began, he was never the same man and died shortly later.

John Sampson, the Chief Constable of West Yorkshire Police, took over both the Stalker Inquiry and the inquiry into Stalker – obviously no-one spotted any conflict of interest there. The subsequent Sampson Report found no irregularities in the conduct of the Northern Ireland security forces.

Stalker was eventually cleared of any wrongdoing and returned to duty, but shortly afterwards took early retirement. The last time I saw him was on TV, appearing in an advert for remote-control garage doors. One line in the advert says, 'And there's nothing worse than coming home on a rainy night and your garage doors won't open.'

Really? I can think of a few things a fucking sight worse.

A year or two later, I got a phone call from Captain Bill, who, for some bizarre reason for an American boat skipper, was working as a postman in Oldham. He said he was thinking of coming back to Spain and would there be a little work for him.

'I think you've got the wrong number,' was my answer.

One of the things I loved about Silks was the table-hopping. On a good night you could sometimes table-hop all the way to the door and hope that the person who hopped into your seat wound up with the bill.

I was having a meal with Jack Trickett one night when a bloke a couple of tables away sent a drink over. We shouted, 'Cheers,' and I asked Jack who he was.

'Not a clue,' said Jack, 'but I'm going for a piss, see if you can find out.'

I hopped over and introduced myself, saying that Jack had neglected to tell me his name. The man's name was Jimmy Quill and he was an ex-publican from London. He had owned the infamous Blind Beggar pub in the East End, the scene of George Cornell's murder by Ronnie Kray, one of the offences that led to the Krays' life sentences. He was currently in the boxing game and that was how he knew Jack.

With his memory refreshed, Jack invited Jimmy over to our table after the meal and the subject of conversation naturally enough was boxing. Jimmy was in the process of promoting a proposed heavyweight title fight between Funso Banjo and Proud Kilimanjaro. You couldn't make it up, could you? Jack can, and frequently does, speak for hours on the subject of boxing, so partly because I was out of my depth and partly to save Jimmy a merciless ear-bashing, when Jimmy mentioned that his main business these days was property development, I jumped in. Just by way of contributing to the conversation, I mentioned a property I had in Manchester.

I had worked, and I use the term in its loosest possible context, on and off for a wealthy Iraqi called Hassan back in Manchester. My actual job description would be difficult to pin down but fell somewhere between personal assistant and errand boy, with a little chauffeuring thrown in. Hassan had bought a new Rolls-Royce but wasn't that keen on driving and I liked making myself a big shot, so the arrangement suited us both.

Hassan's main earner was export to the Middle East but his hobbies were nightclubs, owning them, and poker, playing it. He was also into property in quite a big way. One of the properties he owned was an eighteenth century, Grade II listed building. Apparently the ownership of a listed building carries with it certain obligations, one of which is keeping it in good repair. This place was practically derelict and Hassan was getting threatening noises from people like the Historic Buildings Council saying if he didn't put it in order they would, and would send him the bill. Even the Historic Buildings Council can't get blood from a stone, so Hassan had the building put in my name. In partnership with a pal of mine, Tommy, we got a grant from Manchester Corporation of £43,000 to convert the house into four flats. The work was still in progress when I had abandoned ship and moved to Spain, but was now very near completion and the place was going up for sale.

Jimmy said that, by coincidence, he would be in Manchester in two or three weeks and would have a look at it. I gave him the address and a couple of phone numbers. The talk returned to boxing and I thought no more about it until, three weeks later, I got a call from Hassan. He wanted to know why I hadn't told him 'my pal' Jimmy wanted to buy the house. He had bid £125,000 and what did I think? I thought it sounded wonderful. By the time Hassan got his original outlay back, Tommy got back whatever he'd put in over and above the grant and we cut up the difference three ways, I would finish up with about thirty grand.

For all my ducking and diving over the previous eighteen months, I hadn't accumulated much money. I had about six grand under the mattress, a halfway decent car and a bit of jewellery but not much else. The credit card game was finished. Shops and restaurants were now getting computer terminals installed that gave them instant validation of the cards, so I was forced to spend cash. One pal of mine who owned a clothing shop took me in to show me the new terminal. I felt like the man who owned the gas-mantle factory must have felt the day Thomas Edison displayed his new invention, the light bulb.

Any bits of business I had been doing stemmed from Fuengirola. The Bubble had sailed to the Greek Isles for a couple of weeks three month earlier and hadn't been heard from since. Apart from a few trips to La Linea, I had done very little. Vinny and Steve were thinking of heading home to face the music, as the murk of the Stalker Affair was beginning to clear and they felt they would no longer be used as a political football in the case. An offer had been made for the boat and when that went, much of my social standing would go with it.

I had enjoyed every moment of my time in Banus. The memories will stay with me forever but I had to be realistic and accept that maybe it was time for a move. There was a bar for sale in Fuengirola and I began to think about making an offer.

PART TWO

FUENGIROLA 1985-90

Jim Swords and the Good Times Bar

Having been managing on a shoestring for two years, or in fact all my life, I was reluctant to invest every shilling of my windfall in one project. Ideally I wanted to find a partner and I had just the man in mind. Jim Swords had had a lengthy career as a professional boxer and though, by his own admission, he wasn't world class he did fight many of the top British and European middleweights of the late sixties and early seventies. Had he been fighting them outside the ring, his record would probably have been a hundred per cent. Jim was unbeatable 'on the cobbles'.

Jim had a tough upbringing in the back streets of Ancoats, the old industrial heart of Manchester, and when he first turned pro he couldn't believe how easy this boxing lark was: just get in the ring, knock someone out and pick up a few quid. Of course, as he moved up the ranking things started to get a little more difficult and he was meeting people that were much harder to hit. He described it as like being pecked to death by a duck. But every fight was a war and they were always sell-outs.

His last pro fight, in Johannesburg against Pierre Fareed, was stopped when Jim suffered cut eyes, a problem that had haunted him all his career. Jim was a little aggrieved, thinking the ref could well have given him another round or two so, when a large Afrikaans gentleman came ringside shouting abuse to the effect that Jim was lucky they stopped it and he would have got murdered, things got a bit heated. Jim vaulted out of the ring and, with one well-delivered right hook, knocked the Afrikaans spark out. Joe, Jim's brother and second, asked why he hadn't done that to Fareed, for which he would have been paid something half reasonable. I suppose it goes back to having to be in with someone you can hit.

Outside his boxing career, Jim was heavily involved in the fruit and veg game, having invested in several barrows, and ran much of the street trading in the city centre. When he wasn't doing all that he was buying and selling cars. If you work earning money sixteen hours a day and sleep the other eight you're not left with much time to spend it. Not surprisingly, he had accumulated a fair tank.

Having worked very hard for his dough, he didn't part with it easily. The stories of Jim's carefulness with money are legion but the one I like best is when his daughter, Jenny, was about eight. She lost a tooth and put it under her pillow for the tooth fairy.

'Dad, the tooth fairy never left me my half-crown,' were her first words the next day.

'I know. She said to tell you she had no change,' explained Jimmy.

Another time we were having a meal in Puerto Banus with my Iraqi pal Hassan, who had paid the bill the previous evening. As we finished the meal, Hassan called for the bill again. Jimmy's wife, Lynne, never shy of voicing her opinion, gave Jimmy a kick under the table.

'Sssh,' whispered Jimmy.

'Never mind "Sssh",' said Lynne. 'He paid last night. We're not paupers, you pay tonight.'

'Look,' lectured Jimmy. 'You don't understand. He loves taking people out for meals and I hate spending money. We're both happy so mind your own fucking business.'

At one time, Jim owned a small corner shop which Lynne

ran. One of the products they sold was Burton's biscuits and the manufacturers came up with a promotion whereby a ten-shilling voucher to be used at Burtons the Tailors was included in every carton. Over the following months, Jim accumulated a couple of hundred of them and when holiday time came around he decided to treat himself to some new clobber. He marched in and ordered half a dozen sports shirts, a couple of pairs of slacks and some socks and underwear.

'That'll be seventy-five pounds fifty,' said the salesman, totting up the bill.

'Fine. There you go mate. Take it out of that,' said Jim, handing him the wad.

The salesman looked bemused.

'Well? They're alright aren't they?' demanded Jim.

'I'm sure they are, sir,' replied the salesman. 'But you're in John Collier's.'

Needless to say, the order was cancelled.

If Jim thought the bar was worth a go that was good enough for me. There was one small fly in the ointment with having Jim as a partner. One of his sidelines was the recovery of unrecoverable debts; his powers of persuasion and his negotiating skills were nothing short of amazing. He didn't work cheap, assuming that before anyone approached him for help they had already exhausted every other possible avenue. He worked on the principle that it had to be accepted that half a loaf was better than no bread.

An example of Jim's negotiating skills: one day Jack Trickett was in his hotel, the Acton Court, when three or four gentlemen from the travelling community arrived at the door. They said that they noticed when passing that Jack had a few potholes in his driveway and by chance they had a bit of stuff on the wagon that would only go to waste. Would Jack like them to fill in the potholes?

'How much will it cost?' Jack asked.

'Just a few shillings,' said the head pikey, so Jack told them to go ahead.

An hour later he looked out the window to see the driveway had been tarmac-ed from kerbside to front door.

'That'll be two grand, sir,' Jack was told.

Nimble as ever, Jack explained – lying through his teeth – that he was only the manager.

'I'll have to phone the boss,' he said and rang Jimmy, who arrived post haste accompanied by two or three of the lads.

No-one will ever know the full content of the discussion that followed but suffice to say the head pikey agreed to settle for two hundred quid and remain friends. The pikeys left, Jack made the lads a cup of tea and after about twenty minutes they left too.

No sooner had they gone than Jack looked out the window to see the head pikey marching back up the driveway. More than a little uneasy, Jack went out to confront him.

'I've just cum back, soir, t'tell yer how fecking sorry I am for yer, having to work fer a bastard like that Jimmy Swords,' and with that he turned on his heel and left, never to be seen by Jack again.

So, Jim's negotiating skills established, back to the ointment fly. Jim has very strict criteria as to what debts he'll get involved with. The debtor must have the money, as even Jim can't get blood from a stone, and the debt must be genuine, nothing to do with the likes of gambling or, and here's the rub, anything to do with drugs.

Years earlier Jim had been approached by a firm from Liverpool who were going into the puff business and wanted to use Jim's name to ensure prompt payment. In return Jim would receive a healthy commission. He refused on principle. He once told me, without any sense of regret, that had he decided to go with them he would probably own Spain today, instead of a few apartments scattered along the coast.

So, if he didn't get involved when he could have done with the money, he certainly couldn't get to know about any of my current ducking and diving. Fortunately, due to all his years in the fruit and veg game, he was always an early riser and was often in bed before dark. My extra-curricular activities would have to be confined to after the nine o'clock watershed.

I managed to do a remarkably good deal with Jim. He would put up half the money and draw a small wage, about what he'd get leaving the money in the bank, and be half in to any profit when the place was sold. Partner in place, I went off to make a bid. It was accepted but buying the place didn't turn out to be the straightforward deal I had anticipated.

Ricardo, the South American chap who was selling me the place, didn't actually own it. The real owner was an eighty-odd-year-old Spaniard who lived in Barcelona. His plan was to fly down, pick up his readies and fly back but Iberia Airlines were being very uncooperative and kept going on strike. Also, Ricardo didn't want the Spaniard to know the true price I was paying, so covert plans had to be made with a large brown envelope.

Due to the strike, several signing dates had to be aborted. Then one night Ricardo went home a little the worse for wear. He remembered to switch off the water for the coffee machine but neglected to switch off the power. He was awoken in the small hours by the Old Bill informing him that smoke was pouring out from under his shutters. The damage was only cosmetic and I got a new paint job, which was needed anyway, and a new coffee machine but it did mean another delay.

We finally set a date to sign on the 18th of December and hold our opening night on the 19th. The food was all arranged, curries and paella, the stock was bought and everyone invited. Then Iberia took a hand again. I think Ricardo sensed I was on the point of telling him where to stick his bar because in the end he just gave me the keys and said we'd sign when the old man got there, which he eventually did the following Monday.

The opening night was a great success but then again if you're not busy on opening night you must be doing something wrong. Opening nights are only rivalled on the busy barometer by closing nights. It being Christmas week, a lot of the local expats had friends and family over from the UK and the place was packed.

The Sunday was nearly as good, with a few people showing their faces who couldn't make the opening. Ronnie Knight, who owned The Mumtaz Indian restaurant next door – hence the curries – came in, bringing with him Mad Frankie Fraser. Frankie had just got home after serving twenty-odd years in prison. Two Manchester club owners, Owen Radcliffe and Paddy McGrath, both of whom I had worked for in the past, had opened a place in South London called Mr Smith's. Being pally with the well-known Richardson brothers, they asked them for some help with security and they had sent along Frankie, their main heavy. There was a clash with another gang, shots were fired, several people were badly hurt and a man named Dickie Hart wound up dead. Frankie finished up with five years for affray.

Frankie made it clear from day one he was having nothing to do with prison discipline. One particular bone of contention was Frankie's slippers, which he found very comfortable but the screws didn't think were suitable attire outside the cell. This difference of opinion led to more than one row. He would be charged with everything from assault to inciting a mutiny and that's why it took him so long to get home.

'Our paths crossed once, you know,' I told him. 'Strangeways, seventy-two.'

'You weren't a screw, were you?' he asked, looking appalled.

'No, no. I was doing eighteen months at the time,' I assured him.

Whilst we were discussing the pros and cons of various penal institutions, a bit of a scuffle broke out, Irish Wally v Deptford Dennis if memory serves. It was only minor, some pushing and shoving, a couple of broken glasses and soon resolved. I went back to Frankie and apologised for the disturbance.

'Don't worry, son. I've seen worse than that in my time.'

A master of understatement, old Frankie. Still, nice to get our first fight out of the way.

Carry on Bullfighting

Having had a wonderful couple of weeks over the Christmas, by the middle of January things were getting a bit quiet. We are talking of a village where every second doorway is a bar and, although I had plenty of help from the locals, so did a number of the other bars. With hindsight, after about ten attempts at running a bar without once making one pay, I've decided that if I ever meet a successful publican of one of these small, neighbourhood bars I'm going to have him or her stuffed and put in a glass case in the local Chamber of Commerce. No, we were going to have to do something to put ourselves on the map.

Still, what's the point of having a resourceful chap like Jim Swords for a partner if he can't come up with something novel? Actually, I'm not sure novel accurately describes the idea Jim came up with. Bizarre? Insane? You be the judge.

There is, and I kid you not, a bullfighter who lives in Eccles, just outside Manchester, called Frank Evans. Or as he's known in Spain, Francis 'El Ingles' Evans-Kelly. Suppose we were to promote a bullfight, a sort of challenge match, England versus Spain. That would generate a bit of notoriety, wouldn't it? Well, I should think so!

The first thing we needed was a venue. Frank Evans went and negotiated with the owners of Fuengirola bullring and got us a deal. It seats about ten thousand and is bang in the middle of the Costa del Sol. Perfect.

Next, obviously, some bulls. Frank went off to Seville, the

world capital, apparently, of bull breeding. Bulls are graded by age and weight and above a certain weight can only be fought with the assistance of a picador, the chap on horseback with a thing like a spear. Horses and people with spears are extremely expensive, so Frank was given strict instructions to make sure we wouldn't need any. Being the supreme egotist he is, Frank bought the biggest, fattest, oldest bull that could possibly fall under the limits. The problems this brought about, we'll come too imminently.

We were going to need some publicity if we were going to sell some tickets. I had a pal, Tony Allan, who had the Tall Man pub around the corner. Tony was a mad bullfight fan and was only too pleased to put up a poster and let all his fellow aficionados know of the forthcoming event. Several other bars were inveigled into putting posters up and we got Frank dressed in his suit of lights to go around and get a few smudges done. Everything in hand and all going to plan.

Then we had a stroke of luck. This was the summer of 1986 and the preparations for Sport Aid were in full swing. All sorts of sporting events were planned and donations were to be sent to feed the starving of Africa. Frank got hold of the organisers and offered a percentage of the profits to the cause. He was told they didn't want any of his dirty bullfighting money.

In the meantime, one sponsored event was Myra Hindley, the moors murderess, running around the exercise yard at Cookham Wood prison, whose money was being accepted. Nigel Bowden of the *Sun* got hold of the story and I suppose it was a quiet week news-wise, because a few days later there was a three-page spread in the *Sun*. They even included one of those phone-in polls asking the punters to give their opinion of the rights and wrongs of it all. Another sportswriter who happened to be a bullfight fan gave us a mention on the front page of the *Daily Telegraph*. All in all it must have been the best publicised bullfight, certainly as far as the Brit contingent were concerned, in history. Couldn't miss now, could we?

The problem with the dimensions of the bulls almost brought the whole thing to a halt. I don't know what the weight and age limits are but, for example, say the weight limit was 500 kilos, ours weighed 499 and a bit – if they skipped breakfast on the morning of the weigh-in. Say the age limit was four years, then these were only three but it was their birthday the day after the fight. That's how close we're talking. Frank's Spanish opponent took one look and said no fucking way, José, or words to that effect. He said he was going nowhere near them without one of those chaps with the horse and spear. We were at something of an impasse. Paying a picador was out of the question. Frank threatened to sue since the Spaniard had signed a contract, but he wouldn't budge. Even Jimmy's powers of persuasion fell on deaf ears; the Spaniard seemed more frightened of the bulls than of Jimmy.

Finally the Spaniard came up with a compromise. He'd fight them if we shaved them. Shaving a bull's horns is a very delicate and specialised job. It's also illegal. A day or two before the fight, the bull's horns are shaved down by about an inch. This disorientates the bull, who still thinks his horns are an inch longer than they are. This could be a vital inch when the bull's intention is to ram his horns into your gonads or up your arse.

Frank phoned the breeder to see if he would come and do it but had no luck. He said had we made it a condition when we bought them, he might well have considered it, but as things stood they were now our bulls and we'd have to make our own arrangements.

Patience not being a virtue that Jimmy is known for, he said, 'Fuck it, I'll do it myself. How difficult can it be?'

The answer to that question proved to be 'difficult in the

extreme'. For the benefit of anyone who has never seen a Spanish fighting bull at close quarters, I'll do my best to describe one. If you can imagine a half-ton, armed Rottweiler, you're getting quite close. Not the sort of thing to be trifled with.

With a fair amount of effort, about six of us managed to get a rope around one of their necks and pull its head through the stable window. Jimmy set to work with a hacksaw, which isn't the ideal implement for the task. The bull was quite vocal in his protests and the look in its eye left little doubt as to what would happen to Jimmy if the bull ever got his hooves on him. After a couple of minutes hacking, the tip of the bull's left horn resembled the bottom of a Coca-Cola bottle.

All the noise had attracted the attention of the bullring owner, who soon arrived on the scene.

'What are you doing?' he screamed, 'We're all going to get nicked. On top of that, you've ruined a good bull.'

'Don't worry,' Jim said. 'I'll soon sharpen it up a bit if anyone has a file handy.'

No-one had.

Jim was forced to admit that he wasn't qualified for the job in hand and we'd have to leave well enough alone. Even the Spanish matador reluctantly accepted the fact that the bulls weren't getting shaved and he agreed to fight them anyway. He could have saved us a lot of trouble if he'd done that in the first place.

As things worked out, despite all the publicity, attendances were dismal. Frank reckoned we needed about two thousand to break even but less than a thousand turned up and how many of them actually paid is anyone's guess. The post-fight board meeting was quite a sombre affair. Frankie had the receipts and the few quid for the dead bulls which had been bought by a local butcher. He also had a lengthy list of exes.

The money was heaped up on an upturned beer barrel we were using for a desk. Jimmy swooped across and gathered up anything foldable leaving a smattering of shrapnel behind.

'That's about what I put in, so I'm level on the deal,' he declared.

'What am I supposed to tell my partner back in Eccles?' Frank asked. 'He put in the same amount as you.'

'Tell him he should have been over here, looking after his money like I was,' suggested Jimmy.

As far as the whole business of putting the bar on the map was concerned, I think we can claim some small degree of success. For months afterwards, people would walk past and say, 'Oh, look, that's that bar owned by those nutters who put on a bullfight.'

Friends Old and New

My priority when I bought the bar was to find some staff, little realising that these little bars can't support employees, especially if you try to do it all nice and legal, paying the social security contributions and stuff like that. The general idea is that the person who buys the bar works behind the bar, but never having been a big worker that thought never entered my head.

At the time I had a Spanish girlfriend, Maribel, whose cousin, Juan, was an unemployed waiter. He got the night shift. A pal of mine owned a disco in Fuengirola and, chatting to his barmaid one night, I mentioned I was opening a bar and would need staff. She had a pal, Annie, who had just arrived from Cordoba and was looking for work. Annie got the day shift. Problem solved; or at least it was until it came time to pay them.

It soon became apparent that I couldn't afford them but having given them contracts, letting them go was a problem. Spanish workers, particularly in the south, had historically had a rough time of it. When the first socialist government got into power, sweeping changes were made to workers' rights. That was all very well if you were a Spanish worker but not so handy if you were trying to make a small bar pay. It was all a bit one-sided. The employer was obliged to fulfil the contract for its duration but, should the employee get a more favourable offer, he could pack up and leave you in the lurch and there was little you could do about it.

Come what may, at least one of them was going to have to go. At the time Neil and Micky, they of the Hotel Montariq saga, had taken over the Algarrobo Country Club. Among other things they were putting on fairly elaborate and highly popular Sunday lunches. They would put on bands, singers, comedians, a couple of times even a hypnotist. The star of the show was usually Polly Perkins, who later became famous as Trish Valentine in the soap *El Dorado*, which was filmed locally and is best remembered for its piss-poor acting and appalling scripts. Polly was the only one who came across with any degree of credibility, but then again if you base a character on a local personality and then get that personality to play the part, credibility is almost a given. Anyway, with all this going on they were looking for staff and we managed to come to a sort of free-contract arrangement and off went Juan. By re-juggling the opening hours, Annie and I could manage. This new arrangement worked quite well because, a year the following June, Maribel having got the elbow, Annie and I got married.

One new friendship that sprang up was to prove invaluable. Suntan Tony was a yacht skipper and he was in the business. I was destined to work with him for the next ten years. Suntan's operation was a lot more sophisticated than The Bubble's; none of that crashing onto beaches in the middle of the night, slinging puff into jeeps and hoping for the best. Suntan's vehicle of choice was the cabin-cruiser type of thing, with plenty of room to make a stash where the gear would be fairly safe from anything but the most rigorous of inspections. There is a multitude of small marinas between Gibraltar and Almeria where an illicit cargo can be unloaded if a little care is taken. Suntan was very successful and his percentage of the load was available for sale at an even more advantageous price than The Bubble's had been, or even the gear from old José in La Linea.

Another acquaintanceship was to prove less rewarding and would eventually lead to my first and last, and thankfully very brief, experience of Malaga prison. The man's name might have been, but probably wasn't, Norman Shaw and he was an exception in that he appeared in the bar without any sort of introduction. Normally when a new face arrived on the scene, someone would say this is my pal so-and-so from such-and-such a place, thereby establishing the person's bona fides. Not so with Norman, who was quite reserved and certainly not forthcoming about his pedigree. He was kept pretty much at arm's length at first but he never asked any awkward questions and before long was accepted as a regular. He seemed to have plenty of money and wasn't shy about buying a drink, which suited some of my less affluent clientele.

One day he came to me with a proposition. The story went that he had been in the farming game and was in the process of selling some land but he was in the midst of a very messy divorce. If the wife got wind of the money she'd want half of whatever was left after the tax man got his teeth into it. He wanted to know if he could give me the cheque, which was for £180,000, to cash for him, keeping five grand for my trouble. I asked him to give me twenty-four hours to think about it.

On the face of it this seemed a very low-risk deal. In fact, any risk there was appeared to be on Norman's side but it did ring a bell with a new scam I'd just heard about. A pal of mine, Geoff Lapidus, known to everyone as 'The Poodle' because of his bushy hair, had just arrived from Manchester and told me about it. The Poodle came from a very wealthy Jewish family – his uncle was the Parisian designer Ted Lapidus and his parents owned a very profitable clothing company called Raincheetah. Geoff was doing his utmost to send the entire dynasty into destitution with his gambling and was always desperate for money.

He had met a Londoner who had a pal who owned an industrial cleaners, which gave him access to the office building during the night. If he could get his hands on the company chequebook and any documentation containing the relevant signatures, a cheque could be removed from the rear of the book and deposited in a pre-prepared, hooky bank account. The Poodle had been asked to present one but didn't have the patience for all that nonsense with hooky bank accounts – he knew of a good thing running at Royal Ascot the following week and couldn't get his hands on the money quick enough. He filled out the cheque to himself and put it through his own account. The cheque was paid and The Poodle drew the dough, retaining his percentage. Needless to say, a few days later the Old Bill were kicking down the parents' front door, wanting to know the whereabouts of their prodigal son. Hence Geoff's arrival on the coast.

I made up my mind to confront Norman.

'Look, mate,' I said. 'I've heard all about the crooked company cheque scam going on back home. If this cheque is part of a similar scam, I have no objections in principle but I'll certainly be wanting more than five grand.'

'On my mother's life it is all totally above board,' he swore. He even showed me a passport in the name Norman Shaw, which of course meant absolutely nothing since if the cheque was crooked then so was the passport.

I decided to go ahead, thinking that in any case my situation was very different to The Poodle's in as much as this cheque was already made out to Norman. He would endorse the back and I would present it as a third party cheque, therefore doing nothing illegal if it did turn out to be hooky.

I called in at the bank several times to enquire as casually as possible if the funds had arrived but given the antiquated

Spanish banking system it was always going to take a while. After about three weeks, the bank manager told me that yes, the money was currently in Malaga but wouldn't be in my account until the next day, as today was a fiesta in Malaga.

'Okay,' I said. 'Can I arrange to withdraw fifty grand in readies and a bank draft for one hundred and twenty-five grand tomorrow?' All as per Norman's instructions. Fifty grand was about as much as you could draw in cash at that time.

'If you're taking cash, why have you had the money put into a convertible peseta account?' asked the bank manager.

There used to be two types of account: convertible, where the funds could be changed back to foreign currency, and normal, where they couldn't.

'What difference does it make?' I asked.

'Well, none,' he said, 'but I could do with a few convertible pesetas myself. How would it be if I gave you my cheque for fifty grand of normal pesetas which I'll then cash at the window and you gave me a cheque for fifty grand of convertible pesetas?'

I was only too happy to oblige.

Bright and early the next morning, I was sat in the bank. The manager was writing his cheque out for fifty grand's worth of normal pesetas, his assistant was counting out the readies, his assistant was typing out the draft and I was writing out my cheque. That's when the phone rang.

'Urgent telex from London. Stop payment. The cheque is forged.'

'What part is forged?' I asked.

'All of it,' the manager croaked.

I couldn't get out of the bank quick enough and set off to find Norman back at the bar. He knew by my face that things hadn't gone to plan. I brought him up to date and refreshed his memory that he had sworn blind it was all above board.

Far from breaking down in remorse and begging forgiveness, the nearest I got to an apology was, 'Fucking fiestas, eh.'

Of course the saga didn't end there, although I never laid eyes on Norman, or whatever his name was, again. A week or two later, I got a message to go and see the comisario of group one at the provincial crime squad headquarters in Malaga. Group one turned out to be the fraud squad: welcome home. I had taken the precaution of bringing an interpreter with me to avoid any confusion and the interview went off quite smoothly. I related the tale pretty much as I've related it here, omitting only my knowledge of The Poodle's activities and the bank manager's convertible peseta slush fund. I wasn't asked a direct question with everything going through the interpreter. As I was leaving, the comisario asked if I wouldn't mind coming back on the Friday and I said it would be a pleasure.

On the Friday we went through the whole rigmarole again. I presume this was to see if there were any discrepancies, which I'm sure there weren't. They asked me to wait in an outside office, where I roasted till four in the afternoon. It was at this point that he came in and said he was arresting me on a warrant from Fuengirola for failing to appear on a drink-driving charge. I wasn't too happy but it didn't sound like a matter of life or death. But by the time they got me to court it was seven o'clock and the Fuengirola court was closed. The Malaga judge said he couldn't release me until the Fuengirola judge authorised it so I'd have to go to Malaga prison.

The Malaga prison has since been closed down and they've built themselves a nice new one in Alhaurin. Not before time, in my opinion. I was put in a cell that held eight people, with the only toilet facilities a hole in the corner with two embossed footprints. At least I think they were embossed, maybe they'd just got worn there over the years. The whole system worked solely on the laws of gravity. Fortunately I wasn't there long enough to discover its more intimate details.

I had the feeling that all this messing about was some kind of ruse to keep hold of me whilst they pursued the matter of the cheque but the interpreter was making himself busy, to some effect. In his capacity as official court interpreter he had become quite friendly with the Fuengirola judges, so he went around to the judge's house and put her in the picture as to how an innocent man was languishing in Malaga nick. She was good enough to send a telegram to Malaga night court ordering my release. I was out having a light ale shortly after midnight.

I never did hear another word about the cheque. I think proving any guilty knowledge would have been hard and a glowing reference from my bank manager probably went a long way. The reference was quite understandable when you think one word from me about his convertible peseta slush fund and he'd have been in the cell next to me.

One great character I met was Bing. He was a bank robber by trade and a pretty unorthodox one at that. Most bank robberies are carried out by an organised gang who all have their specific roles to play, one of the most important being the getaway driver. Not Bing. He worked single-handedly and his getaway vehicle was a racing bike.

One time he robbed a bank in Edinburgh, gaining access during the night and tying up all sixteen employees, one by one, as they arrived for work. He pedalled away with a rucksack on his back containing fifty grand and two automatic pistols. A few miles down the road, he came to a police roadblock. Pedalling to the front of the queue, he asked what the problem was and was told, 'Get the fuck out of here. There's a mad gunman on the loose.' He did a quick speed-trial down the road and disappeared into the distance.

He was eventually nicked and got twenty years. All the time he was away he kept hearing what a great game the puff job was and thought maybe that's where his future lay. When he got out, he went around to his mother's house to pick up his bike, which had been hanging on the mother's garage wall for the past fourteen years. He pumped up the tyres and headed for Spain, where some colleague from the bank robbery industry directed him to the Good Times. I sold him five key, which he secreted about his person before jumping back on the bike and heading for Glasgow. I never heard exactly what went wrong but he was arrested near the French border and got three years.

He came back a second time, again on his bike, saying he had perfected his role and this time everything would be okay. I sold him another five key and off he went again. His confidence was not misplaced. This time he got as far as Dover before getting nicked. I've not seen him since but I suppose he's gone back to the business he knows best, bank robbery.

A good few pals from back home found their way over and we were starting to get quite a cosmopolitan mix: Manchester, London, a few from Birmingham, Liverpool and a number from Scotland and Ireland. What amazed me was how well everyone got on. These same people meeting up in England at, God forbid, a football match and fatalities wouldn't be out of the question. Yet here there was very rarely an argument.

I was also getting to an age when some of my pals had sons in their late teens and early twenties and some of these wanted to get into the puff job. I was happy to accommodate them, even though it was only small stuff, because I certainly wasn't going to make a living selling bottles of San Miguel.

One pal of mine, Vinny Mason, came in one day. Vinny was one of the few not interested in the puff job, being quite well off already. I had met Vinny in Featherstone prison; he was quite an upmarket burglar, specialising in stately homes and antiques. He was very knowledgeable on the subject and had a genuine fascination for antiques. When I met him he was serving his third sentence for stealing the same set of scent bottles. They had been presented to Lord Curzon when he was Viceroy of India and were apparently quite valuable but Vinny didn't want them for their intrinsic value, he wanted them … well, because he wanted them.

I worked in the prison education block and one day Vinny came to me asking if I could get him on the pottery class. Certain that he was up to something, I asked him to put me in the picture. It seemed there was a potter called Albert Beardsley who, in the early 1900s, had made these big, chunky vases that were currently fetching big money. Vinny was convinced he could make reasonable facsimiles in the pottery room. I put his name to the top of the list. Vinny began churning them out and passing them out on visits to his pal, or accomplice if you will. The pal then placed them in small, county auctions where they were soon fetching between two and three grand apiece. Before long, Beardsley collectors grew suspicious at the sudden volume of Beardsley's work coming onto the market and the police got involved. The next time the pal entered an auction he was arrested and this led to a visit to Featherstone by the Art and Antiques Squad. They confiscated pots, kilns and any books in the library that had any connection to pottery.

Vinny was charged, and I've never heard a charge like it in my life, with 'obtaining money by deception whilst under the jurisdiction of the crown court'. The papers got hold of the story and this led to a front page headline in the *Sunday Times* reading, 'How to make pots of money in the nick. Throw it yourself.' The article went on to say how pleased the governor of this new, progressive prison was with the sudden enthusiasm for the pottery class. He had on one occasion stood and watched eight of these vases being removed from the kiln. Of course, Vinny denied any knowledge of the pots being sold and claimed he was only making replicas to give to family and friends as presents. He was eventually acquitted. It was nice to see him and talk about all our yesterdays.

Another old face that showed up was Manchester George. I've known some very good card cheats over the years but George was head and shoulders above them all. Most cheats are quite weak players, which is usually why they resort to cheating in the first place, but George was a brilliant hand game player and a more than competent poker player. This meant he only had to cheat very occasionally at a crucial moment and sometimes not at all. If someone became suspicious of his perpetual winning streak and put him under the microscope, having someone watch him play, invariably the verdict would be that he won because he was a very good player.

His biggest asset was his nerves of steel. Most cheats would prefer to restrict their activities to tickling up old ladies in card rooms, knowing full-well that old ladies rarely break people's legs and the worst that could happen if it came on top was to get barred. George didn't care who he cheated as long as they were prepared, and had the money, to play big. So he must be a millionaire, right? Wrong. Like most of us, George had his weakness and his was greyhounds. It wasn't unheard of for him to get in his Roller and drive from London to Newcastle to have two grand on a dog when he could have bought every dog in the race for less. If it wasn't for the dogs he probably would be a millionaire but in the meantime he lived like one. It was nice seeing him too and I hope he's still about.

So, between selling a bit of beer and my other ducking and diving, I was managing to keep the wolf from the door.

Friends Old and New

Speaking of wolves and doors, one new pal I made was Banjo. Banjo was a fairly old and slightly senile German Shepherd who was owned by a bar owner around the corner called Screwy Hughy. I know this because he had a large orange disc around his neck saying, 'My name is Banjo, follow me to Screwy Hughy's fun pub.' Lorna, who worked for me on a Sunday, Annie's day off, had run the place before I took over and had got into the habit of throwing Banjo a few scraps every day. Obviously no-one had informed him of the regime change and he came in most days, wandered behind the bar, snaffled anything eatable and wandered out again.

Besides Banjo's public relations duties, he did the night shift as a sort of burglar deterrent, sleeping in the bar. With his advancing years, Banjo had become a bit incontinent and Screwy finally got fed up with mopping up pools of piss and decided Banjo had to go. One day he loaded Banjo into the Screwymobile, one of those open-top Citroen jeeps that was also bright orange – it must have been Screwy's favourite colour – drove to the far side of the airport and kicked the unfortunate Banjo out. Heading back to Fuengirola, he got as far as Benalmadena when he realised he was near one of his favourite pubs, the Dubliner, and stopped for a pint or two of Guinness.

In the meantime one of the lads, having dropped off a pal at the airport, was returning to Fuengirola when he spotted Banjo ambling along the hard shoulder. Wondering what he could be doing so far from home, he stopped and gave him a lift. When Screwy got home Banjo was sitting, probably in a pool of piss, on the pub steps waiting for him.

A short while later Banjo did disappear and we never got to the bottom of what happened to him but I'd bet big money Screwy knew something about it. The bastard.

Two Weddings and a Failure

With my plans made for a June wedding, I decided to put the Good Times bar up for sale. I had enjoyed my time there, met a lovely girl and established my status as the person to speak to if you were looking for some decent quality puff at a reasonable price, but it was time to move on. I was looking for a business that was a little less time consuming.

Spain had just joined the European Union and part of the deal was a new extradition treaty with Britain, so it was a worrying time for a lot of people. Some were packing their bags and heading for the likes of Costa Rica. Others felt they'd already moved as far as they ever wanted to from the comforts of home. In the main, the attitude was wait and see, as no-one was really sure whether the new treaty was retroactive.

I was one of the least worried, knowing that if my name was on a list at all it would be pretty near the bottom. Besides, my problems were with Britain but I travelled on an Irish passport and was a fully-fledged Spanish resident shortly to be married to a Spanish national. I thought all that would probably make any extradition proceeding too complex for anyone to bother.

We were, however, beginning to hear rumours of people being shipped back. The first one I knew personally was a pal from Calahonda. Through a tapped phone conversation, British police got to know that his girlfriend was travelling over and that he would be meeting her at the airport. They faxed over the flight number and a photo of the wanted man. The Spanish police seemed to have the attitude that they had enough of their own villains to worry about without running around chasing British ones, particularly since most of them were doing little other than spend plenty of money. However, having been given the time and place where he would be and even a photo, they had little choice but to go and nick him. Which they did, and he got a ten.

A good few of the more well-known faces would eventually go home too. Fred Foreman would be literally kidnapped from his apartment in La Alcazaba, Marbella. One lunchtime the porter rang up to say someone was asking for him in reception and he came down dressed in a tee-shirt, shorts and flip-flops. He was handcuffed and bundled into a car. Without seeing a police station, courtroom or judge, he was driven onto the tarmac at Malaga airport and put on the British Airways flight to Heathrow. I was told quite reliably that they administered a strong tranquiliser known as the liquid cosh. I saw him that evening on the news, still in shorts and flip-flops, being driven away from the plane in London. The justification for this cavalier treatment was said to be that Fred was on a crooked passport. He was later given eight years for handling the stolen Security Express money and a year for the passport offence. He was never charged with the robbery itself.

Ronnie Knight went home with a bit more style. The money was beginning to run out, he'd already beaten a couple of extradition attempts and in any case he felt he had a fair chance of getting a not guilty. The *Sun* offered him forty grand for the exclusive story of his surrender and he accepted. He was flown home by private jet from Granada aerodrome. There were photos of him in the next day's papers drinking champagne with the reporters on the flight back. However, when he got back he found things were a bit grimmer than he had imagined. Threats were made to make members of his family co-accused, so when a deal was offered to plead guilty to handling the Security Express money, he agreed on condition no-one else was charged. He also got an eight.

But that was all in the future; for the time being things were ticking over much as before.

Selling the bar was remarkably easy but then again it was one of the very few freeholds on the market. The first people to look at it immediately agreed my asking price. In fact they agreed so quickly I tried to squeeze another few quid out of them but they wouldn't have any. They then, belatedly, tried to chip me a few quid and I wasn't having any either. So we did the deal at £47,500. By the time I had returned Jim's investment, given him his share of the profit and settled any of the outstanding liabilities that couldn't be avoided getting settled, there wasn't a massive earn. Still, I bet a lot of other ex-publicans in Spain would have liked to finish in my position

I spotted an advert in the local paper for a car hire business for sale and when I rang the number, it turned out to be a friend of mine from Manchester, Ernie Press. I went to meet him, taking a deposit with me. Pity I didn't take my brains. The deal was for ten cars on finance and a lease on an office for twenty grand. It all sounded right and I paid the deposit. Then I went to see Jimmy Swords to ask if he wanted to roll over his investment. He looked over the deal and said, 'Quite honestly, I'm fucked if I can see what you're getting for your money. I think I'll give this one a miss.' He did go on to say that if anyone asked, let them think he was still my partner, because I may well need him to do some sorting out at a later date. Very prophetic of him.

A bit of simple arithmetic could have saved me a lot of heart ache. Ten cars at seventy-five quid a week, if they were rented out twenty-four hours a day, seven days a week, which they obviously wouldn't be, would return £750 a week. Out of that I had to pay the rent, the car payments, insurance, maintenance and incidentals like advertising and cleaning. It was just not possible. The only way to make the car-hire job work is to have at least half of the fleet paid for so that they can subsidise the ones on finance but I certainly wasn't in a position to go out and spend fifty grand on ten new cars.

With a wedding to plan I had other things on my mind, and put the car-hire problems on the back burner.

Ronnie Knight and Sue Haylock were married on June 7. Actually the wedding was performed at the registry office on the sixth, but the blessing and reception took place the following day at El Oceano Beach Club. As you might expect it was a very lavish affair, attended by several hundred guests including most of the coast's personalities. Despite the large gathering, the guests were probably outnumbered by undercover Old Bill and paparazzi. One mob of photographers even got hold of a helicopter and flew over the terrace every ten or fifteen minutes, snapping photos. It all made for a very memorable occasion.

Annie and I were married a fortnight later, on June 21. Our wedding, at the Algarrobo Country Club, was a much more modest affair, though attended by much the same guest list. Ron and Sue, Freddie Foreman and Maureen, train robber Charlie Wilson and most of the lads from the VAT swindle were there. The Duke and Jocelyn from Duke's Bar came. Mel Williams was working but sent a greeting telegram. Gilly Burns was over in the States, pursuing some vague offer of a recording contract.

Hassan, my Iraqi pal, brought over a couple of dozen from Manchester. Tragically Vinny's eldest son, Carmen, died that week, so obviously he was in no mood to attend a wedding reception. My two brothers and two sisters came with their respective spouses. My father was already living in Spain at this stage, while Annie being one of eleven daughters meant a large contingent from Cordoba. All my ex-customers and quite a few locals made up the rest of the guest list, probably constituting about two hundred and fifty people.

There aren't many Rolls-Royces on the coast but I did have one pal who owned one and he agreed to lend it to me for the day. Neil agreed to drive it. The wedding was set for one o'clock and I was at the Algarrobo at about ten to make sure everything was in order. By half eleven there was still no sign of the Roller and I was beginning to panic. Surely he hadn't forgotten?

Neil and I began making a few phone calls and it didn't take long to solve the mystery. On the Friday night there had been a major police swoop, Operation Octopus, and nineteen people were arrested, including the owner of the Roller. Most of the arrestees were wedding guests and at that very moment the Roller was sat in the pound at Marbella police station. Hmm, time for Plan B. Except I didn't have a Plan B.

I was scratching my head trying to think of someone who had a presentable car when my eyes fell on Jimmy the Weed sat at the bar. I told him of my plight.

'Here,' he said throwing me his keys. 'Take my Merc.' He added, as an afterthought, 'But be careful, it's a ringer.'

That is, a stolen car which has been given a new identity with new plates, not unusual back then when half of the English-plated cars on the coast were ringers. Most of the other half were drippers, that is, cars bought on HP back in the UK by people who never had the slightest intention of making a payment. Beggars can't be choosers and, as it was the Merc or one of my Seat Pandas, I set to work with ribbons and the flowers. Neil drove me to the church then went to collect Annie and her mother.

After the service, the tradition in Spain is for the bride and groom to drive around town, beeping the horn and everyone gives a clap and a cheer. I told Neil to dispense with all that and get us to the reception before we all got nicked.

The reception is the easy part of wedding planning. Just make sure everyone gets pissed and there'll be few complaints. I had paid for the food, the cake, the flowers, the music and the after-dinner brandy. The only thing I'd owe would be the bar bill. I had put on a free bar but how much could that come to? I'll tell you how much that could come to. Five grand. Now I know there were a few good drinkers there and I know the bar was open from about half two till after midnight, but five grand?

I should point out that by this time Neil and Micky were no longer running the place and I wasn't particularly pally with the new management, so I voiced my opinion. I told him that in the Good Times I could be very busy, sixteen hours a day, seven days a week for ten weeks and not take five grand. And I had some good drinkers there, too. I asked for a reappraisal and got him down to three grand.

Hassan had given me a cheque for two grand as a wedding present so I gave him that and a grand in readies. Hassan, not wanting a cheque of his going into my account, had asked one of his pals to write one that he would cover when he got home. For whatever reason the covering never happened and the cheque bounced. I had the bloke from the club around, screaming, and I told him I'd sort it. By the time the two grand arrived a couple of months later, the last thing on my mind was driving up to the club and paying him, so I suppose you could say the bar bill was very reasonable.

With the wedding under my belt it was time to get the car-hire business in some sort of order. Here I did have one ace in the hole. As part of the deal, I had stipulated very forcefully that a crucial facet was that Ernie get the office phone connected. This was still the period when you couldn't get a phone for love or money but Ernie had assured me it would be on any minute. Six months later it still wasn't. I was paying rent on an office that wasn't the slightest bit of use and had cars sitting about that I couldn't rent because no-one could phone me.

I went to see Ernie, taking Jim Swords with me. After all, he was my partner, wasn't he? Jim convinced Ernie that the only honourable thing to do was to give me two of his cars, which were paid for, as compensation for the rent and loss of earnings. He wasn't too happy but took it on the chin. The cars were worth about four grand each so it brought my investment down to a more realistic twelve grand. Even so, I still would have preferred a phone, as I was in no better position as regards renting them out. Jimmy the Weed had started running a printing business on the coast and took two or three for his reps, and another pal of mine, Wally, a sort of self-employed builder, took another but these long-term deals were only for small money.

I did have the occasional windfall. The legal position in the car job was that I had to submit a form to the Old Bill with the hirer's details within twenty-four hours of the hire. Some people might need a car for a couple of hours, say, to pick up a bit of puff and not want to go through all the legal nonsense. I could rent them one at a very inflated price and if everything went smoothly no-one need be any the wiser. If something untoward happened and the Old Bill came around asking who had hired the car, I could tell them nobody had. The car should be outside my office and if it wasn't, someone had nicked it. Actually, nothing untoward ever did happen so I don't know what the Old Bill's reaction would have been, but I don't imagine they could have done a lot.

Even allowing for all this I was rapidly coming to the conclusion that I had a better chance of making a living not working than working. Far fewer expenses. In the end I sold the two cars that were paid for and sold the rest of the parcel back to Ernie for eight grand. I probably finished close to level on the whole escapade.

Suntan, Fareed and John the Bread

When I sold the Good Times, I took my business and most of my customers to a little bar that had just changed hands around the corner, the Queen Vic. Its new owners, Steve and Pauline, were both ex-croupiers from the UK who had given up the game in England to go and work in the illegal casinos in Amsterdam, where the money was much better. If the gaming board finds out that a croupier has worked in the illegal casinos, their gaming licence is permanently revoked, so when the work in Amsterdam came to an end, they moved down to Spain and opened the bar.

Suntan Tony had been one of my regulars and now moved with me to the Queen Vic. We would meet on more or less a daily basis and did quite a lot of work together. One day he introduced me to Fareed, the Moroccan supplier who he mostly worked with. A bigger nuisance in drink than Fareed would be hard to find in a long day's walk. Later he would discover cocaine which allowed him to drink ever more and become an even bigger nuisance. He could empty a bar by simply walking in and saying, 'Good evening.' Fareed did however have one very important redeeming feature. He brought over, regularly, very large parcels of extremely good puff. I knew his gear was good because it was the same stuff I had been buying from Suntan. I wanted direct access to it, so I palled him up.

After a while he came to me with a proposition. If I would rent a villa, he would give me his parcels to store and I'd be at liberty to sell as much as I was able and return him £650 a key. This left plenty of room for an earn. If he found his own customer, he would put on twenty-five quid a key for me to cover my risk and expense of housing the stash.

On the face of it, it might seem Fareed was taking a terrible chance with a parcel that might be worth half a million or more at any one time, but somebody had to mind it. At least he knew I'd been around a few years and was married to a Spaniard. I was probably as close to a stable character as a Moroccan drug smuggler was going to find.

I did better than renting a villa. I had a pal, John the Bread – apparently he'd been a baker back in England – who had a fairly secluded villa just off the Mijas road. He was stuck for dough and more than willing to make his garage available to me for a reasonable consideration, with no nosy landlords or neighbours to worry about. I bought a transit van to hold the gear and put reinforced doors on the garage. As long as The Bread didn't breathe a word, nobody on the planet, not even Fareed, needed to know where the gear was stored.

I was now in a position where I could supply anything from one key to five or six hundred, virtually at the drop of a hat, any time of the day or night. It was top quality at the most advantageous price I'd ever heard of. Not many people could compete with that.

I dispensed with all the rigmarole of hotel rooms and safes. My system was much more straightforward: give me your dough, take the gear away and if you're not happy with the quality or quantity, bring it back and pick up your money. If that doesn't suit, go elsewhere. Quality was never a problem and since I was loading the gear with my own two hands, I knew the quantity was right. I don't recall any hiccups.

The villa was about a hundred yards above Lew Hoad's tennis village, which was accessed down a narrow lane that led into a large and fairly busy car park. This was the perfect place for a swop-over. The punter could park his car, meet me in the car park and hand over the money. I would drive up the hill, count the money, load the gear and drive back down. Back in the bar, I'd give him his keys and off he'd go. I'd then drive to the Queen Vic which, miracle of miracles, did have a phone where the punter could ring me if he had anything to ring me about.

Before long business was booming.

There had been a shooting in Manchester and the police seemed to think Jimmy the Weed knew something about it. Whilst staunchly maintaining his innocence, Jimmy thought a short break in Spain would allow the dust to settle and give the Old Bill an opportunity to apprehend the true culprit. The Weed sitting about with nothing on his hands but time is a very daunting prospect, so I was pleased when he found something to occupy himself with. One of his sidelines back home was promoting cabaret dinners and he felt it high time the expats on the coast had the chance to experience one.

Jimmy had a very personalised system of book-keeping. He often put me in mind of Yosarian in Joseph Heller's *Catch 22*, who could buy eggs for five cents, sell them for three cents and make a profit. No matter how many times I read it, I can never fully grasp the principle. The theory used by The Weed was only marginally less confusing. If he could rope in three partners and give each, unbeknownst to the other two, a fifty per cent share, then the more money a show lost the better his profit. Of course, should the show make money he had a problem, but with him controlling the purse strings that was very unlikely to happen.

With his partners recruited, the next job was to find a venue.

When he asked me for suggestions, I had to confess to being stumped. He was looking for somewhere that could cater to four hundred people for a sit-down meal. Other than hotel banqueting suites, I couldn't think of anywhere and since he planned the do for New Year's Eve, the hotels would all have their own events to promote. Jim found a place himself and, although I'd lived about a hundred yards from it for two years, I didn't know it existed. La Venta de Torreblanca, apart from being about a mile inland and up a very windy road, was perfect. It would seat four hundred easily in a sort of banana-shaped room with not a bad seat in the house.

The next essential was a headline act. This needed to be a household name who would work for next to nothing; not easy to find. He certainly wouldn't be getting anyone very current. Now, don't be thinking 'past it', 'over the hill' or 'who?' Let's think more 'golden oldie' or 'blast from the past'. 'The long awaited return of ...' works well since it doesn't really specify who's been doing the waiting, the artist or the public. Ever resourceful, Jimmy came up with the perfect answer. Tony Christie had had a number of major hits, was certainly a household name, lived just down the coast in Almeria and numbered among Jimmy's multitude of friends in the entertainment business. Funnily enough, a few years later Tony's biggest hit, 'Is This The Way To Amarillo', was used by Peter Kay in a Red Nose Day sketch and went straight back to number one. He was probably well out of The Weed's budget by then. Anyway, Tony agreed to appear.

Mick Miller, who had appeared regularly on *The Come dians*, came over too, as did a very good female vocalist from Blackpool, Angie Gold. The trio from The Weed's club back home arrived to provide the music and a friend of mine from Dublin, Pearce Webb, who had been singing regularly on the coast and in fact still is today, also appeared. The compère was the Belfast-born singer Johnny Young. These days he's the lead singer with The Bachelors but back then he was playing the cabaret circuit in Manchester. He has a remarkable repertoire and could probably sing for a week without singing the same song twice. All in all, it was a pretty respectable line-up.

On the night, twenty liveried waiters served champagne and canapés in a cobbled courtyard outside the main room. The meal was excellent and the cabaret first class. Everyone thoroughly enjoyed it and the whole thing only lost something small, so the partners weren't too upset and The Weed probably earned something decent.

With the show not long over, I got a message from Jack Trickett to say he was involved with Barry Hearn in promoting a world title fight and needed a little local help. It was to take place at the Torrequebrada Hotel and Casino, seven or eight kilometres down the road in Benalmadena. And not just any old title fight but, for my money, the most prestigious title in boxing, the WBC Middleweight Championship of the World, and I was going to get to play a humble part in it.

I know, I know, when people think boxing the first names that spring to mind are always the great heavyweights – Muhammad Ali, Joe Frazier, Sonny Liston, Joe Louis, Jack Dempsey and, more recently, Mike Tyson. But the fact remains that most people on the planet are not heavyweights, they're middleweights, hence the name. It therefore follows that more boxers are middleweights, making the competition the greatest, so it's the hardest division to win.

Prior to the early Seventies there were eight weight divisions and one boxing board of control, the WBC. This obviously meant there were eight world champions. Today, with the alphabet soup of boards of control and all the split weight divisions, there are several dozen 'world champions', with their number increasing almost daily. Or, to put it another way, there really isn't any such thing as a world champion any more. Anyway, given that the WBC is the original, and many say the authentic, governing body, and accepting all I've said about its difficulty to win, we're talking a very glamorous and historic belt worn by the likes of Sugar Ray Leonard, Marvin Hagler and Carlos Monzon. No small potatoes.

Spain seemed a very strange venue for such an important fight given the fairly limited national interest in pro boxing. Amateur boxing is very popular but try as I might, I can't recall a Spanish world champion. I dare say Jim Swords could reel off a few. As with most things Barry Hearn does, however, there was method in the madness. The fight was to be between Herol Graham, from Sheffield, and Julian Jackson, from the US Virgin Islands. Jackson had undergone a detached retina operation and had been refused a licence to box in the US and England. France was mooted, with a similar result. The Canaries was the next suggestion but Jack said if it was to be Spain then Malaga was the place, as he already had a bit of help there, probably meaning me.

The chances of making a profit in Spain were pretty remote but it was vital for Barry that it went on somewhere. He already had control of Chris Eubank, the IBF world champion. If Graham could beat Jackson, which he had a marginal favourite's chance of doing, the big payday would be two British boxers having a unification fight at the likes of Wembley Arena or Stamford Bridge. If the Graham–Jackson fight cost a few quid, Barry would just have to live with it. Any losses he did make, however, were going to be kept to the minimum.

His opening volley in his meeting with the commercial manager of the Torrequebrada was a work of art.

'How much are you prepared to pay me to put the fight on in this hotel?' he asked the manager.

The manager was a bit taken aback because he had assumed

that Barry would be paying the hotel and said so.

'No, no, no,' tutted Barry. 'I will be filling the hotel in kipper season and publicising it on half a dozen TV networks, which has to be worth a lot of money.'

In the end he got the venue for nothing, six free rooms for the officials and a suite each for himself and Jack. No wonder he's the success story he is.

A very professional team arrived from Romford and took care of the logistics: the ring and seating and stuff like that. My own contribution was confined a bit of PR, putting up posters and doing a couple of interviews on local radio. I sold all the adverts in the programme to local pubs and clubs but the ticket sales were disappointing. I paid $1,200 to sit in row forty-three in Vegas for a Tyson fight when he didn't even turn up, and yet here I was struggling to sell front-row ringside seats for £125. I also did a lot of running about, picking people up at the airport. Don King sent his son Carl over, as Jackson was in their camp, and I picked him up and had a few drinks with him. In fact I had a few drinks with quite a lot of people that week.

The turnout was dismal and on the night we had to do a lot of rearranging so that from the main camera angle the place looked packed. Shame really, because with hindsight it was a remarkably good bill. Julio Cesar Vasquez went on to win a world title, as did Eamonn Loughran. Prince Naseem Hamed, who was only sixteen at the time and still an amateur, was there because he was trained by Herol Graham's trainer, Brendan Ingle, and he got in the ring to do a few somersaults. The main event obviously produced a world champ, so if you count ex-lightweight Jim Watt, who came over to do the commentary, how many boxing fans can say they sat front-row ringside and saw five world champions for £125?

I did even better. Being on a straight ten per cent of ticket and advert sales, I probably earned two grand and was the only one involved who did make a profit. At the time I was making plenty of money and I would have probably put in my small contribution for nothing, just to be able to say I was part of it all. But the two grand was a nice bonus.

When the main event came up, Herol won the first three rounds in a canter and Julian was cut quite badly. I was in his corner when the doctor came in at the end of the third and told Julian that he was only going to give him one more round. Though Herol was nicknamed 'Bomber', his critics have always chided his negativity and said he spent more time avoiding getting hit than hitting. Given the size of the ring – when Jack first saw it he said he thought we were putting on an episode of *Come Dancing* – and Jackson's restricted vision, Herol could have hidden in a corner for three minutes and been world champion. Instead of that he changed a lifetime's habit and came out like a lion.

The right hook Jackson caught him with would later be awarded the punch of the year. Herol was lifted off his feet and collapsed in a heap on the canvas, where he remained for ten minutes. He was driven off to hospital, taking with him any dreams of a unification fight.

After the fight there was a VIP room with a free bar. It appeared that everyone was a VIP and we all went off to drown our sorrows. I got talking to a great character, Alphonso Bailey, who had fought, and I use the term loosely, the Argentinian Julio Cesar Vasquez. Alphonso had once been the top-ranked amateur in the USA in his weight class and was a half-decent pro but was totally outclassed by Vasquez, who as I said went on to win a world title. I'll give you a description of the fight, which if I said lasted thirty seconds I would be grossly exaggerating, in Alphonso's own words.

'When the bell rang he caught me with one on the chest.

I was just thinking what would happen if he landed one of those on my head, when he landed one on my head. I could now see three of the bastards and lunged at the one in the middle. The ref said he'd have to stop it and I said, "Thank you very much, sir."'

I said, 'At least you earned a few quid.'

'Yes, but not much,' he said. 'I was paid two thousand dollars but had had to pay my own exes.'

Since he had flown from Los Angeles, there wouldn't be a lot of change and it seemed a bit parsimonious so I phoned Jack.

He said, 'No, we paid three thousand dollars wages plus the exes.'

Alphonso didn't have a manager, he had an agent, and it would appear the agent had had all four hooves in the trough. Alphonso vowed that if he ever laid eyes on him, he'd break his jaw.

When the free bar ran dry, we headed for the 27 Club in Fuengirola. The first person Alphonso spotted was the agent, and without further ado he walked over and knocked him spark out. We were nearly all dressed in dinner suits for the occasion – a Rastafarian shoplifter from Manchester had acquired mine and I still have it – and when the agent came round I suppose we looked like a posse of doormen. He got a bit brave.

'You'll never fight again,' he told Alphonso.

'Well, maybe just once more,' Alphonso said and knocked him out again.

Since they were both on the same plane back to Los Angeles the following morning, God alone knows what occurred crossing the Atlantic.

Next lunchtime I was awoken by a phone call asking me if I'd mind picking someone up at the airport. Actually, I did mind. It had been my intention to stay in bed until at least Monday. But when I heard the people to be picked up were George Best and his then girlfriend, Angie Lynn, I was more prepared to make an effort.

There had been a bar in Covent Garden, London, called Blondes which most people thought was owned by Besty. They were wrong. Most of the people who knew that Besty didn't own it thought it was owned by two Manchester lads, Mike Tufnell and Joe McManus. They were wrong, too. The real owner and sole financer was my Iraqi pal, Hassan. George had been brought in for his not inconsiderable PR appeal and had no money of his own in it. This may have been because, contrary to popular belief, he never had any weight of money. He could always pick up a couple of grand for opening a supermarket or doing some after-dinner speaking but as regards footballers accumulating money back then, forget it. At the absolute peak of his career I'd be surprised if George was earning £500 a week, when a factory worker might have been getting £50. Today, when a factory worker might be earning £500, top footballers aren't earning five grand, they're earning fifty or a hundred grand or whatever their agents can demand. Different times altogether. The deal when George was brought into the bar was that he'd receive a small wage and a share of the proceeds when the lease expired. It had now expired and it was time for the carve-up, which was why he was over.

I had known Besty quite well back in Manchester in the Seventies but then most people who had a drink in Manchester in the Seventies knew George. I used his club, Slack Alice, a fair bit and he was a regular in Phyllis's. He also used a gambling club owned by a friend of mine, Sid Otty, where I used to deal poker. George's affection for gambling was never as well publicised as his affection for a drink.

Having said that, I'd have to add I would never have put Besty in the class of a big drinker. That sounds such an outlandish statement when you think he went through two livers in slightly less than sixty years that maybe I'd better qualify it. There was an awful lot of drinking went on in Manchester in the Seventies, probably still does. I'll accept that George occasionally broke out and went on thirty-six-hour binges but thirty-six-hour binges were par for the course in those days. I know people who have been on thirty-six-year binges and don't seem appreciably the worse for it. Why booze had the devastating effect on George and didn't on, say, me, is one of life's great mysteries.

Bearing in mind the length of time since I'd seen him and the multitude of acquaintances he had, it's not surprising that when Mike told him I'd be picking him up, he said 'Maurice? How will I know him?'

Mike said, 'For fuck sake, George. I think he'll know you.'

I picked them up with no problems and took them to the Don Pepé. When I'd booked the room in the name 'Best' the manager had asked if I meant George. When I said yes, he immediately upgraded him to a suite. Nice to see he hadn't been forgotten in Marbella.

Hassan had booked a table in Silks for sixteen of us and we all had a great night, though Besty was in one of his dry periods. I think it was the time he'd been to Sweden and had some anti-booze pellets inserted in his stomach. I suppose he spent the whole night waiting for Hassan to tell him how much his share of the defunct club came to. The sad truth was that after Mike and Joe had raped and pillaged the business for whatever number of years it was open, there wasn't much carving-up to do. I suppose Hassan thought it was better to break the news in Marbella than Manchester.

I had lunch with Besty the next day and we chatted for

an hour or so before I made myself scarce. I know if I had a couple of days in Spain with Angie Lynn, I'd have better things to do than chat to George, and I'm sure he felt the same about me. He did come back a few weeks later and there was some talk of him opening a youth academy at the Algarrobo. Kenny Dalglish, Mo Johnstone and a few more came to a meeting there one Sunday but nothing ever came of it and George went home to do other things.

Funny Things Happen With Puff

At the best of times, there are many things that can go wrong in a puff deal. If the people involved are less than proficient, or a bit careless or even unlucky, the likelihood of a hiccup increases dramatically.

Take Mick Murphy for example. Mick had worked for years in the Middle East on pipeline projects. He always claimed his area of expertise was catering but I find that difficult to believe, unless pipeline workers are much less picky about their food than I would have imagined. Having accumulated a few quid, Mick came to Fuengirola and opened Murphy's Bar. It was a pretty seedy place but in an excellent location and soon after Mick bought the place, the landlord decided he'd like to re-develop the site. He offered Mick a deal whereby Mick would vacate the bar, which would be demolished. A block of flats would be built and Mick would get a brand, spanking new bar on the ground floor. Mick agreed but unfortunately very little was done in the way of paperwork. When the new edifice was finished, Mick went along to take possession of his new business and the landlord's attitude was basically 'Mick Who?'

Now without a business and running a bit short of dough, having sat about for a year doing nothing, he thought a little sortie into the puff job might get him back on his feet. Why not? Everyone else seemed to be getting a few quid. He rustled up the necessary, bought five key and recruited his pal Paddy to fly home with it.

A little bit concerned that the smell of the hash might give the game away, Mick thought some form of insulation should be employed. Unfortunately the material he chose to use was aluminium kitchen foil, not one of his better ideas. The twenty foil-wrapped bars were distributed around Paddy's person and off he went to the airport. Of course he only got as far as the airport metal-detector. Ding-a-ling-a-ling. Paddy was nicked and the money lost.

Undaunted by this setback, Mick planned a recovery mission, presumably using a more orthodox form of insulation, and went out and bought another five key – not from me, I should point out. When he got it home, Mick's son Derek rolled himself a joint. This might have been a sort of quality control measure, though it's equally possible Derek just fancied a joint. Either way, Derek wasn't impressed with it and told Dad that the best course would be to sell it in Spain and wait for something better to turn up. Eventually Mick found someone who was less picky than his son and who bought the gear. The reason for his lack of pickiness became apparent when Mick went to change the three hundred and fifty tenners he'd been given. The notes were forged. Mick was arrested and sentenced to three years.

When he came home, his financial straits were even more dire than when the saga began. However, whilst in prison Mick had got pally with some of the local scallywags who were in the heroin trade. They offered Mick some work couriering a bit of the nasty down from Madrid. Mick was to be paid on a percentage basis, in gear, leaving him with the problem of where to sell it. I didn't then, nor do I now, know where I would go to buy or sell a bit of heroin. Apparently, neither did Mick. He did finally manage to make contact with some even bigger scallywags than the ones he was already working with, who agreed to buy it. The meet was set up for, of all places, the Queen Vic and Mick duly arrived with his bag of gear. The buyers arrived but hadn't brought the money. They had, however, brought their badges and guns, being undercover Old Bill. Mick got twelve years.

When he was released, he returned to Dublin where he died not long afterwards. His son Derek also died back in Dublin in a building site accident. So, what was the catalyst for this chain of disaster? Well, I suppose if Mick had just asked a little advice as to what to wrap the gear in, things might have worked out differently.

Slippery was a lovely fella of Danny DeVito proportions, a quick wit and good company, but I could never fully resist the urge to count my fingers after shaking hands with him. He came to me one day saying he had acquired thirty key from somewhere, I thought it best not to ask how or from whom, and he wanted to know if I knew anyone who might want to drive it home. I had just the man. Stan Richie was one of the last of a dying breed: a safe-blower, or peterman as they were known in the job. Stan's trade was lost to redundancy with the arrival of the thermic lance. I dare say even that's been superseded by now.

Stan's last bit of work had been blowing the safe at the margarine works in Eccles for which he'd received his third eight-year sentence. When he came home he was of pensionable age, had a few quid put away and decided to retire to Spain. It didn't take him long to realise that, cheap as Spain was, he was undercapitalised. He was quite friendly with my dad, who was also living here by then, and we would often have a drink together. One night he told my dad that if a bit of work came up he was available, so I went and had a chat with him about Slippery's proposition. He was delighted.

Slippery brought the thirty key around to my lock-up for me to wrap and pack into Stan's car. It was the weirdest bit of gear I've ever seen. Quality-wise it was excellent but it came in 150 gram sheets, which meant you couldn't wrap it in kilos. You could only wrap 900 grams or 1,050 grams. I scratched my head. There were two hundred sheets so the thirty key was all present and correct. I divided it into four stacks of fifty sheets and then wrapped five sheets together and put ten bundles of five into each door. That would have to do, and off Stan went. He made it to the UK with no mishaps. The buyers met him at a service station just outside London, took the car away, unloaded it and gave him it back. He set off for a few days with his pals in Manchester.

A couple of days later, the screams started. The buyers said every packet was light and the parcel only came to twenty-two-and-a-half key. Where was the other seven-and-a-half key? I said no, four packets of seven-and-a-half were thirty. Silence.

The problem with putting gear in a car's doors is that the windows won't open. The sensible thing to do if you're packing thirty key is to put ten in three doors and leave the driver's door empty so the window would open. That's exactly what the buyers had assumed I'd done. Having removed three packets from three doors, they thought they had the lot so why would they open the fourth door. Stan was now unwittingly driving around Manchester with seven-and-a-half-key of puff in his car and I had no way of contacting him. I rang everyone I knew in Manchester that might know Stan but had no luck. I even offered a reward to anyone who could get him to ring me. Still no luck.

Ten days went by and I was driving through Benalmadena when I spotted Stan's car outside his local boozer. I put him in the picture and he wasn't pleased but by now the money had arrived from the gear that had been sold. Slippery acquired some more gear to go with the seven-and-a-half and off Stan went again. So, everything worked out in the end but I can't help wondering what the Spanish Customs would have thought had they nicked Stan bringing the gear back to Spain. It would have had to be the first time in the history of puff smuggling that anyone had ever been nicked for importing puff to Spain from England.

When puff goes missing it's not always as easily explained as in that tale. I really am convinced that somewhere in outer space is one of those black holes full of bars of puff, so much of it goes missing. I can't count how many times I've put gear in a car, sent it up the road to give to someone who gives it to someone else, and when it gets to its final destination there's a few key missing. You rarely get to the bottom of it. In the trade we refer to it as shrinkage.

Another story with Slippery more accurately illustrates how he got his name and to where some of the missing gear finds its way. Slippery got involved with a little mob from Gibraltar and the plan was to send fifty key home. Unfortunately, no-one in the deal trusted anyone else and for fifty key there was an awful lot of people involved. There were the drivers, two of them, and the people from Gib, and Slippery and his partner. Oh, and the buyers. Everyone wanted to be on site when the gear arrived so they were all assembled in the lock-up to meet the car and began unloading it.

They got the count to forty-eight and couldn't find any more, and Slippery was just getting into his, probably well-rehearsed, fanny about a couple of Germans he'd paid to load the car. They must be the culprits. He hadn't got far when the garage doors flew off the hinges and in marched the Customs and Excise. Everyone was lined up against the wall. During the ensuing search, one by one, the missing eight bars were recovered from Slippery's pockets, socks, underpants and I think even one or two from under his baseball cap.

Slippery got five years for the importation charge. I never

did hear what punishment he received for the snaffling.

Another bit of gear that re-surfaced caused me more expense than if it had stayed missing. A pal of mine had two hundred key that he wanted taking to Alicante, from where his transport to the UK was leaving. As an incentive, he told me there was room on the transport for three hundred and if I wanted an interest I was free to do so. I spoke to a couple of people who were interested in an investment and between us we made up the other hundred.

The two hundred was dropped off in a small hatchback, I slung it with my own hundred into the camper van we used to transport the gear and off we went. But when we handed it over, the count only came to two sixty-eight. A bit of shrinkage is one thing but thirty-two key is stronging it. I knew my hundred was right because it was in four of those familiar twenty-five key bales. The rest was loose bars. I phoned my pal. He said there was little that could be done at this stage and told me to carry on and we'd sort it out later.

When I got back to Fuengirola he told me he'd found the missing gear in the wheel well, where I had no idea I was supposed to look. Mystery solved, but he now had thirty-two key and nowhere to leave it. He asked if I'd take it off his hands and return him twenty grand when it was sold. There'd be a bit of profit in that, so I agreed but I was off to Malta the following day. I asked my driver, Irish Gerry, to take it up to the campsite and leave it in the camper, where it would be safe enough if no-one knew it was there. I told Gerry that if anyone was looking for anything small, it was for sale and to go ahead and sell it.

When I got back, Gerry had a story. He said he'd sold one key and the person who bought it must have followed him to the campsite and returned later and nicked the other thirty-one key. I had my doubts but there was little I could do and I paid the twenty grand that was owed. A week or two later, my doubts to some extent were confirmed. Gerry came to me and said he was moving to Tenerife to work in the timeshare game. This struck me as odd since he had been loosely involved in the timeshare game for years in Fuengirola without getting any medals. That's probably why he was prepared to drive a bit of puff up the road.

Apparently things were better in Tenerife and Gerry became a celebrity timeshare salesman. He lived pretty well for a couple of years before returning to Fuengirola. The return was either because the timeshare bubble burst or because he'd exhausted the twenty-odd grand he'd nicked from me. I'll never really know.

With hundreds of cars coming off a cross-Channel ferry, a Customs man is only going to be able to dig out two or three victims. He'll ask a few questions and cast his professional eye over the vehicle. If your answers are satisfactory and the appearance of the vehicle rings no alarm bells, everything should be okay. If it's your intention to convince him you've only been at Disneyland Paris for the weekend, it would be well not to have a straw sombrero and a stuffed donkey with 'Souvenir from Torremolinos' written down the side sitting on your back shelf. Of course, if you're not up to any mischief you wouldn't be bothered about appearance or answering a few questions. Nothing terrible can happen, can it?

I have a pal, Mick Skelly, who's one of those Arthur Daley type wheeler-dealers. One day he phoned me to say he had a Merc and a speedboat on the coast that he desperately needed back in the UK to complete some complicated deal he was in the middle of. He wanted to know if I had anyone to drive them home. My dad was always happy to have an expenses-paid trip home and would also earn a few quid, so he said he'd go.

The trip to Santander went fairly uneventfully except for the brakes on the Merc failing by about eighty per cent. Not a great position to be in when you've got half a ton of speedboat behind you, but still he nursed it onto the ferry alright. At Plymouth the next day he was stopped by the Customs and asked if the boat was on the British Small Ships Register.

'Don't know,' he said.

'Why? Is it not your boat?'

'No.'

'What about the Merc?'

'That's not mine either.'

'Who owns them?'

'A fella called Mick.'

'Mick who?'

'Don't know.'

'What's his address?'

'Don't know.'

'Phone number?'

'Don't know that either.'

'Then how are you going to deliver the car and boat?'

'I'm meeting him at Knutsford services on the M6.'

It's quite difficult to think of a series of answers that would be more likely to get you a spin. That's exactly what happened and my dad was told to drive the car over to the inspection sheds. He is almost sure he heard the Customs man mutter, 'I think we've got a live one here.'

The rummage crew set to work with a will. The boat was taken off the trailer, as were the wheels. Holes were drilled and probes inserted. Panels were removed. Meanwhile the car was getting similar treatment. Doors, seats and the battery were removed. More drilling and probing.

The first Customs man and my dad were looking on and chatting. How long had he been in Spain? Did he live alone? When my dad said that his son lived there, he asked my name and wandered off, presumably to put my name through the computer. When he returned, he shouted to his pals to keep digging.

The search went on for about six hours and it was time for the crew to go off duty. A second shift arrived but the first shift, I suppose out of professional interest, hung around to watch, wondering where the new mob would find the gear they had missed. The second shift toiled away for several more hours before accepting defeat. 'If there's something in that car or boat that shouldn't be there,' said the head man, 'I'm fucked if I can find it.'

They were now faced with the problem of having to re-assemble everything. They had been so sure they would find something that they hadn't been very fastidious about the parts they'd removed, never dreaming they'd have to put it back together. Those little plastic things that hold the window winders on seemed particularly problematical. I'm not convinced they were one of Mercedes' better design features. They eventually got it more or less back in one piece, though there did seem to be a few bits left over. But that's always the way, isn't it? These bits were thrown in the boot, probably with a silent prayer they were nothing to do with the brakes or steering, though by this stage it might well have been a silent prayer they were something to do with the brakes or steering. Dad was waved on his way twelve hours behind schedule. God alone knows what Mick was thinking, sat at Knutsford.

Halfway down the Plymouth bypass, my dad spotted blue flashing lights approaching from the rear and pulled over. It was his pal, the Customs man.

'Look Tom' – they were on Christian name terms by this

stage – 'whoever replaced the light board has put it on upside down. When you put on your left indicator the right light flashed and vice versa. If you drive home in the dark like that you're a certainty to be pulled over by the police. And if you give them the same story you gave us, you'll have another twelve hours sitting about while they pull the car to pieces again.'

They tried inverting it but the brackets didn't seem to work. In the end the Customs man, blue lights flashing, escorted my dad to a service station where he had to wait until eight in the morning for the garage to open.

All in all I think Mick Skelly spent the best part of twenty-four hours sat on Knutsford Services.

Funny Things Happen With Money Too

If there is a black hole full of puff, for sure there's one next to it full of bits and pieces of readies. They disappear even more often. When money arrives it's normally very untidy, with every hundred quid, in assorted denominations, folded up in one of the notes. Ten of these bundles are fastened together with an elastic band. That's a grand, isn't it? Probably not. If you're lucky it might be nine-ninety and if you're unlucky it might be nine and a half.

Similarly to the puff, by the time it gets to me it's been through so many hands you're never going to get to the bottom of it. On thirty or forty grand the shortfall might be anything up to a grand or two, but a little dexterity with the exchange rates can usually make up the difference. If it's massively adrift, plan B comes in, one of those 'Oh my God, that parcel I told you about has gone, there's another but it's a tenner a key dearer' stories. You have to fight fire with fire and it's all part of the job.

The real problems start when entire parcels of money go missing.

I had one pal, Harry Flashman, who came into the job at a very early age. He started off in the traditional way with small stuff, graduated to cars and before long was loading half a ton or more on wagons. This suited me fine, as he bought most of his stock from me and he treated the job very professionally. As Flashy's empire grew, getting the money back over became as much a job of work as getting the gear home. It's all very well putting a couple of people on a flight with thirty or forty grand but when you're talking half a million, things are a bit different.

Flashy had a right-hand man, Roy, and he also had a cousin who was an absolute little stunner. Roy and the cousin fell in love and got married but as is so often the case with two very attractive people, both used to getting their own way, it was a very tempestuous relationship, as often off as on.

Flashy needed £460,000 bringing over to Spain and Roy was delegated to do the driving. At the time, Roy and the cousin were at loggerheads but he told her he had had a bit of a touch and was going to Spain to buy some property. Did she want to come and give it another go? She did.

For security reasons, Roy didn't know exactly when he was leaving or even what car he was driving. One morning he was picked up, driven down the A3 and given the keys to a car. See you in Spain. Roy phoned the wife, did a U-turn and went to pick her up.

At Dover, leaving the wife in the car, he went to buy a second ticket for her. When he got back the wife, the car and the £460,000 had disappeared. At first he thought he was mistaken as to where he'd left the car and it wasn't until the ferry left and he was standing in a deserted car-park that he accepted the situation. It was time to make a few phone calls.

To be fair to the cousin, she hadn't known the amount of money involved and had been under the impression that whatever money there was belonged to her husband and therefore was half hers anyway. All that didn't stop World War Three breaking out, with doors being kicked in all over London and guns getting put to people's heads. It turned out that several people were involved and some took the view that if the real owners of the money ever got their hands on them they were bang in trouble whether they returned it or not, so why return it? In the end the bulk of the money was returned, with Roy's share being confiscated to help make up the shortfall. Roy was reduced to the ranks and faced the prospect of having to go back to working at the sharp end.

By the time the money eventually arrived in Spain, the parcel I had control of was well sold and I couldn't put my hands on the amount Flashy needed. Because of all the dramas, Flashy's next bit of work was thrown together with less than his usual eye for detail. He put a rush deal together to pick up some gear in Algeciras and Roy was sent to oversee the job. It all went boss-eyed and everyone was nicked. Roy got eight years.

A short while later, the cousin's mother – Flashy's aunt – who Flashy had always reckoned was the prime instigator of the rip, lost a long battle with cancer. The aunt was a notorious shoplifter and was known in her own circles as simply 'The Shoplifter'. The funeral was one of those affairs that only Londoners can do well, with the horse-drawn carriages and all the trimmings. The aunt was buried in a Zandra Rhodes original which she'd no doubt nicked from Ms Rhodes's boutique. When asked her opinion of this by the Press, Ms Rhodes said, 'I'm very flattered. The Shoplifter could have been buried in anything she chose – Chanel, Dior or anything else.' A famous soap star did the reading and at one point said that while the aunt may have been a thief, she never stole from her friends. Reading the write-up in the following day's paper, I heard Flashy mutter, 'Wasn't so fucking picky with her family.'

Being the resourceful chap he is, Flashy put these reversals behind him and went back to work. Before long he was up and flying again. By this time I was living in Dublin, and one day I was trying to get hold of him. I tried his mobile numerous times and in the end tried his landline, although I knew he didn't really like using it. He answered halfway through the first ring.

'Sorry, mate. Tried the mobile but it's off,' I said.

'Right this minute I'd cheerfully give five grand to know exactly where my mobile is,' was Flashy's reply.

'Seems an awful lot of money for something you can pick up for a three-er. What's the problem?'

'Well,' he said, 'the last time I saw the mobile it was in my father's hand and my father has now disappeared. So has the four hundred and fifty thousand quid he was minding for me.'

Do I need to point out that the father was the aunt's brother? I think it was Oscar Wilde who once said, during a conversation about orphans, 'To lose one parent is unfortunate but to lose two smacks of carelessness.' I'm sure that was how Flashy's partners were beginning to feel about sacks of readies.

Flashy went for a walk to clear his head and debate with himself his next move. Walking along Marbella's main street, his eyes were drawn to a metal sign attached to a lamp-post advertising a private detective agency. It was only around the corner and, although feeling he was clutching at straws, he went around for a chat. He gave the detective an abridged version of events and asked if he thought there was any chance of locating Dad. The detective said he'd see what he could do and asked for a five grand advance. This was probably the bulk of Flashy's current net worth but, even though guessing he was throwing good money after bad, he paid.

Flashy was stunned a couple of days later when the detective phoned to give him Dad's new address. Apparently he had been in the land registry office a few days earlier signing for his new apartment in the Watersport development in Gibraltar. Flashy set about rounding up the troops.

I think it's fair to say that Dad was less than pleased to see his son and heir, accompanied by several pals, standing on the doorstep, but nonetheless invited them in. The first thing

Flashy noticed was that Dad was wearing a new Rolex, the nice one on the Presidential bracelet with the diamond bezel. You could pick one of those up in the Red House for less than twelve grand in those days.

'Dad, do you really need a twelve grand wristwatch?' he asked.

'Well, you've got one,' said Dad.

Hardly the point.

During a lull in the conversation about the missing money, Flashy cast his eye around the apartment and couldn't help but admire what a nice job Dad had made of the décor, given his very short tenure. Obviously no expense had been spared. In fact the conversation was interrupted by a knock at the door which Flashy went to open, Dad being a little tied up at the time. He was confronted by an Oriental chap with a silk carpet on his shoulder.

'Mr Flashman?' the chap asked.

'Is that paid for?' was the best he got by way of an answer.

'Not yet, sir.'

'Very good. You can fuck off,' said Flashy, slamming the door in the unfortunate chap's face. Shame really, would have gone very nicely with the new velvet drapes.

Once again most of the money was recovered, if you count the Rolex and the apartment. Actually, the apartment was a bit of a bone of contention. Flashy took Dad to a solicitor where Dad signed a power of attorney giving Flashy title to sell it, but no sooner had Flashy left than Dad went back, said he had signed under duress and revoked it. For all I know, Dad's there to this day.

Despite all this adversity, Flashy went on to become a very wealthy man and retired from the job. I lost touch with him until one time, years later, when I wasn't doing so well I got a phone call out of the blue to meet him in Calahonda. He said he'd heard I was having it hard and that he appreciated some things I had done for him in the past. He felt he owed me a drink and gave me a holdall with twenty-five grand in it. He swore me to secrecy, probably not relishing the thought of being known as a soft touch and having a string of strugglers turning up on his doorstep, but Flashy had enough people run him down over the years; I think the good things should be mentioned, too.

Jimmy the Weed, for all his enthusiasm for making money, could be a little careless with it. One time he was driving over from Manchester to Spain accompanied by his consigliere, Wally McNally. After a couple of days on the road, instead of going to his flat and unpacking, they headed straight for the Queen Vic and a gargle. The Weed destroyed the best part of a bottle of brandy and Wally did some serious damage to a litre of vodka before they finally set off for the flat.

The bitching started on the apartment car-park, with both claiming the other had had the keys last. Luggage was pulled out and rummaged through, resulting in socks, shoes and underpants becoming scattered around but with no sign of the keys. Wally's main duty on the trip was to take care of The Weed's briefcase, which contained fifteen grand in cash and about twenty grand's worth of jewellery: chains, bracelets and rings. Wally placed the briefcase on the roof of the car for safe-keeping and the search went on.

The keys eventually turned up, in Wally's pocket as things worked out. The scattered clothing was gathered up and they bickered their way upstairs, The Weed giving Wally plenty of I-told-you-so. No thought was given to the briefcase still sitting on the roof of the car.

They were awoken the next morning by a knock on the

My dad in 1949, when he served with Liverpool Police. Not perhaps the typical parentage for someone who would go on to spend twenty-five years smuggling cannabis.

In Manchester in the early 1980s, on the night I drunkenly bid a small fortune for a fox fur jacket to impress a girl. Soon after, I departed for Spain to escape the attentions of the Serious Fraud Squad.

Puerto Banus, Marbella, the jet-set playground of the Costa del Sol, became my base in 1983 when I fled the UK. I soon found that if you wanted to earn a living in Spain, there was only one game in town: the puff job.

Eddie Avoth, Welsh boxer and owner of the popular Silks restaurant in Puerto Banus, after winning the British title. Eddie knew everyone.

My Iraqi pal, and the ace-in-the-hole for much of my life, Hassan Al-Jaizani: club owner, wealthy businessman and *bon viveur.*

With Bill 'the Duke" Meeks, owner of Duke's piano bar in Puerto Banus, and his wife Jocelyn in the mid-1980s. Bill liked to drop mysterious hints about his 'US Special Forces' background.

Frank Evans, or 'El Ingles' as he's known in Spain, is so far as I know the only professional bullfighter to have been born in Salford. Here he fails to have things all his own way with half a ton of disgruntled bull.

With my bullfight-promoting partner Jim Swords, ex-boxer, Manchester legend and a man I feel privileged to be able to call my pal. The other guy, with the beard, used to play for Manchester United. Now what was his name?

Sharing a drink with singer Mel Williams (right), a fixture in Spain for many years. Mel has never received the recognition his talents deserve.

Annie and I met when she arrived on the coast from her native Cordoba looking for work. We were married on June 21, 1987. Our wedding car, supplied by my pal Jimmy the Weed, turned out to be stolen. Typical.

Jimmy 'the Weed' Donnelly (left), in Spain to avoid questioning over a shooting, with the singer Tony Christie, me and Annie at a cabaret dinner promoted by the Weed.

With Dickie Rock, probably Ireland's best-known singer. One night he came in to see my pal Pearse Webb at Rory's Lounge, then got up and did a forty-five minute spot. It would have cost me several grand had I booked him.

Dining with Gilly Burns, resident singer at the Play Bach bar in Banus and later co-owner of Pinky's in the Port, and her father Ray, who was himself once reputed to be Britain's highest-paid entertainer. The picture was taken at my villa in Mijas.

Barmaids are a little like children, in as much as you're not supposed to have favourites, so here are my two favourite barmaids: Mary from Bulgaria (left), she of the sharp tongue, and the lovely Kelly from Newcastle.

Oh, alright. Put a gun to my head. My very favourite barmaid, Lisa Mernock, princess of the popular Irish Rover bar.

Annie and I with Annie's sister and brother-in-law at Platform 1 in Rio de Janiero. I can't deny that smuggling puff gave me a good life. My problem was not earning money but hanging on to it.

My dad (left), me and Annie with soccer legend Bryan Robson. on a night out at Old Joy's pub. Marbella was a magnet for footballers and other celebrities and I had a drink with many of them over the years.

My Irish friend Gerard 'The Monk' Hutch, doyen of the Dublin underworld, with his famous stretch Hummer.

Jimmy the Weed's son Tony (left) with all-round hardman 'Pikey Mike' McDonagh in Rory's Sports Lounge. We did our best to make a go of Rory's but running a bar in Spain is a thankless task and eventually it closed.

'Gentleman' George Stokes, of the grasshopper mind and crazy smuggling schemes, with his long-suffering partner, Julie Egan

My friend Fritz, 'remarkably adept at getting hold of the artificial stimulant of choice of any particular person'.

Suntan Tony Dawson, yacht skipper, fellow world traveller and pal, propping up the Queen Vic bar. Sadly missed.

Sparking up a fag, my one weakness (well, apart from Jameson's whiskey, and cards, and horses, and one or two other things), outside the famous Sinatra Bar at Puerto Banus harbour, scene of many a gathering.

At the opposite end of the success scale, the disastrous Bromley's, complete with for-sale sign, waiting, like The Creature From The Black Lagoon, to ensnare its next victim.

Conche, the flower vendor and totally 'impartial' witness who offered to help me after an altercation at Ronnie Knight's bar. I ended up with a suspended jail sentence.

Great Train Robber Charlie Wilson, a major player on the Costa del Crime, at his villa in San Pedro. This is the spot where he would be murdered shortly afterwards. One of the dogs was also shot.

With another of the train robbers, Gordon Goody. We are holding, and I'm afraid you'll have to take my word for it, an authentic mail bag from the 1963 infamous robbery. Gordon moved to Spain after serving his sentence.

Sitting by the beach and contemplating my next move after the inconvenience of a three-year stretch in a less-than-luxurious Spanish prison for smuggling puff. Perhaps I'll take up golf.

door and The Weed was confronted by a Spanish chap holding his briefcase. He asked Jimmy if it was his and The Weed dragged him inside. Apparently the Spaniard's son and his pals had been playing football with the briefcase and when it sprang open and the English money fell out, they thought it must be The Weed's since he was the only Englishman in the block. Vague promises of a substantial reward were made but I don't recall them coming to fruition. Some people are just born to be poor, and I don't mean The Weed for losing the bag, that sort of thing can happen to any of us. I mean the Spaniard for returning it. Talk about looking a gift horse in the mouth.

I had my own misfortunes with money now and again. One time I was doing some work in Amsterdam with a couple of lads from Liverpool. We had worked together in Spain during the summer but with the season over their transport was finished until the next year. They had come up with a new scam. They had got hold of a crooked steward on one of the cross-Channel ferries. There was already a sort of mini-mafia operating on board, running cigarettes, booze, perfume and a bit of porn but this steward was prepared to take it to the next level.

At this particular UK ferry port, the Customs inspection for the ferry employees was very hit and miss. One of the merry band would disembark and if he saw the coast was clear, he'd give the nod to his colleagues, who would then disembark with their bags of booty. If there was an inspection they'd just leave the booty on board and try again on the next crossing. The steward could only take what would fit in a small holdall – we settled on fifteen key – so it all sounds pretty small potatoes but he did work five days a week. In fact, he did two crossings a day, so if we got really, really organised we could work ten times a week. Needless to say, we didn't get really, really organised and it never went anything like ten times a week. Not even five but it did go home a huge number of times.

Even so, it was too small to bother bringing the gear from Malaga. Although it was a bit dearer there was plenty of gear available in Amsterdam and I had a connection there, which was why I was invited in. We all met up in Amsterdam and, all of us assuming we were only there for a chat, none of us had brought any money with us.

My Dutch connection was quite taken with the plan. He said, 'Let's do it tomorrow. Or tonight.'

I explained the embarrassment of funds and he said, 'Don't worry, I've got plenty of gear about. We'll sort the money out later.'

I phoned my driver to get up to The Dam and hire a car at Schiphol airport. The Dutchman took away the spare and packed the puff inside. Not very sophisticated, I know, but the drive from The Dam to the French ferry port was pretty low risk. At the ferry terminal car-park the driver slit open the spare, put the puff in the holdall and boarded as a foot passenger without getting a look at. Once on board, he handed the bag to the steward and his work was over. The gear was on the afternoon ferry, in England by tea-time and on the streets of Liverpool by supper-time. We were ready to go again two days later.

The figures broke down to five key between me and the Dutchman and ten key between the Scousers, since there were more of them. The third load was on its way home before the first bit of dough arrived which meant, not counting the third one, we owed Dutchy ten grand for his five and twenty-five times £800, or £20,000, for the gear he'd advanced us.

After dropping off the third load, the driver brought me back the thirty grand from the first load to give Dutchy. He came to the hotel and I gave him a very scruffy thirty grand, tied up in a Safeway's plastic bag. I threw it to him.

'Hang on to it and I'll pick it up after we've had a drink,' he said.

He came to pick me up for dinner that night and I gave him the money again. He said, 'Hang on to it and I'll pick it up after we've eaten.' I threw it in the back of the wardrobe.

After the meal, we went for a drink and a wander around the Red Light. I got back to the hotel, drunk, at about two in the morning. I was on the early flight to Malaga the next day.

The third parcel got home okay but there was a bit of sulking over the quality. I flew back to Amsterdam at the weekend for a board meeting, which was held in a Chinese restaurant. Dutchy looked on the sulking as a ruse to delay things and give the lads time to squeeze the best possible price out of the gear.

'The third parcel was identical to the first two and perfectly acceptable quality-wise,' he said. 'In the meantime, I still haven't seen a penny of your money. Just when is this situation likely to be rectified?'

Everyone looked at me. I looked at Dutchy.

I said, 'But I gave you thirty grand last week.'

'Yes, but I gave it back to you.'

'Yes, but then I gave it back to you.'

'And then I gave it back to you.'

Oh fuck.

Dutchy and I downed chopsticks and headed back to the hotel, the Ascot on The Damrak, which fortunately enough was the hotel I was staying at on this trip, too. We dashed in and asked to speak to the manager. I had scarcely got into my hastily prepared fanny about this car I was buying from Dutchy when the manager stopped me.

'Ah, yes,' he said. 'We have something belonging to you

in the safe.'

He went away and came back with a large, brown carrier bag from which he withdrew the neatest pile of money I had seen in a long time, each bundle of a hundred held together by a paper clip.

'Twenty-nine thousand, seven hundred and twenty. Correct?'

'To the penny,' I said, certainly not wanting to be quibbling about a bit of shrinkage at this stage.

He said he'd tried to contact me at the address I had given but was unable to do so. Hardly surprising, I've never given my correct address at a hotel in my life. Maybe I should think of starting. Apparently the cleaner found it in the wardrobe and, thinking it was rubbish, was on the point of throwing it in the bin when she realised it was readies. She handed it in to the manager. Has to be a moron, but I gave her the £720 as a tip and put a grand on Dutchy's exes. It was in a much more relaxed atmosphere that we finished the Chinese. Even the quality issue seemed to have evaporated.

By the spring, the ferry line had closed down and the steward had moved to a new boat that docked at Dover. Customs inspections at Dover are anything but hit-and-miss, so that was the end of that particular gravy train. Nothing lasts for ever but it was good while it lasted.

Another time, in Brussels, things didn't work out quite so well. I had a pal flying over from Dublin with forty-two grand and another driving over from Manchester with thirty grand. I went to the airport and picked up the first bit and then took another cab back to my own hotel. Once in the room, I put all the money in a briefcase which I put inside a suitcase. I locked it, put a second suitcase on top of the first and threw an overcoat over the lot. Time for a bit of lunch.

Jolly nice lunch it was, too. Smoked salmon and prawns, a peppered fillet, a half-decent bottle of Chablis, all rounded off with a couple of Irish coffees. Just as well I enjoyed it, it cost me seventy-two grand.

When I got back to the hotel room, the briefcase was lying open on top of the pile of luggage. Hmm, I wonder who the beneficiary could have been. An unscrupulous cleaner? An extremely fortuitous hotel thief? The shadowy figure from the grassy knoll? Colonel Mustard in the bedroom with the screwdriver? Or could it have been the only person on the planet that knew I was in Brussels to pick up a few quid. You be the judge, answers on a postcard please.

Around this time there was an incident in Manchester that, whilst nothing to do with the business, does show that when money goes missing someone, somewhere knows something about it. Vinny's brother, Louie, was driving into town one lunchtime when, for some reason, he was pulled over by the Old Bill. During the ensuing search a couple of expensive wristwatches were found in the glove box, which the police jumped to the conclusion were hooky. Louie was arrested.

At the police station, Louie explained that he had the watches on sale or return from Phil the Barber. Phil's brother, Artie, owned a barber's shop in Moss Side where Phil had worked in an earlier incarnation, hence the nickname, but now he worked as a freelance jewellery wholesaler. The Old Bill were having none of this and put Louie in a cell, first relieving him of his personal possessions. These included two grand in readies.

The desk sergeant began to carefully count the money and make out an itemised receipt. Midway through, he was distracted by a colleague asking him something and glanced away. Louie, purely out of devilment and not dreaming he'd get away with it, flicked ten £20 notes from the counted stack to the uncounted stack. The sergeant turned back and resumed the count, re-counting the ten scores. Louie was sitting in the cell for a couple of hours, complete with his itemised receipt for £2,200.

Phil was eventually tracked down, most likely in Gus Demmy's betting shop on Cheetham Hill Road where I would have looked for him in the first place. He confirmed that the watches were his and were straight as a die. Time to release Louie, and he couldn't wait. The envelope with his possessions was thrown to him.

'Sign here,' he was told.

'Thank you very much, sir, but just to be on the safe side would you mind if the money was counted?' said Louie.

The sergeant heaved a sigh, slit open the envelope and began counting. Then he started counting again. The third time, he carefully flicked each note, I suppose to make sure eleven £20 notes hadn't got stuck together. On the fourth count he held each note up to the light, I suppose to make sure he hadn't mistaken a £20 note for a £220 note.

Finally, he said, 'Well, you can fucking search me.'

'It's all very well searching you, sergeant, but I know where I've been the past couple of hours. I don't know where you've been.' Louie was magnanimous enough to add, 'I'm not suggesting you went anywhere, like to the bank for instance.'

A search was instigated with all hands to the pump, about seven officers by this stage rooting through desks, drawers, waste paper baskets and each other. They even searched Louie, the only person in the building with an alibi. The sergeant was faced with no choice but to inform head office, who dispatched an inspector to investigate. He took the sergeant into the office next door where Louie couldn't hear the conversation but he could read the body language through the glass partition. The gist of the chat seemed to be the inspector suggesting that if he had had it, now was the time to come clean, and the sergeant swearing on his mother's life he knew nothing about it.

Deciding it was time to bring things to a close, Louie asked to speak to the inspector.

'Look it's only a two-er. I'm prepared to forget it. I'm the last person who wants to see anyone getting nicked.'

This was ironic, since the other eight people in the room had the sole ambition in life of seeing people getting nicked.

'However,' said Louie, 'I have got a few motoring summonses that I've been a bit concerned about. I wonder if we could do any business.'

A deal was struck and Louie resumed his journey to work feeling reasonably content with the afternoon's events.

Having mentioned Amsterdam it seems a shame not to give it a bit more space, with it being such a great town and a place I've visited on many occasions. I think what makes it so good is their very liberal attitude to booze, gambling, puff and prostitution. They take the view that if an adult wants to drink, play cards, smoke puff and rump whores it's nobody's business but their own. Couldn't agree more.

Landing at Schiphol there's a wonderful feeling of relaxation, knowing that nothing terrible can happen law-wise for the next few days. Make no mistake, if the Old Bill fall over you with a wagon-load of puff you will go to prison, but not for long. I had one pal nicked with eleven-and-a-half tons of African grass and he got two years, three months. Back home he'd be lucky to get a twenty but nevertheless he appealed against severity of sentence. He got nowhere but with remission he was home in a little over a year. And they really do have to fall over you. Dutch police devote their resources to more important matters.

My favourite hotel is the American but it seems it's a lot of other people's favourite and you can't always get a room at short notice. There are half a dozen rooms on the first floor with terraces overlooking the Liedseplein that give a perfect view of the street entertainers, who are usually very good. The Moonlight bar on the ground floor is a little haven of peace and quiet and the ideal spot for a clandestine meet. Straight across the square from the hotel is the Bulldog, which is an Amsterdam institution and where the expats, particularly the Brits, meet. The ground floor is a sort of disco bar which gets very loud and very packed at night. The basement is a coffee shop. The term coffee shop has a very explicit meaning in Holland, since besides selling coffee they can sell spliffs and 'space cakes' loaded with hash. Visitors to Amsterdam are often like kids in a sweetshop, feeling like they should try all the flavours. There are dozens and dozens of coffee shops scattered all over town but the Bulldog would be one of the best and certainly the best known. To the left of the hotel is another small square where you'll find the Oyster Bar, one of Amsterdam's best seafood restaurants. There's also a couple of good Irish pubs there.

A five-minute walk takes you to the start of the Red Light area. This is full of pubs, cafes, coffee shops and porno book shops. There are live sex shows, the most famous being the Casa Rossa. There's one place called Bananarama where you pay about twenty quid for half an hour drinking what you want and watching girls doing strange things with fruit and vegetables. There are places for people who like being tied up and places for people who like tying people up. There are places for people who like to wear leather or plastic or nothing at all. There are tattoo parlours and places that do body piercings. I sometimes wonder how some of those people get through an airport security gate.

Of course the most famous thing about the Red Light is the

windows. There are rows and rows of shop fronts along both sides of the canals, each one with a single girl behind the glass, and you walk along and take your pick. Sounds wonderful but the funny thing is, no matter which side of the canal you're on, the pretty one always seems to be on the other side. You find a bridge, cross over and walk back only to find when you get close up she's got varicose veins and droopy tits. But, wait a minute, that doesn't look a bad shout on the other side. You cross back over only to find she's worse than the one you've just passed on. It must be something to do with the subdued lighting.

As far as brothels go, the best in Amsterdam, possibly in the world, is the Yab Yum. No varicose veins or droopy tits there, but at their prices there wouldn't want to be. A friend of mine had his coming-out-of-prison party there and ran up a bar bill for thirty grand. Mind you, I'd imagine a bit more than drinking went on. I seem to recall something about a caviar smearing competition. Thirty grand hardly seems feasible, but it was a party. Say there were thirty of them. Ironing out a grand a head on food, beverage and sexual favours would present little difficulty in the Yab Yum. A couple of girls each, a bottle of champagne, a few light ales and a cheese and tomato sandwich would leave little change. And that's without the caviar smearing, so maybe there were only twenty-five of them.

Amsterdam is a very cosmopolitan place. Don't forget Rotterdam, just down the road, has been a major North Sea port for five hundred years and the Dutch weren't behind the door when it came to a bit of colonisation: South and West Africa, the Carribean, Surinam on the South American mainland and the likes of Indo-China in the Far East. But it's a very integrated town. There's no Black Quarter, no Chinatown, no Latin Quarter or Irishtown. Everyone is everywhere. In the bars there's a mixture of every colour under the sun. Nowadays there's a fair sprinkling of Eastern

Europeans, whose arrival started with the Yugoslavs, followed by Bulgarians, Romanians and Russians. There's also a lot of Moroccans and Algerians, Turks and Greeks, and of course all the Northern European neighbours, the Germans, the French, the Belgians and the Scandinavians.

Amongst all this racial cocktail are some of the world's leading dope dealers. There are a few reasons why so many congregate in Holland but one is that, unlike the situation in Spain, a number of the big players are Dutch nationals which means there's always stock on hand. The fact that the penalties for slip-ups are so much more lenient is an incentive too but the fact that spending a few quid isn't frowned upon is a major attraction. If someone spent thirty grand in a brass-house in Manchester or Dublin, the Assets Recovery mob or the Criminal Assets Bureau would be kicking their door down the next morning wanting to know where the money came from. That doesn't happen in Amsterdam, and you can bet your bollocks that if I know that story, the Dutch Old Bill know it.

Likewise the casinos. It's fairly common to see people with wads of cash, night after night, playing blackjack and roulette with nobody batting an eyelid. Back home anyone performing like that wouldn't have long to wait for the early-morning call. You see people pulling up outside the Bulldog in Merc Sports and Porsches without a care in the world. Back home it's not unheard of for someone to be pulled over, have their car keys confiscated and be told they can have their car back when they can prove where they got the money to buy it.

Just recently a well known football player from Manchester, who happens to be black, was driving along the M61 in a fancy sports car. He got pulled over, apparently because he was black and driving a fancy sports car, and the police found thirty grand in the car.

'Why are you driving around with thirty grand in cash?' was

the officer's, I suppose fairly legitimate, question.

'Because I can,' was the reply that very few other people in the country could have got away with.

One group of big-hitters you don't see much of in Holland is the Colombians, who generally work worldwide through local agents. I think they have things pretty much their own way back home when it comes to enjoying their few quid.

For all its good points I couldn't see myself living in Amsterdam, though I do know people who went for a few days and stayed forever. The one thing that puts me off is the weather. Eight months of the year a brass monkey could be at serious risk. Mind you, I suppose that applies to a lot of places. Paris can be quite depressing in the winter and Brussels can be quite depressing at the best of times. All the years of Spanish sun have probably spoiled me.

All in all I think the Dutch have got it right. Do what you want as long as you're not hurting anybody. Live and let live, that's the way to run a country. It might not be Utopia but it's headed the right way.

The Exception that Proves the Rule

I did start off by saying that major drug busts are rarely the result of sophisticated undercover work or diligent surveillance. Of course that implies that occasionally they are.

Micky Reilly and Neil Robertson had been pals for years, stolen eiderdowns notwithstanding, both of them coming from west London: Mick from Paddington and Neil from Chiswick. At one time they had run Streisand's Bar together in Puerto Banus. Mick was having things a bit hard but had come across what appeared to be an exceptionally good bit of transport. Things are a lot different today, where Customs have all kinds of fancy equipment to scan and x-ray vehicles. I've even heard of a gadget that sucks air from a container and can detect drugs, explosives and even carbon dioxide from people smuggling, but back then Customs relied very heavily on profiling to decide which wagons to inspect. The three most important criteria were: origin of the load, value of the load and length of time the company had been operating.

To take the two extremes, suppose there is a wagon load of watches coming from Switzerland being carried by a company that has been in business since they used horses and carts. Then there's another wagon carrying a load of oranges from Valencia being carried by a company set up a week last Friday. I know which one I'd want to search if I was a Customs man and I know which one I'd like to have my bit of puff on. Transport rarely gets as good as the Swiss watches but unfortunately often gets as bad as the Valencian oranges. I once read somewhere that one particular year there was more gear captured in Valencian oranges than every other cargo put together. Don't say you haven't been warned.

Mick's transport leaned more towards the watches. The story went that it was computer equipment carried by a company that had been running for donkey's years. It left from Zaragoza which, though still Spain, was inland, which is lower profile than coastal Spain. You don't get much more inland than Zaragoza.

Mick's problem was that the transport people were insisting on a minimum of three hundred key and he had no money. This sort of minimum requirement wasn't unusual and, at £200 a key, the transport people knew they were on at least sixty grand. On this occasion the true motivation was a little more sinister. The charge for importing less than three hundred key is 'importation'; the charge for importing more is 'mass importation' and the penalties go up significantly. Since everyone involved on the transport side was undercover Customs, they wanted to make sure of thoroughly nailing everyone's hat on, the cunning bastards.

Good as the transport sounded, a bit over two hundred grand was still a massive investment on an untried run. A syndicate was needed. I was approached partly to see if I wanted a share and partly because I had the facility to get the gear to Zaragoza. All in a day's work; I joined in. Even so, we fell a bit short of the three hundred and in the end only about two sixty went. That was probably the only lucky thing that happened in the whole scam.

Irish Gerry and I got the parcel up the road and Mick was waiting to hand it over. This must be the point where Gerry and I got our get-out-of-jail-free cards. Since the intention was to follow the gear home and nick everyone involved, they couldn't nick us because it would mark Mick's card that there was skulduggery afoot. Equally, they couldn't get the Spanish Old Bill to nick us since their Spanish counterparts had never been put in the picture that there was an operation going on. Smacks a bit of rule-bending but who am I to criticise.

Mick flew home to pass the gear from the transport to the buyers, who were very professional people and were equipped with scanners to listen in to the police and Customs. No sooner had Mick left than a message was broadcast.

'The targets are splitting up, follow the white vehicle.'

Since they were in a white van, evasion tactics were called for: a few quick lefts and right and into a lock-up, where the doors were slammed down. Out the back window they went and down the pub to await developments.

First suspicions fell on Mick but a few phone calls established his bona fides. That night a little firm went in and moved the parcel to a second lock-up without anything untoward occurring. No-one knew that a tracking device had been put in the gear and the Customs could follow it at their leisure.

It was beginning to be assumed that there had been a bit of over-reaction. After all, there are a million white vehicles in London. The following day, the buyers were driving to the second lock-up and when they turned onto the street they heard their own car registration being read out over the scanner. All thoughts of over-reaction went out of the window. They drove straight past the slaughter, abandoned the car and six hours later were sitting on the beach in Marbella.

Mick was less fortunate. Not knowing of the latest developments, he went down the pub.

'What a fucking day I've had,' he said to Neil. 'One minute it's home, the next it isn't, the next it is. Thought it was on me for a while, but everything seems okay now.'

No sooner were the words out of his mouth than the doors flew open and in stormed a combined force of Customs and armed Old Bill. Everyone in the pub was nicked – it was that sort of a pub – but the only one charged was Mick.

At his trial, Mick used the did-he-fall-or-was-he-pushed defence. If Mick asked the transport man to bring the gear home he was guilty but if the transport man asked Mick to put some gear on his wagon, then it was entrapment and Mick was not guilty. The jury was having none of it and found him guilty. He got ten years but of course he appealed, primarily against sentence, which was a bit on the strong side, but also, as a sort of makeweight, against conviction.

The appeal court took the opposite view to the jury and said at the very least the undercover man should have been required to give evidence.

'In the event that I ordered a retrial,' asked the judge, 'would the Customs be prepared to produce the undercover man?'

'We'd be opposed in principle,' said the prosecution, 'but in any case he is unavailable as he is on another operation.' No doubt luring some other unfortunates into the net.

'That being the case,' said the judge, 'I have no alternative but to dismiss the charges.'

A few minutes later a very bemused Mick, whose most optimistic expectation was getting the ten cut to a seven, was standing on the Strand scratching his head.

Sadly, the saga doesn't end there. Mick's financial position was, if anything, even worse than before it all began. He needed to get a bit of work done and got active with some people grafting from the West Indies. They had a crooked baggage handler at Heathrow. Now I've no doubt there are crooked baggage handlers but I've never heard a success story with one. How much clout can a baggage handler have anyway? Surely they can't walk about, willy-nilly, with trolleys full of gear? If someone told me they had the head of security crooked I might be a bit more interested. Anyway, this next bit of work came a tumble and Mick got another ten. This time he was unable to wriggle out of it.

Incidentally, Mick's case set a precedent and is quoted in Archbold, the book of case law. Under English law entrapment isn't a defence, it's only mitigation. A defendant has to plead guilty, saying, 'Yes, I did the crime but those unscrupulous bastards lured me into it.' In Mick's case the argument was whether the undercover man should appear to testify and he wouldn't or couldn't, so the charges were dropped.

came a tumble and I got totally [illegible] he was unable to [illegible] out [illegible]

[illegible]

[illegible]

[illegible] Accounts [illegible]

other [illegible] possible. But frequently [illegible] there has ever been a [illegible] regular [illegible] than this one.

As soon as things were going this way [illegible] too big for me [illegible] as far as [illegible] had [illegible]

The World's Biggest Kalooki Game

Getting plenty of money from the puff game for little effort, and having no other business to occupy my time, allowed me to indulge myself in a few hobbies, one of which was playing cards.

Kalooki is a variation on the game of gin rummy. Without going into the technicalities, it is normally played four-handed but can be played three- or five-handed. Two-handed is very boring. John and Steve were two wealthy characters who played every day, with whoever was available taking the third, fourth or fifth seats. They were eagerly trying to recruit a third regular player. The game is played for units of one, two and four. Their unit was a £100, which means, with five players, there's two grand in the pot before a card is dealt and a potential six grand in the pot by the time it's finished. Plus call-ups, the one or two units paid for each hand. It was customary to play the last game for double stakes and far from unusual to play the very last game for double-double stakes. That means £8,000 at the start and possibly £24,000 at the end.

I can't positively say that there has never in the history of the world been a bigger game. I suppose the likes of J.P. McManus could have bumped into Kerry Packer on a plane going somewhere and played a few games for bigger stakes to pass the time. Anything's possible. But I seriously doubt there has ever been a bigger regular game of kalooki than this one

As good as things were going, this game was just too big for me, much as I'd have loved to have played. A bad week could have wiped me out. Then one day, John came up with a suggestion. I could play for twenty-five per cent of the stakes, still a more than reasonable game. If I won a game the other players would take back seventy-five percent of their investment. If I lost the winner took the whole pot. I thought I'd give it a go.

Things went very well for a few weeks and I also had a couple of tickles in my own business, so I offered to play fifty per cent stakes. Another few favourable weeks and I decided to take the bull by the horns and play the full whack. I never looked back. One disastrous day I lost twelve grand and one fantastic day I won twenty-three grand. Most days weren't as dramatic as that, two or three grand one way or the other with many more winning days than losing ones. All in readies. Pretty scruffy readies right enough, but readies none the less. A pot could contain any combination of sterling (English and Scottish), pesetas, guilders, Swiss francs, lira and the odd Irish punt.

It wasn't that I was any better than the others, we were all much of a muchness, but I did have a couple of things in my favour, not least that the money was much more important to me than it seemed to be to the others. John and Steve particularly had bundles, though it turned out later a lot of the time Steve was juggling with other people's dough.

John loved a bit of puff and would smoke joints the way I smoke cigarettes, which is to say quite a lot. He also enjoyed a drop of good brandy and would often down several coffees and brandies through the course of the afternoon. I didn't drink when I was playing. Steve was a phoneaholic and would often play cards with the phone clenched between his left shoulder and his chin. I switched my phone off. Most of the casual players were wealthy people over for a few days' break and had their holiday head on rather than their kalooki-playing head.

John was also taking a few bets on the racing, principally from Steve, and the English racing commentary would be playing on the Gibraltar TV station. I rarely had a bet on the horses when I was playing cards. One day, by chance, I heard of a horse called Atoll, Atoll running at Haydock Park and knew it was owned by Jim Swords. Then I remembered that there had been a missed call from Jim on my answerphone the previous night and jumped to the conclusion he had been ringing to tell me to back it. I did. It won. That night I rang Jim to see how much he'd had on it and he said, 'Not a penny.' He had tried to get me the night before in case I saw it running to let me know it hadn't got an earthly. So much for tips.

With all this going on, my opponents' concentration had to be a bit suspect and, while kalooki isn't rocket science, the one vital ingredient is concentration. If you don't know what cards have been discarded you can't possibly know what cards are left to come. I'm convinced I was a little ahead in the concentration department.

By its nature, kalooki often gives rise to a situation where a decision has to be made whether to play conservatively or go for the biggie. Since the other players were playing principally for the excitement, and there's less excitement in playing conservatively, they habitually went for the biggie. Of course this would occasionally come off but I'm not convinced it is the best long-term strategy. I played ultra-conservatively and fuck the excitement.

I did have one other major advantage. There are two variations of kalooki, London Rules and Manchester Rules. There may well be others but these are the two I'm familiar with. Manchester Rules, though I'm sure some Cockneys would disagree, make the game infinitely more difficult. I'd go as far as to say the gulf is as wide as the gulf between snooker and pool. Whilst the fundamentals are the same, an over-the-hill snooker player like Steve Davis in the twilight of his career can and does go out and win serious pool tournaments. The best pool player in the world would have little or no chance in a major snooker event. Having been brought up on the Manchester Rules, I found converting to the London Rules a refreshing change. The proof of the pudding is in the eating and over the next twelve months I won something over a hundred grand.

Every silver-lining has a cloud and the snag with getting big money, easily, doing something you enjoy is that it can't help but lead to losing respect for the money and forgetting how hard it has been to get in the past. For example, one day when we were playing, Steve's phone rang, not an unusual occurrence. This time it was a bloke called Henry Brown, a Londoner who organised junkets to the States, particularly for boxing events. He was running one for a forthcoming Tyson fight and wanted to know if any of us wanted to go. We all did. So did Annie. And Suntan. The decision to go was made with about as much consideration for expense as you'd give to ordering a Chinese takeaway.

The charter was leaving from Heathrow which, for various reasons, excluded a number of us. We did a deal whereby Henry would book the hotel rooms and arrange fight tickets and we would make our own arrangements about getting there. I had a little bit of business to tidy up in Amsterdam, so I booked Annie, Suntan and myself into the American Hotel in the Liedseplein. We would then fly from Schiphol to Los Angeles for four nights and a hire car. A four-hour drive through Death Valley would find us in Vegas.

This would be the point when Tyson got himself nicked for rape or one of his other transgressions and the fight was cancelled. Henry was in a bit of a bind since his cancellation insurance didn't cover rape charges and he begged us all to go ahead, assuring us there would be plenty of boxing anyway. As it would turn out, there wasn't but most of us did go ahead, having made all the bookings.

In Los Angeles we stayed at the Holiday Inn on Sunset Boulevard, which sounded a fairly tourist-friendly location. Not according to Wayne, who was the six-foot-six black guy with the pump-action shotgun that did the greeting at the hotel.

'I wouldn't go out there after dark if I was you,' he advised when we said we were going out to find a pub. 'Or at any time on foot.' Apparently we were in the middle of a street-gang warzone.

Suntan Tony was adamant and went in search of a pub. Accepting that Wayne knew what he was talking about, Annie and I went to the hotel bar. This was on the top floor and called Windows On Hollywood. It was a lovely revolving room which about every hour gave a great view of the famous Hollywood sign.

When Tony walked into the pub he found and said he had crossed over from the hotel unaccompanied, the barman couldn't have looked more surprised if he had said he'd just beamed down from the Starship Enterprise. Tony had his few beers and got up to leave.

'Wait a minute, I'll check if the coast is clear,' the waiter said, sticking his head out of the door and looking both ways. 'Okay, walk very briskly and don't stop for anyone.'

Welcome to LA.

The next day we picked up the hire car and did all the touristy things: toured a film studio one day, took a drive out to Santa Monica another and a trip to Malibu the third day. There's a restaurant on Malibu pier called Alice's and we went in and ordered three beers. The waiter put two beers on the counter and demanded to see some ID before he'd serve the girl. Since Annie was thirty at the time she was very flattered and fell in love with the place.

The last night we drove over to Beverly Hills and had a drink in the Beverly Wilshire, the hotel used to film *Pretty Woman*. Claude, the waiter, couldn't have been nicer and spent a few minutes chatting and telling us all the places to visit, which was a bit late since we were leaving the next morning, but still. Claude was only doing the job temporarily, filling in a lifetime waiting to be discovered as the next Tom Cruise. I ordered a bottle of champagne, Californian but champagne none the less, and three smoked salmon sandwiches. I was about to get my grounding in American tipping protocol.

I've always considered myself to be a very good to excellent tipper, having worked, admittedly briefly, in tip-related employment. In fact it's probably being such a piss-poor waiter, taxi driver and poker dealer that led me to fraud and drug smuggling in the first place. The bill came to $91 and I gave Claude $100, telling him to keep the change. I thought $9 was ample for walking six feet with one tray. Claude didn't agree and metamorphosed into the waiter from hell. Tipping in America is strictly on a percentage basis, with fifteen per cent being the minimum. If the waiter does something other than waiting, like chatting for a few minutes and telling you what sights not to miss, twenty or twenty-five per cent would be more the norm. Nine point eight nine percent doesn't cut it. I suppose had I ordered three beers and three cheese butties and given a $9 tip he'd have wanted to take me home to meet his sister. Or his brother. You live and learn.

Next day we set off for Vegas, a remarkably uninteresting drive. Once you leave LA you see nothing but sand. Americans in general are a pretty law-abiding bunch and if they're told to drive at fifty-five miles an hour that's exactly what they do, so you rarely pass another car and another car rarely passes you. Even in daylight you can see the lights of Vegas from fifty miles away so it still took us another hour to get there. We found the hotel easily enough, another Holiday Inn but in Vegas, so naturally enough it's called the Holiday Casino. It was easy to spot because it's shaped like a Mississippi paddleboat.

If you're not a gambler you'll never have a cheaper holiday than Vegas. The shows are fantastic and cheap: we saw James Brown at Bally's and Gladys Knight somewhere downtown. I'd happily pay good money to hear Gladys Knight reading the telephone directory. The hotels cost next to nothing and the food costs half of nothing. Driving along the Strip you see sign after sign advertising lobster. Why lobster is so popular in the middle of a desert I don't know, but it is. The further you go along the Strip the cheaper the price: $9.99 … $8.99 … $7.99. One place right at the end of the Strip, obviously having given up all hope of making a living, has a sign saying eat as much lobster as you want for $5.95.

The hotel did one of those all-day, eat-what-you-want buffet breakfasts, my favourite meal of the day, for three bucks. The first morning I thought I'd wandered into a pancake eating competition. These Yanks seem to mistake eat-what-you-want for eat-what-you-can. I've never seen so many obese people in one room in my life.

It's difficult to go to Vegas and not gamble. I played a fair bit of craps and a little blackjack without any dramatic results one way or the other, Annie loved the slots and Tony, who is practically a non-gambler, got hooked on keno. If they've invented a game with less chance of winning than keno I haven't found it yet. The one thing I didn't like was the lack of any sort of daily finishing line. Most gambling venues close at some time and you can have a roll-call and know your profit or loss situation. Not Vegas. You don't really know if you've won or lost till you leave.

Having seen the best of the shows, flown through the Grand Canyon and visited the Hoover Dam, and with no boxing on the agenda, we had all more or less had enough after five or six days, and headed for San Francisco. In Frisco we did all the tourist bit again, rode a cable car, saw Alcatraz and had clam chowder and lobster on Pier 39, Fisherman's Wharf. The live music in the bars was fantastic; there was just so much talent around. We sat in one bar and about every hour the band would pack up, pass around the hat and leave to be replaced by another band equally as good. We must have sat through six or eight acts. I liked Frisco, very relaxed with no street-gang wars to contend with. Apparently they do have a bit of aggro now and again from the Hells Angels but I didn't see any myself. All the bars had notices banning the wearing of motorcycle club colours.

After a couple of days it was time to head back to LA and the plane. The drive took two days down the Pacific Coast Highway, stopping the night in Santa Barbara on the way. At Annie's insistence we had to stop at Alice's for lunch. We arrived at the airport with about four hours to kill, which was handy because I had one more visit to make. We returned the hire car and took a cab out to Hermosa Beach. The cab driver had one of those Eastern European names that don't go in much for vowels and didn't speak a lot of English but he eventually got us to where we wanted to go.

When George Best had signed for the Los Angeles Aztecs, he had made it a condition of the deal that they sign his pal, Bobby McAlinden. Bobby might have played a little Sunday League stuff and that would be the height of his football pedigree but that didn't matter. In those days in America to play pro-soccer, being a young, good-looking man about town was miles more important than any soccer expertise. Bobby and George shared an apartment and did all the things reasonably financially sufficient young men would do in LA, including buying a bar which, naturally enough, they called Besty's Bar. I wanted to have a drink with Bobby before we left.

We found the bar alright but the barmaid told us Bobby only came in at weekends. We ordered a drink anyway and a few minutes later the barmaid put up another round saying it was on Bobby. Next minute the phone goes and the barmaid said it was for me. Annie muttered the Spanish for 'I don't fucking believe this'. No lo me coño creo, I believe her exact words were.

I presume the barmaid rang Bobby saying someone was asking for him and this was him ringing back. As it turned out he lived too far from the bar to get there before we had to leave, so I made tentative arrangements to ring him next time I was over. I never did see him again in the flesh but I did see him twice on television. One night I was flicking through the TV channels in a Dublin hotel room when I came across an episode of *This Is Your Life* featuring Besty. His surprise guest from the States was Bobby. The second time was at the opposite end of the happiness scale when Bobby, introduced as simply a family friend, did the reading at George's funeral. With the possible exception of Princess Diana's, I don't know of a funeral to get more TV coverage than that one did. I was delighted to see Gerry Adams sitting next to John Hume, apparently able to put aside their political differences for the occasion as George did all his life.

People whose opinions carry a lot more weight than mine, not least of all the likes of Pelé, have said George was the greatest player ever to kick a football. Admittedly, when they said it they hadn't yet had the chance to see Leo Messi, but still.

I suppose the whole escapade to the States, flights, hotels, car hire, food, drink and a little bit of gambling set me back about ten grand. Plus a fortnight's loss of earning at the kalooki. A mere bagatelle. Or, slightly more than I could earn for helping to hump a ton of puff off a beach in the middle of the night, four times. All a matter of perspective I suppose.

How Much is Enough?

One day Fareed came to me with a deal that confirmed what I had always suspected: these Moroccan agents got a hell of a lot more gear on the move with the upfront money they were given than they'd have you believe. There was fifteen hundred key waiting to be picked up by Suntan but one of the investors had reneged and the gear was going nowhere until thirty grand was found. I've no doubt that Fareed could have easily pulled it up himself but that wasn't how he worked. He never put a penny piece of his own money into any job.

The deal was, if I could find someone who would buy a hundred key for thirty grand Fareed would put a hundred on for me on credit. If the job was a success I would pay him thirty grand. If it went tits-up the thirty grand would stay on the backburner and I could pay it off out of future commissions. I was in a position at the time where I could have pulled up the thirty grand myself, though I certainly wasn't going to let Fareed know that. He seemed to be doing alright working on credit; I'd take a leaf out of his book. I went to speak to Neil Robertson, who I knew was searching high and low for a bit of gear. There was one of those rare droughts on at the time.

Neil and his pals were interested but, after Suntan's transport fee, their hundred would become seventy and they needed a minimum of a hundred. I told them I was having a hundred on myself, feeling no obligation to inform them of the credit element, which would also become seventy after transport. I offered to sell them thirty of mine for twenty-one grand on condition they took my remaining forty home and sold it for me. This seemed to suit everyone and the thirty grand was pulled up and paid to Fareed. Suntan worked with his usual professionalism and two nights later the Cockneys had the hundred and forty key. Putting nine grand of my own with twenty-one grand they'd paid me I went and levelled Fareed up.

About a week later Neil phoned to ask me where I wanted my seventy-two grand dropped off. This puff smuggling job is great when things go right.

You might well think, in light of this windfall, my relationship with Fareed would be on the up and up. Nothing could be further from the truth. His natural paranoia coupled with his stimulant abuse was making him harder and harder to work with.

One day he introduced me to two Dublin lads and asked me to take care of their requirements. I can only assume he didn't do it himself because he was a little wary of them. There was some talk that they had connections to the IRA. Personally, I would have thought that if the IRA were interested in getting in the puff job, they'd have a better way of going about it than sending a couple of lads over to the Queen Vic to ask if there was any puff about. The lads themselves did nothing to dispel the rumours, probably thinking they'd be a big disincentive to any rip-offs.

We had a chat and arrangements were made for them to drop off the dough and pick up the gear the following day. They duly arrived but only to tell me that there was a problem with their transport and the deal would have to be put on hold. Fair enough, these things happen and off they went.

Thirty seconds later Fareed, who must have been lurking around the corner, was at the door looking for his money. I brought him up to date and he threw a tantrum.

'You've served my customers with someone else's gear,' he accused me.

'Where the fuck am I supposed to get gear cheaper than I am getting it from you?' I asked him

'You didn't do it for the money, you did it because you knew I needed money to pay Suntan. If you could embarrass me and cause a fallout you could nick Suntan away from me and have him working for yourself.'

Well, anyone who could come up with such a Machiavellian scheme, at the drop of a hat, must have totally lost it to paranoia or else it was the sort of stroke he'd come up with himself. I decided, rewarding though they had been, it was time to severely limit my dealings with Fareed. In any case, Suntan, who wasn't getting any younger and was quite a wealthy man, was seriously talking of at least semi-retirement. He expenses weren't great, though he did occasionally enjoy the company of girls that, well, could be said to have lost their amateur status. He only drank Guinness or Heineken and drove a fairly elderly car so how much money did he need?

If I lost my supply from both Suntan and Fareed I'd be losing all the advantages I had over my rivals. I went for a drink and a bit of a think.

There had been a few other disquieting developments. Quite a number of people fairly close to me had been getting nicked and I'd have to be very naïve to think the local Old Bill didn't know at least as much about me as the landlord of the Queen Vic did. One particularly worrying incident was when a pal, James, came and said he had a customer looking for twelve key. I gave it to him at a price where he could earn a drink. He probably got between three and six hundred quid out of the deal. The buyers got nicked in France and immediately told the French police that their supplier was a bloke called James who lived in such and such an apartment block and drove such and such a car. On this very tenuous and uncorroborated evidence the French police asked the Spanish police to arrest James, which they did. Even more amazingly the French managed to win an extradition case and James went to France, where he got twenty months and a fair-sized fine.

Taking this a step further, all James had to say was that his supplier had, in fact, been me and I would have been in the cell next to him. Taking it even one step further, I could have then said that my supplier was the Archbishop of Malaga and they'd have had to go and nick him, too. Given that the puff job is just a game, if you make a bad move you have to expect to get huffed but all this smacked a bit of kangaroo courts. Maybe it was time to move on. Time for a roll-call.

I had a little over £200,000 in readies. I had a couple of Mercs, a 230E and a 380SE, neither of them new but both pretty presentable. I had some good jewellery, including a 1.7ct solitaire diamond ring and a gold Rolex, almost compulsory for any self-respecting puff dealer. Annie had some nice stuff, too, including a very nice tennis bracelet with forty .10ct diamonds in it.

There was a bit of a story with the bracelet, since it came from The Weed. He had been on holiday in Cyprus and gone on a day trip to Haifa that included a tour of a diamond factory. Having seen the cutting and polishing and setting rooms, the last stop was the salesroom. Jimmy was admiring the bracelet and the matching earrings and said he'd love to buy them but hadn't brought his credit cards. They said they'd take a cheque but he hadn't brought his cheque book either. They said they had blank cheques and he could just fill in his details and that would be fine.

He had to fill in his correct name to match his passport but the bank account number was the first dozen numbers that came into his head. He guessed that more than likely they'd want to wait for the cheque to clear before parting so he was pleasantly surprised when he got to the exit to find a girl waiting with his purchases in an envelope. She even had a form for him to present at Customs to recover his purchase tax.

A few years later he applied for a licence for the Brown Bull Hotel in Salford, only to have it denied. Apparently he had a county court judgement against him from some Jewish jewellers in Hatton Garden, something to do with some earrings and a bracelet sold by their relations in Haifa. He had to settle. I never did find out who got the earrings but Annie still has the bracelet.

I also had a little studio apartment down at Las Chapas. Another story. One night I got talking to a Dublin fella in the Queen Vic and he told me he was over with his mother who was trying to sell a studio she had bought five years earlier. The paperwork was a bit hit and miss and she didn't have the title deeds but when he said she'd take what she'd given for it, my ears pricked up. They were staying across the street at the Hotel Angela and I went over to see exactly what they did have in the way of paperwork. She had the original receipt for the deposit and she had the cancelled IOUs proving she had paid off the mortgage to the builders. These, with a purchase-sales contract between myself and her, would pretty much give me ownership. We met at a pal's estate agency the next morning. He drew up the contract, I gave her six grand and, without even seeing it, I owned an apartment.

When I did see it several weeks later, it looked pretty much how you'd expect an apartment to look when no-one's been near it for five years. I called a builder who put in a new kitchen, new bathroom, new floor, new front door and new patio doors. Satellite TV and fifteen hundred quid's worth of furniture gave me a place a lot more comfortable than many a hotel room I've stayed in and certainly worth more than the twelve grand I had in it. Very handy if I ever had to make myself scarce for a while, though I don't recall ever having slept there up to that point.

So, all in all, I had a net worth of something over a quarter of a million. I suppose that does beg the question, if someone like myself, in my own bumbling, half-hearted, amateurish way could accumulate a quarter of a million – not counting what I'd spent, which wouldn't be insignificant – what were people getting that treated the job seriously? I guess Harry Flashman would be the person to answer that.

It had never been my ambition to be the richest man in the graveyard, much less the richest man walking around the exercise yard in Malaga prison. I had been invited over to Dublin for a wedding and decided to drive over and stay a couple of weeks for a look around. Maybe there was something less precarious I could get into, now that I had a bit of a float behind me.

PART THREE

DUBLIN 1990-92

Back to Ireland

Andrew and Sarah's wedding was everything you would expect of a very-nearly-society do. Andrew's position as a university graduated, nightclub owning, general man about town and Sarah's job as a flight attendant put them firmly in the upper echelon of Dublin society; not quite on a par with the offspring of senior politicians and captains of industry or celebrities from the music and film industries, but well above your average pecks. The newlyweds flew by helicopter – coincidentally, owned by the offspring of a senior politician – from the ceremony in Sarah's local village church to the reception at the Killiney Castle Hotel in Dublin. A good part of the several hundred guests had booked rooms there, which allowed the festivities to continue well into the night and recommence the following lunchtime. It took me a couple of days to recover.

With the wedding over, I set about contacting a few pals to see if there was anything of interest afoot. Peter Carroll was my first target but all I knew of his whereabouts was that he lived in Bray, twelve miles from Dublin. Bray isn't a big place so I called into the local police station on the chance that an officer with some local knowledge could point me in the right direction. He did what I should have done in the first place and looked in the phone book. A minute later I was talking to Peter's wife, Maggie. After all the hellos, how-are-you, I'm-fine and stuff, I told Maggie I was in Bray Garda Station and she asked me what I'd done. Why do people always think the worst of me? I explained I was only there to establish her address, which she gave me and five minutes later she was making us a cup of tea while we waited for Peter to get home from work.

I had met Peter when he came to Spain to open a bar and an agent brought him around to look at the Good Times, but I was already in the middle of the deal to sell it. He found another place around the corner and bought that. I'll tell you a little about Peter's bar because it illustrates perfectly the total futility of trying to make one of those little bars pay.

When Peter bought the place it was called Billy Jean's. It had been called numerous things before and Peter renamed it The Jug of Punch. The next owner called it The Bar With No Name and the next owner, a Welshman, called it the Red Dragon. He put a sign in the window saying Welshmen were the best drinkers in the world and to come in and prove him wrong. Apparently not enough people did and the next owners called it The Cork. The next owners renamed it El Corcho, not very original being Spanish for The Cork. Tweetie's came next which, unsurprisingly, didn't last long; who's going to drink in a bar called Tweetie's? Today it's called Bromley's. No doubt I've missed out a few and more than likely it changed hands a few times without being renamed. The thing that all these ex-publicans, with the exception of Peter, have in common is they all went home wiser, poorer ex-publicans.

Peter and his wife, whose third child had just arrived, had gone through the usual spectrum of emotions – wild enthusiasm, enthusiasm, slight concern, deep concern – and were at the desperation stage when out of the blue an American called Bill put in an appearance. He very quickly became known to everyone as the Barmy Sherman, as in Sherman tank – Yank. Barmy agreed Peter's asking price of twenty-seven grand, which was nearly twice what Peter had paid for the place and about four times what he would have accepted had he been pushed.

Even if Barmy had been the most genial bar owner on the coast, his chances of success were limited, but he wasn't. He was one of the most obnoxious people I've ever met so his chances were, well, I don't think there's a piece of paper in the world big enough to write down the odds. Barmy went through the spectrum of emotions quicker than most. He skipped straight from wild enthusiasm to desperation without pause and even added a new stage, suicidal. After only about six weeks in business, one morning he went into the Hotel Angela, drank several brandies, paid his bill, took the lift to the top floor and jumped off. That was the end of poor old Barmy.

In the meantime Peter had headed for the Wicklow hills with his twenty-seven grand and gone back into his old business of shop-fitting. He'd arrived just in time for the start of the Celtic Tiger economy boom, the biggest boom in the history of the state, and he was doing extremely well.

We left Maggie and Annie to chat and went for a drink. I told Peter that I had a few quid and of my plans to look around for some sort of venture and he asked what sort of venture. I said I didn't really know but the only straight business I knew anything about was bookmaking so perhaps something along those lines. By remarkable coincidence, Peter's ex-partner in the shop-fitting business, Eugene Kidney, was now in the bookmaking game and owned two shops, one of which was for sale. We set off in search of Eugene and found him at the third attempt, sat at the bar in the Golden Ball.

Eugene was known to everyone as Mr Bean and he did bear a striking resemblance to Rowan Atkinson. In fact the resemblance was so striking I'm half-convinced he practised Mr Bean impersonations every morning in front of the bathroom mirror. He certainly didn't seem to object to being called

Mr Bean, though his wife Judith, who came from a very good south County Dublin family and owned a beauty salon in Foxrock, did take umbrage at being called Mrs Bean. Eugene came from a very good family, too, and all his relatives were professional people. His grandfather had founded the Jurys Hotel chain and the family were still large shareholders and owned privately the Kenmare Bay and Sligo Park hotels. I think it's fair to say that Mr Bean was the black sheep of the family.

One of the shops he owned was in Crumlin, South City Dublin, and the other was in Dean's Grange. The Dean's Grange shop was much more in keeping with Mr Bean's ambition of being known as bookmaker to the gentry and it was the Crumlin shop he wanted to sell. This was the area my mother came from and I knew some people there, so we agreed to meet the next day and I'd look the place over. The shop was on Captain's Road, two doors from the Black Horse pub and twenty yards from the Kimmage Cross Roads Industrial Estate. The place had most of the fixtures and fittings you'd expect and it all seemed fine to me, so I gave Mr Bean a deposit.

I phoned Andrew and told him of my progress and he told me I would need a solicitor and an accountant. And a doctor and a dentist. And a few other professionals. They all turned out to be around Andrew's age and I suppose this was some kind of old boy network with some mutual back-scratching going on. Very handy person to know, was Andrew. I went to see the solicitor, Peter Silvest, and instructed him to proceed with applying for the licence and to sort out the lease. I gave him a deposit. The accountant, Colin Waters, advised that the best route was to form a limited company. At the time a rather futile attempt was being made to gentrify the Captain's Road area and the name had been changed to

Ravensdale Park. Ravensdale Racing Services Ltd was born. I gave Colin a deposit.

Next I needed somewhere to live. The house Peter was living in was only rented while the one he was having built was completed. Against all odds, the builders were ahead of schedule and Peter's rented place would be available in the next few weeks. We went to see the estate agent; I signed a six-month lease and gave him a deposit. Just as well I had brought a few quid with me.

For someone who is not used to getting anything done with any degree of despatch, I was absolutely stunned at what I had managed to achieve in a little over a week. I had a new, straight business, somewhere decent to live, money, cars and jewellery and above all, a beautiful wife who, for reasons best known to her, loved me to death. Now, if I could just get the odd parcel of puff home from, say, Amsterdam to the UK whilst living in Dublin and commuting to Spain, I'd have to be pretty much bulletproof.

I still had a few days left to re-acquaint myself with some of Dublin's better watering holes before it was time for the ferry and back to Spain to pack.

Packing up was a bigger job than I had envisioned, bearing in mind I'd arrived in Spain six years earlier with one small holdall. I had to hire a van to move three-quarters of the gear to my dad's garage and most of the rest went to the studio flat which we'd be using on trips back to Spain. There wasn't all that much to take to Ireland, we didn't have a lot of winter clothes and Spanish TVs and videos don't work in Ireland. A bit of shopping would have to be done.

I drove to Gibraltar, where I deposited a hundred grand in the Bank of Credit and Commerce International – where it would be nice and safe, wouldn't it? Then I packed the rest of my liquid assets to take with me. I decided to drive over in the 230E since it was right-hand drive and leave the 380 parked up at the studio. Being right-hand drive was about all the 230 had in its favour. It was metallic gold and had the AMG body pack with all the fins and spoilers, not the perfect tool for someone wanting to keep a low profile in north County Wicklow. Before long most of the locals were referring to it as the Pimpmobile. The drive back was uneventful and we arrived at the house to find Peter shampooing the carpets, probably not a wasted effort since his fifth child had recently put in her appearance.

We did some shopping, bought a TV and video, had the cable connected and Annie cooked our first meal in our new home. On the Monday I went to see the accountant who had been beavering away and had the articles of association ready for me to sign. Ravensdale Racing Services Ltd was up and running.

The solicitor hadn't been making parallel progress. There was a problem with the lease. The landlord was reluctant to put it in a company name unless I signed a personal guarantee, which I agreed to do, for what that's worth, bearing in mind my only asset in Ireland was the very lease we were arguing about.

The next problem was the licence, which had to be in an individual's name, and it certainly wasn't going to be mine. God knows what can of worms could be opened if I started going for interviews with police and magistrates. Up stepped my cousin Colm and the application went in in his name but it was all very time consuming. Adverts had to be placed in three editions of the morning papers to give any neighbours the opportunity to object. Since the shop had been a bookie's for years I wasn't expecting any objections and in any case, given the area, if I said I wanted to open a crack-house I probably wouldn't have had any objections. In the end it was all getting a bit expensive and I was sitting around for six weeks.

Another unexpected expense was the satellite racing coverage. The company SIS is the sole supplier of the service and as it's impossible to work without it, they can pretty much make up any rules they want. One of the rules is that they'll only install it if you pay a year in advance. They do two packages, the basic for five grand a year, and the full service, which eliminates the need for a boardman, for ten grand. I opted for the basic which meant I did need a boardman and at a tenner a day and twenty quid on a Saturday it was only marginally cheaper but at least I didn't have to pay him a year in advance.

To pass the time and justifying the expense, as a sort of market research I started attending the local race meetings. One Sunday afternoon at Punchestown I bumped into Mr Bean, who had been haunting me for the rest of the money for the shop. He wasn't getting it until I got what I was paying for, a shop with a licence. Anyway, we went for a drink and a chat, during which I began to tell him of my exploits on the turf back in the UK.

Most on-course bookmakers are ordinary working men who get up every day to travel, often by train, to distant race meetings in the hope of getting a day's wages, which they generally do. My own adventures were much different. Hassan, my wealthy Iraqi pal, would put up the float and we'd take a share with a slightly impoverished bookmaker who happened to have wonderful pitches, mostly on the rails, at all the top meetings. We'd travel, usually by Rolls-Royce, and stay at the Dorchester for Royal Ascot, the Chase for the York meetings and the Hilton at Stratford-upon-Avon for the Cheltenham Festival. We'd go to the two big Chester meetings, some of the Newmarket events, the Grand National at Aintree and most of the Haydock Park meetings. Since money wasn't an obstacle, we were able to play quite big and, as is so often the case when the money isn't a matter of life and death, we usually won.

Mr Bean asked me if I'd considered working on-course in Ireland and when I said nothing would give me more pleasure, he said he had a pal, David Maloney, who was an on-course bookmaker looking for a partner. We went over to speak to him and arranged to meet in a pub in Blessington after the races. Dave clarified his situation. He wasn't so much looking for a partner, as he found it difficult to work with one, but was in a position that he was prepared to allow someone to have a share on the understanding that David had the sole say. Bookmaking is a seat-of-the-pants job and decisions have to be made in a split second. There really isn't time for a board meeting before deciding which way to go, so, assuming that Dave knew what he was doing, we struck a deal and I was an on-course bookmaker, or at least an on-course bookmaker's partner. We were destined to work together for a couple of years and I can't remember a cross word. We're great pals to this day.

I eventually got the shop licence through and went in to give the place a bit of a spruce-up. During the sprucing-up I accidentally touched the panic button but it only rang the once and I thought no more of it. A few minutes later, two carloads of Old Bill, armed to the teeth, screamed to a halt and stormed in like the Keystone Cops. I told them it went off accidentally and they got all grumpy. The boss told me that if it happened again I must ring them and I said sure and asked the phone number. He bawled, 'Fucking 999!' A few days later I got a letter from the local inspector saying that he was of the opinion that the alarm was set off deliberately to test their response time and that if it happened again they would stop responding. Yet another bastard thinking the worst of me.

With my new on-course commitments I was now in the same position Mr Bean had been in and had to re-employ the manager whose services Mr Bean had dispensed with. More expense but still, things seemed to be coming together quite nicely. Maybe now I could start earning a few quid.

At the Races

I had travelled over for the Irish Derby numerous times prior to acquiring my bookmaker status. It's the social event of the year as far as the horsey-crowd is concerned and even for quite a few that aren't part of the horsey-crowd. I loved it. By lucky fluke David had some long-standing arrangement with his wife, Anna, that on Derby Day the pitch was hers, which meant I couldn't work. This was fine with me and allowed me to enjoy the day to the standard I had become accustomed.

Back in the days when the race was sponsored by Budweiser, getting a place to sit was reasonably easy. Knowing several publicans, I was usually able to finesse my way into the Budweiser tent, where you got free booze all day and a decent bit of grub. Later, when the sponsors changed, I had to make my own arrangements. Getting somewhere to sit is of vital importance and the only way you can be sure is to book a table in one of the marquees. It's not cheap but after all it's only once a year. Normally it's tables of ten so if you don't want any strangers on the table you have to book the whole table, at about £250 a head. For this you get entrance to the enclosure, a three- or four-course lunch, afternoon tea and free booze all day. And somewhere to sit, so it's not really bad value.

Actually getting to the races is another problem and I've tried every conceivable means. I tell a lie. I've never tried the bus or train, maybe one day I will. But I have tried taxi, minibus, private car and one year we even hired three helicopters. Taxis have the problem of capacity and we'd need three, and then you have to find another three to get you back. Private cars mean three designated drivers who then can't partake of the free booze. The helicopters sound a bit extravagant but for £150 a head, which included champagne breakfast and a meal when we got back, they brought fourteen of us. The problem with them was we missed the traditional after-race drink at the Keydean Hotel in Newbridge. Also they dropped us at the Mountain View pub's pitch-and-putt course in Step-A-Side, leaving a ten-mile drive back to Dublin. So, I suppose the best answer is the minibus.

One of the things I like best about racing is the characters you meet. There are a fair number of characters amongst the bookmakers, as you might expect from a group of people who get their living in such a precarious manner, but the real characters are the auxiliary workers and grafters: the barmen, the fruit and flower sellers, the spivs and tipsters and even the pickpockets. They are all part of the great tapestry that makes up the racing crowd. I've been racing all over the world, places as diverse as the States, Panama, Dubai and most of Europe and I've met their counterparts everywhere I've been. Maybe I have some sort of sign on my forehead that attracts them.

One person I rarely went to a race meeting without having a drink with was Dennis Byrne, or Dennis the Boxman, as he was known. His game was renting out the stools that the bookmakers stand on, which are really only glorified orange boxes. At a big meeting, with seventy or eighty bookmakers having two or three boxes each, at a pound or two each, he took some money. Not one penny of this significant income was squandered, it was invested in its entirety on gambling and booze.

One time I was on my way to Naas, for some reason that escapes me not working, just for a day out. On the way there my phone went and it was someone from Spain giving me a tip for a horse running, ironically enough, in the second race at Naas. I told him I was on my way there already and I'd certainly back it. I got on the course as they were going down for the first, a small field of five runners, and invested fifty quid on a forecast. I was delighted when it obliged, paying six to four, put the ticket, now worth £125, in my pocket and went for a drink where I bumped into Dennis.

We got a drink and I told him about the tip which he said had no chance. Nonetheless, just before the race I went out to back it. It turned out it was a sixteen-to-one chance but the favourite was odds-on and, as is usually the case with an odds-on favourite, I couldn't find a bookmaker prepared to lay each way, so instead of having £100 each way I had £200 to win. Walking back, I spotted a bookmaker betting without the favourite and I could have taken ten-to-one about the tip to win or come second to the favourite but didn't, thinking I had enough on it.

I was doubly gutted after watching the race where the tip ran a very close second to the favourite. Had I been able to back it each way as I had planned, I'd have won a three-er instead of losing a two-er, but worse than that, had I taken the ten-to-one without I'd have won two grand. I went to re-join Dennis and have another drink.

Glancing at my watch I saw it was five past three and suddenly remembered that Jim Swords had a horse, Heidi III, running in the Great Yorkshire Chase at Doncaster in five minutes. Giving Dennis the £125 ticket I said, 'Draw the money and put it on Heidi.'

He ambled off and returned a couple of minutes later with the money in his hand asking, 'What was the name of that horse?'

'Oh, for God's sake! Liven yourself up a bit or they'll be off. Heidi III, three ten, Doncaster.'

He wandered over to the first bookmaker on the rails, one of the Graham brothers, Kevin I think, shouted the bet and gave him the money. With hindsight I'd have to accept that probably Dennis wasn't the best emissary to use. For Dennis to be having one and a quarter on a horse, the bookmaker must have assumed it would be a short-priced one and, not bothering to check, simply scribbled the bet at the top of his ledger.

We sat and watched the race and Heidi duly obliged at twenty-to-one. Now letting Dennis out of my sight with one and a quarter was one thing but to send him to pick up £2,625 was a different proposition altogether. I tailed him out.

He shouted up to the bookmaker that the horse had won and the bookmaker nodded and asked what price it was. Dennis enlightened him.

'What fucking price?' he howled. 'I think you'd better come back after the next race.'

I tried to intervene and explain that the bet was in fact mine but he was having none of it. We adjourned to the bar. In the meantime the bookmaker was on the phone trying to establish exactly what time the race was off, if anything had fallen early on or any other evidence that would confirm his suspicions that Dennis was having him over. Evidently he was unsuccessful because when we went back he threw the money at Dennis saying, 'Tell your Brit pal to take his bets elsewhere in future.'

'He's not a Brit, he's from Crumlin,' Dennis informed him.

I don't think Mr Graham found that a lot of consolation. Obviously Dennis extracted a healthy commission, my girlfriend got a new pair of boots and the rest of the windfall was reinvested or drunk.

Another time, we were at an evening meeting at Limerick Junction in Tipperary. In those days the big racing pub for Dublin racegoers before and after meetings was the Poitin Still on the Naas Road. They had a sort of unwritten law that if you got back before ten-thirty you could stay as long as you liked and the landlord would put up a few sandwiches. Arriving after ten-thirty was unacceptable. As everyone knows, it's a long way to Tipperary and as soon as the last race was over the car-park was like the start of the Le Mans twenty-four-hour race, with parched bookmakers bumping and boring their way out in an attempt beat the watershed. As luck would have it we had arrived at Tipp a little late, so our car was quite near the exit and I got away pretty much in pole position. The drive went remarkably well, one of those nights when all the traffic lights were green and people in front only need slight encouragement from the horn and lights to pull over. Hurt ling through Kildare town Davey Keogh, our clerk, remarked, 'We could well be in line for our first chequered flag.' The lights stayed favourable all along the Naas dual carriageway and I screamed into the pub driveway a comfortable fifteen minutes on the right side. I can't describe my frustration when I spotted Dennis the Boxman's flatbed truck, complete with several hundred orange boxes, sitting in the car-park.

There are twenty-eight racecourses in Ireland and, barring Down Royal and Downpatrick, the two in the occupied territories where I couldn't go, I've worked all of them. The festival meetings at Punchestown, Galway, the three in Killarney and the Christmas meeting at Leopardstown constitute about twenty per cent of the working year and bigger booze-ups don't happen anywhere on the planet. I thoroughly enjoyed every minute, win or lose. Having said all that, if you put a gun to my head and made me pick my absolute favourite meeting, I'd be forced to admit that my heart belongs to the Cheltenham Festival, which has to be as near as you can get to an Irish meeting not actually in Ireland. Sadly, for judicial reasons, I've not been able to attend since 1983 but Punchestown runs a pretty close second.

The '83 Cheltenham Festival is a meeting that will stick in my mind for as long as I live. I was there in my bookmaking capacity, using Hassan's money, and we showed an eight grand profit, which was very nice but we must have been the smallest winners amongst the twenty-odd party that travelled down. A friend of mine, Geoff Kessler, was a very big player and had some sort of a bet every day of his life but every year he sorted out a mega-bet. His coup in '83 was Gay Brief to win the Champion Hurdle and he'd backed it all winter at big prices. Come the day of the race it stood to win him £105,000.

I was standing next to him when it won and he said, 'It's not the money, you know. It's the being right.'

With me, I think it would have been the money.

At the time I had an amusement arcade and I had a partner called Dave Trotter. Trotter's sideline was advertising as a racing tipster in the *Sporting Chronicle*. There was a whole page of these tipsters, all with an advert about the size of a business card. Most of the advertisers gave themselves a military title and an address in a racing centre: 'Major So-and-so, Newmarket', 'Colonel Such-and-Such, Epsom'. Not to be outdone, Trotter's advert read: 'Capt. Kilty, Chorlton-cum-Hardy – Novice Hurdle Specialist'. Since The Triumph Hurdle is little more than a glorified novice hurdle, Trotter felt obliged to give his followers a selection, which was Saxon Farm. He, like Kessler though to much smaller stakes, had been backing it all winter, having tenners and scores at big prices whenever he had a touch. He'd also had the double with Gay Brief. When it won he got about £25,000 and this to a lad who'd probably never had more than £2,500 at any one time in his life.

Most of the rest of our merry band seemed to have similar stories. The Gold Cup was won by Graham Bradley on Bregawn. This was the year Michael Dickinson trained the first five home, an unheard-of accomplishment. Brad had a lot of friends in Manchester, I came to know him quite well in later years, so this result was fairly lucrative for our mob. Funnily enough, when Brad wrote his autobiography he called it *The Wayward Lad*, which was one of the other Dickinson horses that finished behind him.

One pal, Peter Jacobs, whose wife was French, was reading through the race card when he came to a horse called Corbier. His wife said it sounded like the French word for dustbin and Peter said that was probably where we'd all finish up and went off and had £500 each way at twenty-to-one. Not only did it win but a few weeks later it went to Aintree for the National. I was there in my bookmaking role; we put a line through Corbier and laid practically every other horse in the race. When it won we had a clear book, barring a few bits and pieces of place money.

Maybe one day I'll get to visit Cheltenham again but in the meantime I usually get to watch it on TV, which is what I normally do when I'm at a race meeting anyway. I never could get the hang of those binocular things.

[illegible]

[illegible]

[illegible]

Heat

Irish unmarked police cars are very nearly as conspicuous as their marked relatives. They are always the very basic model of a cheap family saloon, unusually lacking hubcaps but always with some sort of antenna. They are usually occupied by two men, sometimes by a man and a woman, rarely if ever by two women. All Irish police vehicles are registered at Dublin Castle so all carry Dublin registration plates.

Spotting a vehicle that fitted the above criteria at Sligo races, I took little notice. When I saw it again at Wexford a few days later, I was only slightly more interested. The third time it made an appearance was at Navan and then I did begin to wonder who, other than myself, had been at all three venues. Well, all the other bookmakers for a start. And their clerks. And the stall-handlers and all the catering staff. And Dennis the Boxman. It could be anybody. There was a little rumour at the time, which was subsequently proved to have some foundation, that the turnstile attendants were up to some skulduggery. Perhaps they were getting a look at.

On the Saturday morning all doubts were dispelled. By this time I was living on Rock Road, Blackrock, which is a clearway and therefore impossible to park on. Not a problem for me with my handy underground car park but not so convenient if you are two garda trying to be unobtrusive. They were parked across the road in the driveway of Blackrock College. I gave them a beep and a wave and set off for the Curragh.

The last race was five-thirty and I wanted to go home, get

changed and be at Shelbourne Park greyhounds before seven-thirty, so I was in a bit of a hurry. Turning onto the Naas Road, I saw blue flashing lights approaching from the opposite direction and automatically slowed a bit. Then I saw blue flashing lights coming up from behind and slowed a bit more. Nearing the traffic lights at Kill a squad car drew alongside and waved me into the slip road.

'Do you realise you were travelling at a hundred and three miles an hour?' asked the officer, a Garda Butner by name.

'Surely not,' I said.

He was adamant and said he had me on video with his calibrated speedo and all that.

'Fair enough. Give me a ticket and I'll see you in court. I'm in a hurry, I've got a greyhound meeting to get to.'

But no. He placed his hand on my shoulder in the old 'feeling one's collar' tradition, a gesture that I've not seen since the days of *Dixon of Dock Green*.

'I am arresting you for dangerous driving,' he said, and took me to Kill nick.

I sat twiddling my thumbs for twenty minutes until the desk sergeant announced, 'Sorry, I can't deal with the matter. You will have to go to headquarters in Naas.'

Well, if they don't let him deal with a speeding ticket, what do they let him deal with? Off we all trooped to Naas. They put me in a large office with a dozen desks and two or three detectives beavering away at their paperwork. Or checking their football coupons or the results from the Curragh. I was reading the *Evening Herald* and wondering what the results from Shelbourne Park would be like.

After about forty minutes, about the time it takes to drive from Dublin, three detectives came in as if by chance. One of them started chatting to me.

'Howeryer?' he said, which is North Inner City-speak for

'How are you?', confirming my suspicion that they had just travelled out from Dublin.

'Fine, thank you,' I said.

'Aren't you the chap driving the English-plated car?' he asked and I confirmed that that was indeed the case.

'Well, being Irish, why are you driving an English reg?'

'I bought the car, on English plates, in Spain, where I live, and in the fullness of time or when I get around to it, I will either transfer it to Irish plates or take it back to Spain,' I said.

'Oh, you live in Spain,' he said in feigned surprise. 'Whereabouts?'

I now felt we'd passed the point where my active cooperation was obligatory and told him so. I went on to say that if he had any more questions I'd like my solicitor present and gave him Peter Silvest's name. Peter has probably never seen the inside of a court room, let alone a police station, in his entire career but I hoped the Jack didn't know that and might think giving him a Dublin solicitor's name gave me some sort of clout.

He laughed and said, 'I was only asking because I get over to Spain now and again myself.'

Really? What was he suggesting? We go for a pint or something?

With that the conversation drew to a close, Dave Maloney arrived and paid £100 bail and I was released but the whole scenario mystified me. I'm totally convinced it was no routine traffic stop but if they just wanted a close look at me they could have done that much more simply any day of the week at whatever racecourse I happened to be at. Maybe, in light of my beep and wave that morning, they thought it was time that all parties were fully aware of the status quo. That is, they were watching me, I knew they were watching me, they knew that I knew they were watching me and now I knew that they knew that I knew they were watching me. Always nice to know where one stands.

I resolved to make some enquiries and try to find out where all this heat was coming from. I had a friend in Manchester whose father was on close terms with a high ranking police officer and I asked if I could be put through the National Criminal Intelligence computer to see if there was anything I should be aware of. There was and it was alarming in the extreme.

There was a supergrass in London with the unlikely name of Michael Michael whose evidence led to a whole series of trials. There's a basic flaw to the supergrass system, which is probably why you don't hear much about it these days. The supergrass is not given immunity but is guaranteed a vastly reduced sentence and, during his period of usefulness, will be held in relative luxury somewhere like Paddington Green or some other secure police station. There he will have the benefit of food, booze, women and maybe even the odd line of charlie. Once his usefulness comes to an end, he will be transferred to the likes of Wandsworth, where he will serve the rest of his sentence on protection under Rule 43, surrounded by rapists, perverts and child molesters. Obviously he's in no hurry to go there, so when he's exhausted his supply of genuine information he may well be tempted to be inventive. Meanwhile, his handlers are never satisfied they've got the lot and always feel there's a little meat left on the bone. They might suggest people, places or events that the grass could know something about. Eager to be cooperative, the grass might well say, 'Why yes, now you mention it, I do recall so-and-so doing such-and-such.'

The problem with all this is that if any one of the numerous defence barristers catches the grass out in one single little fib, his entire testimony is tainted. And that is exactly what happened: many of the defendants Michael grassed up were acquitted. I wouldn't flatter myself that it was the lies he told about me that led to the acquittals but he certainly didn't do me any favours.

I wasn't aware that I had ever met the man but I was later told that he had been on a table, with nineteen other people, at an Irish Derby one year. I wouldn't know the bloke if I tripped over him. He had some interesting things to say about me though. The file sent by the British police to the Irish police was stamped 'for information purposes only' and contained a list of people I knew and countries I had visited. These included England, Ireland, Scotland, Holland, France, Belgium, Spain, the Caribbean and the US. All places I have been to, but so what?

The frightening part was his invention of one particular deal I was supposed to have been involved in concerning a parcel of cocaine coming from South America. The yarn went that I was involved with two other people, one of whom would only have a financial interest. He allegedly didn't like being in deals with me because of my connections with the terrorist organisations.

Fucking marvellous. Now I've been elevated from a small-time puff dealer to a big-time coke smuggling terrorist. To the best of my knowledge I've only ever met one terrorist and he'd been an awful long time in retirement. Is it any wonder the Irish police thought it worth their while sitting on me? Still, as I say, it was inventions such as these that led to the acquittals, so some good came of it. Even so, I had to accept that my card was firmly marked as far as the Irish Old Bill was concerned.

The speeding charge eventually came to court in Naas where I was up in front of Judge Johnson, a renowned crank who had a particular vindictiveness towards any member of the racing fraternity. He said it was his intention to ban me for six months – this was my first ever motoring offence in Ireland – but he was prepared to be more lenient if I would make a donation to charity. I offered £200. In response,

Judge Dread addressed my solicitor, as if I wasn't there or I was deaf or something.

'Tell your client,' he said, 'that if he thinks he's at an auction he hasn't come close to the reserve yet. The figure I had in mind is fifteen hundred.'

I gasped and my brief whispered, 'You'll have to pay it or take the ban.'

I whispered back, a lot more loudly, 'Make sure you get a receipt.'

Charitable donations are deductible, aren't they?

The Monk, the CAB and Veronica Guerin

Terrible as it was, I could never fully understand why the murder of journalist Veronica Guerin in June 1996 was considered so much more heinous than a number of other murders that happened around that time. I know she was a married woman with a young child, but some of the other murder victims were family people. I also know the crime was a revenge killing committed by a hired hitman but some of the other killings had a revenge motive and hired hitmanship had become something of a growth industry in Dublin. It may well be that because some of the other murders were regarded as criminal-on-criminal they were considered somehow more trivial. Okay, what about the plumber shot dead in Finglas because he happened to be changing a washer on a tap in the wrong place at the wrong time? What was he, collateral damage? I can appreciate that, being a reporter, her murder got more coverage by her colleagues, even her rivals, than it might have done had she been a bank clerk or a school teacher. But surely, if you choose as a profession to be an investigative journalist, going into the trenches on a daily basis, writing exposés on the most dangerous people in the country, it carries with it a certain risk element. Unlike say a bank clerk or a school teacher. Or a plumber.

Let me make one thing perfectly clear. I'm not trying to justify or minimise Ms. Guerin's murder. All I'm trying to say is that I really don't understand why this particular murder was the catalyst for the events that followed. Be that as it may, the fact remains that the vast majority of Irish people did see it as the worst crime in living memory and a direct result of it was the setting up of the Criminal Assets Bureau, or the CAB. This was destined to have a devastating effect on the finances of the Irish underworld. The new unit comprised police, Customs, tax experts and forensic accountants and they were given unprecedented powers to investigate anyone they thought had assets purchased with ill-gotten gains. It was a totally new concept where the boot was put on the other foot and suspects had to prove their assets were legitimate instead of the police having to prove they weren't. The initial targets were drug dealers and bank robbers.

I had quite a number of acquaintances in Ireland, amongst them self-employed builders and tradesmen, publicans and even a few professional people, who would consider themselves to be totally law abiding citizens. They all, to a man, greeted the new legislation with whole-hearted approval, apparently able to overlook the fact that the basic principle of Irish justice, innocent until proven guilty, was being trampled in the mire. A few years later, after the CAB's overwhelming success, it began to run out of drug dealers and bank robbers and broadened its terms of reference to include self-employed builders and tradesmen, publicans and even a few professional people. This led to an outcry that the basic principle of Irish justice, innocent until proven guilty, was being trampled in the mire. Too late, of course the genie was out of the bottle.

One of the first targets of the CAB was a friend of mine, Gerard 'The Monk' Hutch. There had been a robbery at the Allied Brinks cash deposit at Dublin airport in which apparently £4 million went adrift. The job was done with such military precision that at first it was thought to be the work of the IRA, but suspicions later fell on Gerard. I have no personal knowledge of the robbery; I've never discussed it with Gerard since it's none of my business. He's never discussed it with me either because it's none of my business or because he didn't do it. So, in actual fact, I only know exactly as much as anyone else who's read the *Sunday World*.

What I do know is that, subsequent to the *Sunday World* articles, any time there was a robbery of any significance anywhere in the Republic, the first words on everyone's lips were, 'That'll be the fucking Monk again.' He'd have had to be the most industrious armed robber since Dick Turpin to get through a fraction of the work attributed to him. I mean, did he never take a holiday, take the kids – he had five of them – to the zoo or the beach? Did he never sleep?

Actually, I know he takes holidays because he was on holiday when I first met him. Every year there's an amateur boxing tournament, Ireland versus Spain, at the Alay Hotel in Benalmadena and Gerard was over supporting a Dublin team he sponsors, the Corinthians. We were introduced by some fellow boxing fans. One night we went for a drink at a bar in Los Boliches, the Dragon's Cavern, where a friend of mine, the Irish singer Pearse Webb, was appearing. I was fairly sure Gerard's attendance would pass unnoticed since the *Sunday World's* circulation didn't encompass the Costa del Sol in those days but I'd reckoned without a Dublin girl who happened to be in. She must have had access to some sort of airmail edition. She came over to ask if that was the Monk I was drinking with and I said it was. She said she thought so, she'd seen him in the lift at the hotel where she worked and where Gerard was staying. She said she had been tempted to ask him to hold a strip of black paper over his eyes so she could be sure it was him. When the *World* published a photo of a suspected robber, as opposed to a convicted one, they blacked out the eyes as a sort of concession to anonymity. Not very effective, obviously.

When the CAB's hammer finally fell, Gerard finished up with a bill for £2.7 million. A lot of people on the list, or who thought they were on the list, or even thought they might be put on the list, salvaged anything portable and headed for sunnier climes. Gerard felt he'd moved as far from the inner-city as he ever wanted to when he moved to Clontarf, so he stayed and fought. Bear in mind this was new legislation and Gerard became a bit of a test case, appealing the ruling through every court in the land. All the appeals fell on deaf ears and in the end he had to pay.

The CAB was magnanimous enough to allow him to pay in stages, which led to a farcical situation, as reported in the *Evening Herald*. They published a photo of Gerard walking across O'Connell Bridge with a haversack containing the last payment of half a million quid, en route to the CAB's bank. When he got there, the manager refused to accept it. Most likely he recalled an incident a few years earlier with Martin 'The General' Cahill. Martin went into his own bank and deposited seventy grand and asked for a bank draft to purchase some property. Two or three minutes after he left, two masked gunmen entered the bank and relieved the manager of the seventy grand plus whatever other few quid was lying about.

This manager was taking no chances and phoned Pearse Street Garda Station, who dispatched two armed detectives to oversee the transaction. The money was counted and Gerard was issued a receipt. As he was leaving one of the jacks, never short of a bit of witty banter, shouted 'Here, Gerry. It wasn't that long ago you were walking out of banks with haversacks full of money.'

These days Gerard runs a highly successful limousine hire company. He calls it Wecarryanybody.com.

Another pal of mine, Micky Green, came to the attention of the Assets Bureau under tragic circumstances. Mick had led a life of adventure, travelled the world and accumulated a sizable fortune but, well into his fifties, he had retired to Ireland and bought an estate in Kilcock. One Saturday night he was driving along the Quays in his Rolls-Royce when he was in collision with a taxi cab. The taxi driver was killed and Mick, dazed, left the scene but was arrested several hours later leaving the River Club. I have no knowledge of whether Mick had been drinking before the crash but, then again, neither has anyone else. I do know that when Mick was intending to have a drink he habitually employed a driver, and had a relative on more or less permanent standby for just such an occasion. Anyway, since there was no argument that he'd been drinking in the River Club a breath test was academic. He was arrested, charged with leaving the scene of an accident and remanded to Mountjoy.

During the couple of weeks on remand, the *Independent* did a bit of digging and came up with some snippets about Mick's pedigree, much of which was highly inaccurate. However, this gossip coupled with his car being a Roller was enough to attract the attention of the CAB. Being well aware that there had been very little in the way of success stories from anyone having dealings with the CAB, Mick decided to err on the side of caution. Leaving the house, an apartment on the Quays and whatever money he couldn't get out of the bank before the embargoes started flying about, he packed his bags and headed for Marbella. He probably left about two million behind. I thought Mick's tribulations were particularly unfair in as much as, wherever his money came from, it certainly wasn't generated in Ireland.

One little sequel to the story. A feature at Mick's house was an ornamental pool which he stocked with koi carp. Apparently run-of-the-mill koi carp can cost up to a grand apiece and these were top-of-the-range koi carp, so God knows what they cost. One night some members of the travelling community were passing and wandered in, possibly looking for somewhere to park their house. Spotting the carp, they fished them out and fried them up for a snack. The *Herald* described it as the world's most expensive fish and chip supper.

There were countless other victims on a smaller scale and a vast amount of assets were seized but, at the end of the day, I really do believe the Criminal Assets Bureau did more harm than good to the country. We went from the biggest boom in history to the deepest slump and I blame it all on the collapse of the black economy. The boom years only came about through politicians like Charlie Haughey and Bertie Ahern turning a blind eye to the black economy. In fact, Bertie Ahern half-admits that he rarely did a deal that didn't involve a brown envelope stuffed with readies, so you could say he actively contributed to the black economy.

In the good old days, if you wanted your car re-sprayed or your washing machine repaired and you weren't fussy about a receipt, you could get a substantial discount and avoid the VAT. The car-sprayer or the plumber had a few quid that only he and God knew from where it had come and could pop down to the boozer. The pubs were doing a roaring trade and the landlords, entrepreneurial types as a rule, had a few quid to throw into the construction of a shopping centre in Limerick or holiday homes in Kinsale. This kept the builders employed, amongst whom it was not unusual to find the odd good drinker. And so it went on.

Nowadays everyone is terrified of doing anything without receipts and VAT and paying the income tax in case they appear to be living beyond their means and get the CAB on their backs. Ironically, the Government would probably get more from indirect taxation, with all the drinking, gambling and smoking going on, than they would ever have got in direct taxation.

I'm afraid without a black economy the future for all of us looks grim. Come back Bertie, all is forgiven.

Drinking and the Law

For a country with such a big reputation for enjoying a drink, the intricacies of actually getting one were hard to believe. Most pubs opened at about half ten in the morning and served until half ten in the evenings. Except between two and three p.m., the holy hour, when they stayed open but stopped serving. This stumbling-block could be circumvented simply by ordering two or three drinks at five to two and making them last until three. On a Friday and Saturday they stayed open for an extra half hour, except in summer when they opened until eleven-thirty. On St Stephen's Day, December 26, and Good Friday they didn't open at all. This is probably why the St Stephen's Day meeting at Leopardstown was so popular, with the bars open all day.

Restaurants very often only had a wine licence, so no coffee and brandy or Irish coffee after a meal. Having said that, most places kept a few bottles of spirits stashed away for the convenience of valued customers. Nightclubs were a law unto themselves and just getting into one wasn't a formality. If a doorman tells you they only admit regular customers it does make you wonder how you become a regular customer. Once inside, the drinks they'll serve you seem to depend on the time and their mood. One night I was in a place in O'Connell Street and ordered a pint for my friend and a whiskey for myself. I was told they don't serve beer after midnight. Whether this was for legal or economic reasons wasn't revealed. Good Friday was a particular problem for clubs. At midnight on

Thursday it became Good Friday so they had to stop serving but at midnight on Good Friday it became Saturday and they could serve, thus creating two nights of disruption.

Years earlier I'd discussed all this with my grandfather, Bertie O'Brien, and he pooh-poohed all my grievances, claiming that he could drink twenty-four hours a day, any day of the year in Dublin.

'Prove it,' I challenged.

He gave it some thought and came up with a compromise. 'I'm too old for twenty-four-hour sessions these days,' he said, 'but would you accept that anyone can get a drink from eleven in the morning to eleven in the evening?'

'I would,' I said, 'assuming they knew the ropes about the holy hour and it was summer or a weekend in winter.'

'Right,' he said, 'meet me tomorrow night outside the Ole Dub in Fleet Street and we'll drink till eleven in the morning.'

Bertie was in the printing trade, working as a linotype engineer for the *Irish Times*. This was back in the days when the print unions were all-powerful and Bertie was earning about forty quid a week when the average wage was about twenty. You only got to be a linotype engineer if you had a relative that was already a linotype engineer. I think it's fair to say he liked a drink. There are clubs with special licences to cater to print workers and their unsocial hours, so our first port of call was the Press Club.

Bertie rang the bell in some sort of coded sequence and a matchbox on a string descended from a first floor window. Bertie opened the box, removed the key and let us in. The place was packed but even here there were rules as to who could drink dependent on what shift they were working and every now and again the barman would shout that people on such-and-such a shift had to leave. No-one took a blind bit of notice, any more than they took any notice that I wasn't a printer at all.

We left at one-ish, ambled back down Fleet Street, across Westmoreland Street and found ourselves outside an apparently deserted pub off Pearse Street. More coded taps on the window gained us admission. Inside it was like New Year's Eve with people six deep at the bar. Bertie ferreted his way through and returned with four drinks, he said to save having to ferret back in ten minutes. Twenty minutes later I ferreted back for four more.

We visited another pub or two and a couple of dives. Around five in the morning we took a taxi out to an Italian café in Ranelagh. Here they served whiskey and Coke, or anything else you wanted, in a teapot. We had several pots. At seven we took another taxi back to the Quays, where there are a few pubs, known as early houses, that open at six and have special licences to accommodate the market workers. They serve anyone. We lingered around there having a few pints of Guinness for breakfast until it was time to stroll over the Halfpenny Bridge back to Fleet Street. They were just pulling up the shutters on the Ole Dub and we finished our last pint on the dot of eleven, Bertie having proved his point.

We shook hands and I was on the point of leaving when Bertie said, 'Do you not fancy a pint?'

'No,' I said. 'I'll have a whiskey.'

When my grandfather died, having, against all odds, reached the age of eighty-seven, I was in Spain but felt it was the least I could do to travel over for the funeral. The Mass was at eleven at Glasnevin and when we were leaving we all agreed to meet at The GAA Club in Drimnagh, which was Bertie's last local and opened at four o'clock. Annie, myself and a friend of mine, Joan Gallagher, arrived at about twenty to four and a chap mowing the lawn asked if he could help us.

'I'm Bertie O'Brien's grandson and we've come for a drink with the family,' I explained.

Abandoning his mower he opened a door that led to an upstairs bar above the gym.

'What can I get you?' he asked, pulling up the shutters.

I gave him the order. Whilst he was pouring them, the doorbell rang and he asked me to answer it. On the doorstep was my Uncle Teddy and a couple more relatives.

'How did you get in?' he asked. It being a members' club, Teddy had assumed he'd have had to make some sort of introduction.

'I told him I was Bertie's grandson,' I said. 'Bertie always told me that if I ever got stuck for a drink in Dublin to mention his name.'

'Yeah, but he's been dead for a week,' said Teddy.

Not the point.

So, I wasn't exactly a novice when it came to finding a watering hole and I did have a card or two up my sleeve. Being pally with Gerard Hutch gained me admission to a few pubs that might not be on the tourist's normal itinerary. One night I got in a cab at the Westbury and asked the driver to take me to the Blue Lion on Parnell Street. The driver asked me if I was sure. I didn't know whether to be flattered or offended that I didn't seem to fit the prototype of a Blue Lion regular.

The Blue Lion was one of a few pubs in the North Inner-City where you might get an after-hours drink, much on the lines of the South Side places Bertie had taken me to, but it had a slightly different system. It was called a lock-in and at the end of the official hours the shutters would be pulled down and some privileged patrons could stay for afters. Pulling the shutters down served two purposes: protection from the prying eye of the licensing inspector and deterrence to interlopers who might have been spending their money elsewhere. These lock-ins had one very firm rule: anyone who stayed was committed to staying until the last man wanted to leave. No excuses were tolerated from renegers. Work commitments – 'Jesus Christ, I've a new job to start tomorrow' – fears of spousal abuse – 'For fuck sake, the wife will kill me' – or upcoming court appearances – 'Oh God, I forgot I have to renew my bail tomorrow' – all fell on deaf ears. Even a feigned heart attack earned little sympathy from the diehard at the bar insisting we all had just one more for the road.

Joan Gallagher was another great pal of mine, one of those salt of the earth characters that abound in the North Side Inner-City, who came from the Gardiner Street flats. I'm sure there are countless perfectly straight, law-abiding people in the area; I just didn't seem to meet any of them. Joan got up every morning to make her contribution to the black economy, working as a market trader, and had a drink most days of her life. She never seemed any the worse for it. Her sister, Rosie, was married to Charlie Dunne who was one of the family of influence on the South Side all through the 1960s and '70s. Joan's favourite watering hole was a pub on Talbot Street and one night I was desperately seeking a late drink and was driving around looking for the place when I was flagged down by the Old Bill.

'Good evening, officer,' I said. 'I'm looking for Talbot Street.'

'You're on Talbot Street and you're driving the wrong way,' said one of them.

'Oh, I beg your pardon. I hadn't realised it was one-way,' I apologised. 'I was looking for number seventy-eight.'

He shrugged and looked at his pal.

'It's a pub called Cheers Bon,' I tried to help him out.

'Oh, that fucking place. Turn around and follow me,' he said.

Nicknames are very common in Dublin pubs. Nearly everyone has one, although you might not always know your own. They often stem from a physical characteristic. There's a Fatso, a Fat Fred and numerous Fatties. There's a Shorty because he's tiny and a Tiny because he's huge. There's a Mr Kingsize, partly because he's big and partly because he gets his living in the cigarette game. There's a Two Bellies and a couple of Four Bellies. I think there's even a Six Bellies but I couldn't swear to it. There's a Hoppy because he lost a leg and a Wingy because he lost an arm. There's a Happy because he's grumpy and a Grumpy because he's grumpy. There's a Dr Zhivago because he's got a Russian girlfriend and a Micky No-Shirts for reasons I was never able to fathom. There was Mick the Russian who was Scottish but had such a strong accent no-one could understand a word he said, except when he was singing, which he was quite good at. After him repeating a remark several times without me understanding a word, I'd ask him to sing it to me. There's Billy No Mates because his only friend on Facebook is his probation officer.

Then there's Fat Neck Carl from Manchester who can get where gas couldn't go. His best claim to fame was the time he got himself into the United team photo at Wembley. You can see Cantona giving Giggsy one of those who-the-fuck-is-that looks and Giggsy giving Cantona one of those not-a-fucking-clue looks. He also came out in all the gear to open the batting for England at Headingley and had a warm-up on the centre court at Wimbledon just before the men's singles.

The Monk was a teetotal non-smoker though later he discovered Smithwick's shandy, then neat Smithwick's, and these days the odd vodka isn't out of the question. Still, he'll always be the Monk. My personal favoutite was a chap who got himself in so much financial difficulty he faked his own suicide. He was spotted a few weeks later in a South Side pub and from that day to this has been known as Lazarus.

Over in Spain there's a bloke known as Les the Butcher. One day he walked by a bar and I pointed him out to a friend, Mary from Bulgaria, mentioning his nom de guerre.

'Oh my God!' she said. 'Why do you call him the Butcher?'

'Because he owns a butcher's shop,' I said, which seemed to relieve her. I suppose there could be more macabre reasons for being known as the Butcher.

As I say, very often you don't know your own nickname and I only discovered mine by chance. Being a bit older than most of the lads I worked with in the puff game, I was referred to as 'Junior' after Tony Soprano's uncle in the TV series *The Sopranos*.

Even the statues in Dublin have nicknames. In 1988, Dr Michael Smurffit commissioned a monument in memory of his father. The Anna Livia Fountain, also known as 'the Spirit of the River Liffey', portrayed a reclining woman with water running down behind her. It immediately acquired not one but two nicknames: the Floozie In The Jacuzzi and The Whore (pronounced who-er) In The Sewer. Far from being offended, both nicknames were encouraged by the sculptor, Eamonn O'Doherty. The site, on O'Connell Street, was available thanks to the ministrations of the IRA. Nelson's Column, The Pillar, had occupied the spot for a hundred and fifty-eight years until they blew it up in 1966. The Floozie has gone now too, moved to Croppy Acre Memorial Park by Heuston Street station to make way for the Millennium Spire. This quickly became known as The Spike because, well, it does look like a two hundred foot hypodermic.

North Earl Street was the site chosen for the statue to Irish author James Joyce, complete with walking cane. It soon became known as the Gimp with the Limp. Molly Malone, who wheeled her wheelbarrow through streets broad and narrow selling her shellfish, was sited at the bottom of Grafton Street. She's known as the Tart with the Cart. The most recent addition is a statue to my pal Phil Lynott, erected outside Bruxelles pub in Harry Street. To the best of my knowledge it hasn't yet got a nickname. If I'm not getting above myself, might I suggest the Rock Star with the Guitar?

The North and South Sides of Dublin are about as different as two sides of the same city can possibly be. I don't think I'd be offending anyone if I said the South Side is a bit more yuppyish, the sort of place where you're more likely to meet a crooked accountant or stockbroker than a crooked used car dealer. I had a bit of help, drink wise, on the South Side, too. I had met an Irish couple in Spain, Robin and Phyllis, whose knowledge of my pedigree stretched no further than that I was an ex-publican who had returned to Dublin to go into the bookmaking business. They owned one of the best big pubs on the South Side, Bruxelles. I say big as opposed to mega. Nowadays there are places like Break for the Border and the Café en Seine that go to five or six floors and cover several acres but back then Bruxelles was about as big as pubs got. Mind you, you wouldn't have thought it from the outside since eighty per cent of their business was done in the three subterranean bars.

A few years later, Robin bought Lillie's Bordello, far and away the best nightclub in Dublin. By that time it had become one of my favourite watering holes but I had my doubts when he told me he'd bought it. It was a massive undertaking for a man approaching his sixties who was already fairly comfortable financially. Firstly, if you buy a very successful business it can't be cheap. Secondly, if a business is taking every shilling it's possible to take then the very best you can hope for is to keep it doing so. There's very little room for improvement. On top of all that, club-goers are a pretty fickle lot and clubs come into favour and go out of favour for no apparent reason.

As usual I was wrong. Ably assisted by his sons, David and Christopher, Robin did manage to improve Lillie's, subtly revamping it without losing its original character. They found a little extra space on the second floor, to where they moved the VIP lounge, which was called The Library. In there they installed a grand piano and employed Paul Harrington, a pianist who'd had a number one hit and won a Eurovision Song Contest with 'We Were the Rock And Roll Kids'.

Anyone of any significance appearing in or around Dublin would generally turn up in The Library: Westlife, Boyzone, Samantha Mumba, the Stereophonics. Joe Elliott of Def Leppard was a regular, as were Formula One driver Eddie Irvine and golfers Lee Westwood and Darren Clarke. Liam Neeson and Pierce Brosnan put in appearances. Eamon Dunphy, the football pundit, was in most nights making a nuisance of himself. His playing career at Old Trafford must have spanned one of my periods in prison because I don't recall him. Paul Harrington would play requests and people would get up and sing. A pal of mine, Jason Titley, who won the Grand National on Royal Athlete, would get out his bongo drums and join in.

One night my pal and I were seated at a table for four. As the place got crowded the hostess, Jean, asked if we'd mind if she put another couple on the table. No problem. The couple joined us and before long we got chatting, bought each other a few drinks and the girls exchanged phone numbers. Into the small hours, two quite large chaps with bulges under their left armpits appeared at The Library door. The lady apologised and said they'd have to go as their escort had arrived. It was only after they left that I found out we'd passed a few hours with Miriam Ahern, the estranged wife of the then Prime Minister, Bertie.

If there's a better bar in the world I haven't found it yet.

Another pal's pub was on the South Side too, Scruffy Murphy's. This was famous for being the place, before my pal owned it, where the plot to win the National Lottery was hatched. In those days the lottery only had thirty-six numbers and the organisers came up with a promotion that on bank holiday weekends anyone selecting three correct numbers would be guaranteed a tenner. One of the regulars was a maths lecturer from Trinity College. He took out a pen, pulled over a beer mat and began scribbling. He very quickly came to the conclusion that if you covered every combination you were certain to win the jackpot plus numerous lines of five and four. The number of lines of three, with their tenner guarantee, would cover the whole investment.

A syndicate was formed, funds were scraped together and the next bank holiday the investment was made. They were unlucky only in as much as two other people, by chance, had the winning combination but they showed a significant profit. The next bank holiday they were fortunate enough to be the sole winners but the organisers were beginning to smell a long-tail. By the third bank holiday they began adding extra numbers to the draw, first thirty-nine, then forty-two and eventually the current forty-nine. This increased the possible combinations to slightly over seventeen million and made the whole scheme unviable. The maths lecturer went on to write a book entitled *How to Win the Lottery* and probably earned more from it that he did from the coup itself.

There was one very uniquely Irish solution to getting a late drink. Well, if not a solution certainly an option. Somebody, and to be fair I think it was Maurice Boland much as I begrudge giving him credit for anything, came up with a ruse. The regulations for obtaining a restaurant licence were fairly minimal and apparently didn't even include such basics as a kitchen. If you opened a place that to all intents and purposes was a disco, called it a restaurant and got a restaurant licence you could serve wine until the cows came home, or at least till four or five in the morning. The first place opened on Leeson Street Bridge and before long every second cellar in

Leeson Street was one of these wine places. A pal opened one of the better ones, called Legg's, which kept a better-than-most selection of labels but even there the majority of punters' sole concern was that it be wet and alcoholic.

I've nothing against wine. I don't think I've ever been to a restaurant and not ordered some of the stuff but after a night on whiskey I'd find it hard to revert to wine. Legg's did however stock a few of the better brands of champagne and I've always been quite partial to a cocktail called a Queen of Spain, which is champagne, fresh orange juice and a drop of brandy. By smuggling in a few miniature brandies, I could make a half dozen of these from a bottle of champagne. The problem with a Queen of Spain is that you seem to get drunk from the foot up. The first thing that stops working is your legs and you have to sit down. Unfortunately the last thing that stops working is your mouth so on the occasions that I got into my second bottle, I probably resembled a babbling blancmange. Anyone reckless enough to accept a lift home was in for a hair-raising experience.

Of course people leaving a wine bar at five in the morning get peckish and an old Polish bloke took advantage of this and began parking up a mobile hamburger van. It was only after he retired that anyone realised how much money he was making, selling several hundred hotdogs and burgers a night earning about a quid apiece. This gave rise to the Hamburger Wars, when about a dozen itinerant burger salesmen began to appear on the street. Several vehicles were set ablaze and on more than one occasion shots were fired. Then the General, Martin Cahill, got involved. His sister owned office premises on Leeson Street which gave him access to electricity, a vast improvement on butane, and before long he'd taken control of the burger franchise and ran it until his demise.

Though last I heard Legg's was still going strong, most of the wine places have gone now because of an even better ruse that came along. If you could obtain a theatre licence you were allowed to serve anything you wanted until half an hour after the last performance. By stretching credibility to its limits and claiming that lap-dancing and pole-dancing were theatrical performances, just such a licence could be obtained. Today most of Leeson Street is lap-dancing clubs.

Despite all my research I still found Sundays problematical. Some places opened early but turned it in at two in the afternoon, others didn't open till three but closed early, and some didn't bother at all. Then I discovered that if you crossed the county line into County Meath, the rules were different and the pubs served till two in the morning. A drive out to the Coolquay Lodge became the order of the day. Before the days of karaoke, they'd have a live band and everyone took turns at doing a song. The amount of talent amongst the punters was amazing. It was always a great night but did leave the problem of getting home. Limping from Leeson Street to Blackrock was one thing but a drive back from County Meath was a much more daunting prospect.

One night, and it must have been just before or just after my period living in Dublin because I was driving a hire car from Dublin airport, I had meandered my way back from the Lodge into the city and for some reason I was on Summerhill when I was pulled over by a squad car.

'Papers for the car,' asked the garda and I gave him the hire agreement with my Spanish address.

'Oh, you live in Spain,' he said. 'When are you returning home?'

'Tuesday,' I told him.

'In that case I don't see much point in nicking you. Move over.'

He got in and, with his pal following, drove me to Blooms Hotel in Angelsea Street where I was staying. He parked the car up nice and neat and took me inside.

'Does he live here?' he asked the receptionist.

'Yes, officer. What's the problem?' she said.

'There's no problem but take these car keys and don't return them to him before lunchtime tomorrow.'

I slipped him a hundred quid which would have been a small price to pay had things gone the other way, bearing in mind the £1,500 I'd been hit with over the speeding. A minute or two later he was back.

'Thanks very much all the same but we can't take that,' he said and gave me the one-er back.

Discussing all this the next day with my father, an ex-Old Bill himself, he said I'd done two things wrong. Two tenners or two scores would have been 'thank you very much' but two fifties smacked of a bribe. The fact that they were two English fifties made it worse. Had I been the sort of ungrateful bastard who had second thoughts and made a phone call resulting in a search, careers and pensions would have been going out the window.

Another morning at about five I was driving through Ballsbridge when I came upon a garda control, complete with illuminated batons and cones and all that stuff.

'Good evening, officer,' I said, winding down the window.

'Good morning,' he corrected me. 'Have you been drinking?'

'No, I've been playing cards,' I lied through my teeth.

'Yes, and I suppose you had people in the car earlier who had been drinking and that's why the car stinks of booze? On your way.'

This sort of thing couldn't happen today, attitudes have changed. When the breathalyser first appeared if someone was nicked the conversation in the pub the next day would be, 'I see poor old so-and-so got nicked last night.' Today it's more likely to be along the lines, 'I see that dirty bastard so-and-so was pissed again. About time he was nicked. They should throw the key away.'

Another massive nail in the coffin of the pub trade was the smoking ban. I know it's in almost everywhere these days but Ireland was the first in Europe, following the example of the goody-goodies across the Atlantic. Any concession to the comfort of smokers was frowned upon. A shelter could have a roof or walls but not both. One pub, Johnny Fox's, up in the Dublin mountains – a more windswept place is hard to imagine – installed an old bus on the car-park for the benefit of smokers but since it did have a roof and walls it had to go.

The logistics of running a pub are quite straightforward. Say a decent neighbourhood pub is taking a grand a day, it's probably earning about a two-er after all exes: £1,400 a week or seventy grand a year. Not bad, and on the five-year buy-back principle worth about £350,000. Such a landlord would have little difficulty in getting £100,000 from his local bank to throw into one of those building projects. However, should a few of the regulars take umbrage at being asked to stand out in the rain with their pint and fag and decide to patronise the local off licence the takings may drop to £800 a day. Not the end of the world, it's still earning about £160, isn't it? Well, actually no, it's probably earning nothing since, apart from a little less stock to buy, none of the exes have changed.

It was assumed that there were vast droves of people who had been sitting at home for four hundred years waiting for the smoking ban to come in before they'd set foot in a pub and these people would rush in to take up the slack. Evidently they failed to appear. The landlord can now forget about any hundred grands dropping through the letterbox from his local bank. In fact, should he currently be behind with the bank, he may well get one of those letters saying that Section 39, subsection (iii), paragraph (c) of the loan agreement was being invoked. This is the bit that says the bank has the right to demand instant repayment.

There's not much a landlord can do about rent, rates, electric or maintenance, so his only area of economy is staff. I'm reliably informed that the redundancy rate averaged slightly more than one employee per pub. That's a thousand people in Dublin alone; a thousand people that were happily earning about £400 a week and contributing to the economy being on the dole and costing a two-er a week. That's a six hundred grand a week, or thirty million a year, turnaround. Throw in the cafes and restaurants and you could probably double it. Multiply it by Galway, Limerick, Cork and the rest you're probably in the region of £300 million a year out of the window. Is it any wonder we're in the shit?

I must admit, I pine for the good old days. Today the pubs open until two or three in the morning, the clubs until more or less when they feel like it, the Temple Bar area is referred to as Dublin's Left Bank and everything is very continental. Anyone but a complete moron can drink twenty-four hours a day. But what about the intrigue? What about the romance? What about the, well, is excitement too strong a word? I can't help feeling an illicit drink tasted so much better than when you were drinking legally, doing something the civilians couldn't do. Maybe I should have been born in a different place in a different era. Maybe Chicago in the twenties when speakeasies were all the rage. I'd have loved to see someone telling Al Capone to put his cigar out.

[illegible]

Bad Day at Blackrock

Back to business, and everything was going swimmingly, wasn't it? Well, not exactly. The uninitiated always think that a betting office is a licence to print money and to a certain extent it is. In the trade the rule of thumb is that a shop will win ten per cent of turnover on single bets and fifteen percent on multiple bets. The vast majority of my turnover was small multiple bets or, as we called it in the trade, shit. This meant my profit ratio was quite good but I just wasn't turning over enough money.

On a good week I would turn over four grand and win between five and six hundred quid. Sounds great, but out of that I had to pay the manager a two-er, SIS a hundred, the boardman seventy, newspapers and wall strips a hundred, rent, rates, phone and electric. And sundries, betting slips, pens and microfilm. All of which meant I had to have a good week to finish level. The main problem with the on-course side of the job was that we quite simply weren't playing big enough in relation to our expenses. If we were standing a favourite to lose five hundred we had the exact same exes as the fellow next to us who was standing it for five thousand. It was very easy for me to stand up like a lion when I was playing with Hassan's money but when it was my own it was a different matter.

Another important point was that your average Irish race-goer is vastly more knowledgeable and better informed than his British counterpart. In all the races I attended in

Britian I never once got on nodding terms with a jockey or a trainer and I met very few people that actually owned a racehorse. In Ireland most pubs of any standing have a racing syndicate where any number of regulars throw in a few quid and buy a horse. This gives them access to jockeys, trainers and other owners. If a short-priced favourite put in a poor performance on the gallops the week before a race, everyone in Ireland knew about it and the horse wouldn't be touched with a bargepole.

The last big difference between Britain and Ireland was the market itself. I once made a book at a four-day meeting at Newmarket and throughout the twenty-odd races there wasn't one where we struck more than four or five bets. These bets were almost exclusively large bets from other bookmakers whose job it was to reduce the prices of certain horses on behalf of the big off-course chains they represented. A few grand scattered about amongst the rails bookmakers could reduce the off-course liabilities by millions. This didn't happen in Ireland because there weren't sixty million people cramming themselves into off-course betting shops. Nearly every penny invested on Irish racing is invested on-course by genuine punters, which means you can't always take as much money for a horse as you'd like, no matter what price you go. Particularly if it's one of those dodgy favourites that didn't perform too well on the gallops.

As if things weren't bad enough, this was the time I picked to rediscover poker. My poker playing career began at age eight. The family holiday every year was a fortnight over to Dublin to stay with one of the grandparents, usually Bertie. There wasn't much in the way of television in those days and the custom in most households was to get the cards out after the evening meal and play poker, which is probably why the standard of poker playing is so high in Ireland. Bertie's house was no exception and the game of choice was five-card draw, as seen in all the cowboy films. A less skilful version of poker is hard to imagine. Still, this was just my apprenticeship.

Years later, when I worked as a poker dealer, the game was five-card stud as played by Steve McQueen and Edward G. Robinson in *The Cincinnati Kid*, though we played short-pack. In this game the twos, threes, fours, fives and sixes are removed, meaning it's very difficult to be dealt an unplayable hand. This of course was the very object of the exercise. Since the house took a small percentage of each pot, the more people who played a hand the bigger the pot and the better the commission. Often dealing an hour on, an hour off for twenty-four or thirty-six hours at a stretch, I couldn't help but become fairly well acquainted with the game.

The two games that were all the rage in Dublin were Omaha and Texas Hold'em. Omaha is unquestionably the most skilful of all the variations of poker and I have to admit I never really mastered it. I fell in love with Hold'em. Unfortunately, I employed the same strategy at Hold'em that I'd employed at short-pack five-card stud. As they're totally different games I rarely, if ever, won.

The sensible answer to all this is perfectly clear, but I didn't get where I am today by being sensible. What I should have done was give up poker, retire from on-course betting, sack the manager of the shop and run it myself. By cultivating a few healthy phone accounts, I could have generated enough turnover to earn myself three or four or five hundred quid a week. Needless to say, I did none of that; I was enjoying myself too much. Getting the odd parcel of puff home would have eased the pressure but when you're not on the ground you only get invited into the high-risk, untried ventures. I had a few sorties, with mixed results, and probably earned something small overall but the bit of heat I had been getting was making me ultra-careful.

Mind you, it wasn't all doom and gloom. I had bought a few books and watched a few videos and my poker game was improving. Perhaps I could stop haemorrhaging money there. The festival season was coming up and if you can't take money at the festival meetings, you're never going to take money. There was only one thing for it. I was going to have to fly to Gib and relieve the Bank of Commerce and Credit International of some of my nest-egg. I resolved to go the following Monday. Awful shame I didn't decide a week earlier because the very day I decided to go was the very day BCCI ceased to trade.

I wasn't aware that banks could cease to trade. I thought there were all kinds of bodies like the International Monetary Fund, the World Bank and droves of auditors and inspectors to make sure everything was above board. And anyway, how do banks get in trouble? They take money off A and give him a bowl of soup and lend it to B and charge him an arm and a leg, having first established that B is more than capable of repaying it. Sounds like a good game to me.

Apparently BCCI had some swampland in Argentina on its asset sheets valued at three or four hundred million. When someone found out it was worth about four pence the balloon went up. Even so, the place was owned by one of the richest families on the planet. Surely they'd pull up the few quid and everything would be fine in a week or two? Wrong again. I did hear years later that people got most of their money back in dribs and drabs but I never did. Just one of the pitfalls of opening an account with a snide passport I suppose. By the time they were paying out, the passport had expired and the money was gone.

Now there really was only one answer for it. Back to Spain and back to work. I gave the shop to Dave, sold the Pimpmobile to Peter and let a pal of mine who was between addresses move into the apartment. I packed my bags and headed back to Fuengirola with my tail between my legs.

PART FOUR

SPAIN 1993-present

Starting Over

Starting over, I at least held a few advantages. I still had the 380 Merc, and I had probably salvaged about twenty grand from the wreckage in Dublin. Also, this was the point when Flashy came to the rescue with the twenty-five grand I mentioned, so I had been in a lot worse situations in my time. I just had to get my nose to the grindstone and get a bit of work done.

The studio had been fine for trips back but it wasn't big enough to live in, so I went looking for somewhere to rent. I found a town house at El Castillo which was handy enough and had the added advantage of a vast underground car park which hardly anyone seemed to use. I bought a couple of old bangers and parked them up under dust sheets for when I had the need of a bit of storage, always assuming I got my hands on a parcel of gear to store.

Had I run into Fareed, I'd have had to swallow my pride and get back in bed with him but there was no sign of him around the Queen Vic. Poor old Suntan was in full retirement. He'd had a bad car crash and broken both his ankles. They hadn't made a wonderful job of setting them and they had to be re-broken and re-set. Very painful and he still could hardly walk. On top of that he'd been diagnosed with both Alzheimer's and Parkinson's. I suppose the only good thing about having Alzheimer's and Parkinson's is you probably forget you've got Parkinson's. He died back in England a few years later. If everyone in the job was as straight as Suntan the game would have been a lot easier.

I did have another Moroccan pal, Musa, who, unlikely enough, had been introduced to me by Slippery. I'd done a few bits and pieces with Musa but the last I'd heard he'd been nicked with a forged identity card and got himself eighteen months. He'd be well home by now. I set about trawling the bars of Torremolinos and Arroyo and eventually tracked him down. Musa, at the time, wasn't as big a player as Fareed but he was much easier to deal with and it wasn't long before he was flying.

So, with access to a bit of gear, all I needed to do was find some customers and/or a bit of transport. Both arrived quite promptly. A pal of mine came up with a particular vehicle that had a readymade stash that would hold a hundred and twenty key. If I could supply him with the hundred, he'd take the other twenty home for me. Getting the gear from Musa at six-and-three-quarters and serving it at seven-and-a-half meant my twenty only stood in at six grand, which was just about the size of investment I was looking for at the time.

Things worked well enough without any major hiccups but the transport was a bit on the dear side. Any transport that works can't really be said to be expensive, particularly at my discounted purchase price, but it wasn't something that would go on for long. The driver couldn't keep coming over in the same vehicle so we had to keep changing it. When we wanted to buy one it was the most sought-after vehicle on the planet and when we wanted to sell one it was a petrol guzzling monster that no-one would touch with a bargepole. Still, I suppose everyone has to get a living, even the secondhand car dealers.

So I seemed to be getting back on an even keel. I had retired from poker and gone back to kalooki, with much more favourable results. Maybe the few quid I was getting from the transport had given me my confidence back. Musa was happy I was turning over a bit of tackle for him and his prestige with his suppliers was growing by leaps and bounds. Besides all that, Annie was a lot happier to be home. She'd been a bit of a fish out of water in Dublin, not speaking much English although she had picked a fair amount up from my cousin Colm's wife, Sandy. People found it amusing, her speaking with an Irish accent.

One big change I did notice coming back was the amount of violence that had crept into the job. The advent of the Robbery Squad and the Armed Response Units in the UK in the Seventies and the Eighties had largely led to the demise of the professional bank robber. On top of that, there just wasn't the volume of cash in transit as there used to be, what with credit cards and people getting paid by cheque. Banks held less cash and department stores and supermarkets took less cash. With the best will in the world it was nearly impossible to find enough money to rob. The robbery teams that had been nicked earlier on were now coming home having heard little else throughout their sentence but how much money there was in the puff game. They now wanted to be in it and, being people who had been fully prepared to risk life and limb robbing a bank, they weren't likely to accept wishy-washy stories if a bit of gear went astray. A body was found in the boot of a Merc in Puerto Banus and another in the back of a Range Rover at Malaga airport. Several other people disappeared.

The climate back home was much the same. I had one pal, John, who was a big hitter in West London and regularly got big parcels home. The puff market works very much on the same lines as Lloyd's of London, where members pledge their worldly assets to honour any deal they enter into. Say John got a ton of puff home, as he frequently did, he would give two hundred or two fifty to four or five people who would each give forty or fifty to five other people who would each give five or ten to several people who would go out and sell anything as small as a tenner's worth. The money then worked its way back up the chain, but this all took time. In the meantime John might well have got another ton home, so there was money flowing up the chain and gear flowing down, which is fine as long as everyone honours their pledge. Of course you always get the odd rascal so John employed a sort of accountant chap who kept a slogger on who owed what and for how long.

One Christmas Eve they were having a board meeting and discussing any matters that needed tidying up before the festivities began. The accountant mentioned one habitual slow payer who needed a wakeup call, and I mean that quite literally. Not sticking a gun in his ear, putting him in the boot of a car and leaving a message for his friends and family that they could have him back when his account was settled; more like, 'Come on mate, do the honourable thing.' The accountant said he would call in at the delinquent's local on his way home.

No notice was taken of the accountant's absence until December 28, by which time his wife had given up thoughts that he had fallen asleep in a drunken stupor on someone else's sofa and had begun to worry. She phoned John to see if he knew anything of his whereabouts. John didn't but said he'd make some enquiries and headed off to the boozer that was the accountant's last known port of call. The delinquent wholesaler was sat at the bar and confirmed that he had indeed seen the accountant on Christmas Eve, at which point he had levelled him up every penny that he owed. John smelt a long tail since this particular wholesaler had never once levelled up every penny he owed in their entire working relationship. John's suspicions weren't allayed when the wholesaler went on to add, funny you should mention it, but there were a couple of very dubious-looking strangers in the bar that night who left immediately after the accountant. John went away to mull over the revelations but was a bit at a loss with evidence being on the slim side.

The next day, having got no further forward, the wife went to the police to report the accountant's disappearance. Contrary to what we'd all like to believe, the Old Bill aren't complete fools and probably knew as much about how John, the accountant and the wholesaler got a living as they all knew about each other. They worked their way around to interviewing the wholesaler and were just as sceptical as John had been. Unlike John, they were in a position to pursue the matter and went and got a search warrant. Spotting a recently re-tiled patio they got out their picks and shovels but found no trace of the missing accountant. They did, however, find the remains of two other accountants from two rival organisations. The delinquent wholesaler is currently serving two life sentences and is unlikely to see the light of day but the accountant's family have still had no closure.

With all this in mind, and much as I needed the money, I resolved to be a little circumspect about who I got into bed with.

Smuggler Ted

I had to make a couple of trips back to Ireland to tidy up some things, and on one of the trips I got a phone call from a yacht skipper, Ted, who I'd known in Puerto Banus. Ted had spent most of his adult life on and around boats in the Med and the Caribbean and, if you believed his stories, a good part of his time smuggling: cigarettes from Gib, brandy and perfume from France, even arms to Yugoslavia and Algeria. Funnily enough he never mentioned puff but that was about to change. He was phoning to ask if I could do him a favour and drop off £80 with his wife in Dublin. I told him I was flying back the next day and if she wanted to meet me at the check-in I'd give her the money. She was there waiting and I paid her, flew home and in the Queen Vic there was Ted sat at the bar. He proceeded to tell me his tale of woe.

He had been skippering a boat in Banus for an English company and a cheap secondhand car had come up. Being a bit of a mechanic he knew there would be some profit in it if he put in a bit of work. Unfortunately he had no money, so he borrowed it from the boat's float. As luck would have it the next day the company accountant arrived to do a call-over and discovered the money was missing. Ted was sacked, thus also becoming homeless, and his name was mud amongst the tight-knit boatie community. He said he'd asked me to give the wife £80 because that was all he had, and offered me it. I told him he'd better hang on to it and asked where he was going to stay. He said that now he had £80 he would book into a hostel for a couple of nights. I took him home and put him in the spare room.

Before long Ted was coming home with yachting magazines and brochures and telling me how easy it would be for a man with his qualifications to charter something decent and get to work with a bit of puff. I think it's fair to say that he recruited me rather than I recruited him. Some pals and myself threw a float together and sent Ted off to the Balearics, where he knew some brokers he could have a deal with. He found us something we could charter for six months for twenty-five grand. When I eventually saw it I wasn't sure I would have wanted to give twenty-five grand to own it, but by then the deal was done.

The twenty-five grand turned out to be only the thin end of the wedge. I did some reading up on sail boats and discovered that they travelled at 1.2 times the square root of the hull length in feet at the waterline. This one being thirty-six foot meant it would travel at eight knots and cover about two hundred nautical miles a day. The Balearics are something less than a thousand miles away, so allowing a bit of leeway and assuming I had my sums right, Ted should be in Fuengirola in five or six days. But no.

The first call came from Valencia, followed by calls from Alicante, Murcia, Almeria and Granada. What all these calls had in common was requests for more money for unexpected expenses and necessitating lengthy round trips with more funds. In Granada I told him to give Fuengirola a miss and take the boat straight to La Duquesa. I didn't want to become the talk of the wash-house with people in Fuengirola knowing I had a boat and guessing what was afoot.

In Duquesa we set about making a few modifications to the boat. This thing had one very unusual feature for a boat its size. It had a full-sized bath, whereas the most you'd normally expect would be a shower. By removing the bath and installing a partition with a shower in front of it we were left with a space about the size of a telephone box. A bit of tiling and we had a stash that was bang on the centre of gravity and very difficult to detect unless you were very familiar with the particular model of boat. It would hold eight hundred key, not a vast amount in boating work but if we managed half a dozen trips through the summer it would come to big money.

Musa went off to Larache to prepare the gear for loading and a few days later Ted was on his way to pick it up. The next morning I got an irate call from Morocco wanting to know why the boat hadn't turned up. I had no answer to give him and set off for Duquesa to find out. Ted told me that he couldn't get through the Straits because the current was too strong. I was beginning to have my doubts about Ted's enthusiasm but asked him what the solution was. He said he'd leave that night, travel through the Straits on the ebb tide, hang about in the Atlantic all day and be at the pick-up point the following night. Fair enough, off you go, and I went to ring Musa with the new arrangements.

If the call two days earlier had been irate, the one the next day was verging on the homicidal. The boat hadn't turned up again. Back to Duquesa and a confrontation with Ted but there was no sign of him. That night I got a call from him saying he was in Gib with engine trouble. I told him to meet me at a pub in La Linea and off I went, taking a pal who was a mechanic. Ted and the mechanic went to survey the damage, which appeared to be to the oil filter. The mechanic's opinion was sabotage. Judging by the oil splatter, he came to the conclusion that a sharp instrument, possibly a screwdriver, had been stabbed into the oil filter while the engine was running. I decided to go and look for myself, for what that was worth.

Alright, how much can an oil filter cost? We went around to

the Volvo dealer in Shepard's marina to find out. Not much as it happened and he could certainly supply one: two to three weeks delivery from Sweden. I looked around and spotted a new engine complete with oil filter and asked if he could remove that one and sell it to us and replace it when the new one arrived. He said that the oil filter wouldn't fit our engine so I asked how much he wanted for the whole thing and he said four grand. I asked how long it would take to fit and he said that if Ted and the mechanic gave him a hand they could do it in twenty-four hours. I threw him the four grand and told him to get on with it. He said, 'Fucking hell. You're in a hurry. Where are you going? Or shouldn't I ask?' I suppose paying him with twelve thousand-guilder notes didn't make my behaviour any less suspicious.

One of my favourite authors is a chap called Donald Westlake who writes very funny books about a gang of bungling robbers led by a man called Dortmund. One of his books, *How to Steal a Diamond*, was made into the film, *The Hot Rock*, with Robert Redford playing Dortmund. The gang are recruited by an African prince to recover a diamond that the gang had stolen and then lost. Apparently the diamond had some sacred significance to the prince's tribe. Most of the film is taken up by Dortmund returning to the prince with ever increasing lists of ever increasingly expensive requirements he's going to need to complete the job. I was beginning to appreciate how the prince must have been feeling.

Twenty-four hours later, Ted set off for the third time and it was with some trepidation that I awaited the inevitable phone call from Musa. When it did arrive I was more than a little surprised to hear that everything was hunky-dory, the boat had been loaded and Ted was on his way back as we spoke. I left for Duquesa and parked on a hill above the port with my binoculars and waited to watch Ted tie up. And I waited and I waited. Come late afternoon, I drove down to a bar to check the teletext and see if there was any newsflash about a boatload of puff having just been captured. Nothing. Not even a little snippet about a small sailboat getting run over by a petrol tanker in the Straits.

I went home feeling rather dejected and not really sure how to break the news, or lack of news, to the partners. No sooner was I through the door than the phone rang. Ted was in Gibraltar. I told him to meet me, again, in the pub in La Linea and off I went. The story went that he'd had a chase from a Spanish Customs cutter but had managed to escape into Gib harbour. This all sounded a bit thin because I had established that the boat only did eight knots and a Customs cutter did about eighty so any chase would be pretty shortlived. My own opinion is that Ted felt, being quite well known in Gib having sailed in countless times, that he was less likely to get a looking at there than in Duquesa. He probably also thought that if the worst came to the worst he'd sooner be nicked by the British than the Spanish.

Ted seemed quite pleased with himself. 'You've got the most valuable boat in Gib marina,' he told me.

'Quite honestly, I can't really see how the gear is any more use to me in Gib than it was in Morocco. When can we move it?' I asked, thinking tonight would be good and if not, tomorrow would do fine.

'Everything should have cooled down in a month or so,' he said.

I don't know how I kept my hands off his throat. I told him I was off to Fuengirola to give the matter some thought and told him to meet me the next morning at ten.

Captains fall into two main categories. Total professionals very often lacking in resolve, and self-taught cowboys usually game enough for anything. It's very rare to get someone like

Suntan who knows what he's doing and has nerves of steel and, even if I did, what would he need me for? Driving back to Fuengirola I was flicking through my mental Filofax under the heading 'Self-taught cowboy'.

Arriving at the Queen Vic, lo and behold who's sat at the bar but Bullets – he had several firearms convictions – who, whilst falling squarely into the cowboy category, was more capable than most and a very adaptable chap. He was a big bloke with a shock of bushy white hair. He often dressed in army fatigues and drove an ex-army jeep, still painted in camouflage colours, all of which made him a very recognisable local character. I brought him up to date on my current predicament and asked if he'd be interested in moving the boat from Gib to Duquesa and if so for how much. Fifteen grand. Hmm, £18.75 a key. That didn't sound out of the way in the greater scheme of things.

We met at eight in the morning and drove to La Linea, where we met Ted. I left them to discuss the practicalities and went to wait on my hilltop at Duquesa. At a quarter to one the boat came into sight and at half one it was moored safe and sound in its berth and by half two we were unloading the gear.

Without blowing my own trumpet, I think I came up with a very ingenious system for the unloading. Across the road from the port is a golf course with an underpass linking the two. I hired a golf buggy and bought two secondhand sets of clubs which I chopped the heads off, leaving three or four inches of shaft. I impaled these into two wooden discs which I glued into the mouths of the golf bags. This left a space that would hold thirty key, and by Ted and his pal Micky playing, or not playing, two rounds a day we had the boat unloaded inside the week and the gear stored in a villa I'd rented close by.

It was patently obvious that Ted wasn't cut out for this work and it was now time to pay him off. I knew he wasn't going to be happy. His twenty grand wages were reduced by the fifteen grand I'd given Bullets, which thinking back about it may have been a little hard. On the other hand he'd lured me into an investment of the thick end of three hundred grand to finish up with a parcel I could have bought for a touch over half a million and not had all the dramas. He'd had his exes paid for a couple of months, including a flight back to Dublin to visit his wife, and when he met me he had £80 in the world, which he owed to me. I did promise that if the gear got home there'd be another few quid for him and if Bullets could get a few trips done in the five months we still had of the charter, I'd give him ten grand a trip. After all, if it hadn't been for Bullets the gear would still be sat in Gib and there'd be no wages for anyone. He went away about as happy as I could have expected him to be.

If Bullets had one major failing, and he had many failings, it was his almost pathological hatred for anyone in authority. If the person concerned happened to be wearing a uniform, the hatred was compounded. On his first trip it was decided, to save all the worries about getting through the Straits, that he would leave from Gib. He sailed in and tied up at the fuelling berth and on the next pier someone who was either police or Customs spotted him.

'Don't forget to book in,' he shouted over.

'Yes sir, I was on the point of doing that very thing,' would have been a good response. Not Bullets.

'I'm fucking busy and I'll be round to see you in my own sweet time,' was Bullets idea of diplomacy.

To be fair, I think if you just pull into a port for fuel there's really no reason to check in but who ever won an argument with one of these officials? With his back firmly up, he phoned for reinforcements and the next thing a Customs rummage crew was on board giving Bullets a hard time. British Customs rummage crews are reputed to be the best in the world but they never found the stash. What they did find was the charter agreement in Ted's name, which led to Bullets being arrested for being in possession of a stolen boat.

I got hold of Ted, who sent a fax to the Old Bill with a copy of his passport and a letter with a fanny about being back in England because his mother had taken ill. He said he'd asked Bullets to move the boat to Portugal where the people who had paid the charter wanted to spend a few weeks. This led to Bullets's release but the Old Bill, looking for their pound of flesh, had contacted the brokers who said the charter agreement was violated and sent a skipper to repossess the boat.

The skipper was a Dutchman and obviously knew the boat inside out. He went on board and flicked all the trip switches in the right order and pointed out that a torch was missing from a shelf. He wandered around to check things out and amazingly enough never mentioned the missing bath. Now, I've nothing against Dutchmen, Holland being a place where I've had many pleasant experiences. But I think it's fair to say that Dutch people are vastly more knowledgeable about puff than their European neighbours. This Dutchman was a yacht skipper based in the Med so his knowledge would be better than most. I'm sure he couldn't wait to get out to sea and find out what booty was concealed behind the new shower.

This wouldn't be the last time that I would swear on everything holy never to have anything more to do with boats.

The Brick

I hope no-one is under the misconception that I was part of some sort of organised gang. No, probably not. The truth was that dozens and dozens of people were getting a living one way or another from the puff job. Most of us knew each other and would bump into each other in pubs, clubs and restaurants. Inevitably the conversation, sooner rather than later, came around to the job: current market prices, quality and quantity status and any gossip about recent technical advances by Customs and Old Bill.

These occasions were also an opportunity for anyone short of a particular link in the chain to explore possibilities of a solution. My own areas of expertise were the ability to source gear at reasonable money and to find a driver desperate or reckless enough to take a bit of gear to some obscure departure point of someone's transport. A wagon routed from Manchester to Alicante couldn't come to Fuengirola to pick up the gear; the gear had to be taken to the wagon. I frequently had a contribution to make to these conversations.

One day I got talking to someone and the subject of boats came up. I related my experiences with Ted, telling him it was one area of activity I was having nothing more to do with.

'All you need is a competent captain with a bit of bottle,' he said.

'Yeah, I know,' I said. 'Try finding one.'

'I've got the perfect man,' he said. 'Clive.'

Apparently Clive lived for two or three or four years at a

time on a boat in the Caribbean enjoying the boatie equivalent of a county squire lifestyle. When his money ran out he'd sell the boat, return to the UK and let it be known that he was available for a bit of graft. He was in just such a position at the time and the only thing my pal needed was a few investors to help bear the cost.

'Okay, but even when these things work, there are no fortunes to be earned,' I pointed out.

'There is if you take the gear direct from Morocco to the UK, and Clive's prepared to do that.'

This was detail that put a whole new complication on the scheme.

'I'll have a word with some people and get back to you,' I said.

Several of us agreed to give it a go and threw in a few quid. Clive was flown out from England and I was quite impressed by him. With his plummy, upper-crust accent and his debonair style, he was a lot less likely to get a spin than the sort I usually came across. I gave him instructions to go and find a suitable craft, which needed to be dual purpose. It had to be big enough to hold a ton and, since it was to be part of Clive's remuneration, something he'd feel comfortable sitting on in Barbados, sipping his pink gin. He found just the thing in Tenerife – for eighty fucking grand. Still, in for a penny. I told him to buy it and dispatched Musa to Morocco to prepare the puff.

Leaving Tenerife, getting loaded in Larache and sailing to the UK would take something like a fortnight, so obviously Clive couldn't do it single handed and would need a crewman. I suggested Bullets. With hindsight I probably should have kept my mouth shut. The only thing worse than not having a captain is having two captains, both of whom want to be boss. Clive and Bullets were at loggerheads from day one, each accusing the other of getting drunk and blabbing of the forthcoming venture to anyone who'd listen.

In desperation I told them to bring the boat back to the coast, hoping a few days at sea with their hands full and without the booze might enable them to get on. When they docked in Estepona port they were greeted by a horde of police and Customs that proceeded to turn the boat upside down. One or both of them had been talking out of school and the eighty grand's worth of boat was now seriously compromised. On top of that, Musa was getting a bit grumpy, saying that it was costing him money to store the gear and when were we coming to get it? I went to Tangiers to meet him and apprise him of the situation. He said that if a customer came along he would have to sell the parcel and in that case he would need a couple of weeks to replace it. I could not give him much of an argument. Clive was still keen to get the work done but obviously he couldn't use the current vessel; we'd just have to buy another one. Thoughts of the African prince returned.

Another problem was timing. We'd all agreed that the job had to be done and dusted by the autumn equinox, September 21, after which the weather became a major concern. Here we were in November and we didn't even have a boat. The first boat would still serve the purpose of a floating gin palace in Barbados, so at least Clive could be a bit less picky in the vessel he chose for the work. We sent him off to Portugal to look at one he'd heard about. Micky, who'd done the trip with Ted, went along as crewman. The thing they bought had to be seen to be believed. I never realised that you could build a boat from concrete, or knew why you'd want to, but apparently you can and we had one to prove it. It was immediately nicknamed The Brick. All my misgivings about the success of the venture had been dispelled, to be replaced by a deep and knowing certainty that the whole escapade was doomed to failure.

The Bay of Biscay was a very daunting prospect in the winter. I remember one time Jim Swords had travelled over by car using the Plymouth–Santander ferry about the same time of the year and claimed the trip was so bad he kept getting up to read the abandon ship instruction and his temper was verging between the homicidal and suicidal. This was a man who could leap, probably has leapt, tall buildings in a single bound, travelling on a purpose-built, state-of-the-art, ultra-modern ferry. And these two were going to make the attempt in The Brick.

As far as the crew went, I was prepared to accept that Clive knew more or less what he was doing but Micky was another story. Apart from his couple of jaunts over to Morocco with Ted, the sum total of his maritime experience was a few trips on the Isle of Wight ferry to visit his pal in Parkhurst prison. I tried to think of any additional handicap that could be heaped on the shoulders of these two unfortunates to make their success even more unlikely but I was stumped. I tried to think of things I could vow to do if they were successful but could think of nothing dramatic enough; certainly something more dramatic than eating my hat or going to the foot of our stairs. I tried to think of comparisons along the lines of 'They've got as much fucking chance of …' but again I was stumped. Phrases like walking on water and swimming the Channel came to mind but smacked a bit of tempting fate.

I was at the point where I would have sold my involvement for a very small consideration but I could think of nobody I disliked enough to inflict such a deal upon so I rolled the dice and let them fall where they may. In any case, I was booked on a Christmas Caribbean cruise and wasn't about to let concerns over The Brick spoil it. I resolved to put it all out of my mind until I got back.

The Brick

In Victorian times, passengers wishing to avoid the baking afternoon sun in both directions of their journey to the Far Eastern colonies would request a port cabin on the outbound trip and a starboard cabin on the homeward trip, presumably paying extra for the privilege. Their ticket was stamped POSH, hence the word. All that may or may not be true but it sounds plausible enough.

In any case the trip we had planned could fairly be described as posh. If you live in Bolton or Barnsley it's not hard to find somewhere better to go on holiday; maybe Blackpool or Bridlington would make the cut. But when you live on the Costa del Sol you get a bit more picky. My pal Danny's wife, Christine, was celebrating her fiftieth birthday on Christmas Day and Danny wanted to do something special so had booked himself and ten of his family on a holiday of a lifetime, cruising the Caribbean. He asked if I wanted to go, and me, Annie and my dad made the group up to fourteen. By the time we upgraded the flights and hotels and booked the seven best cabins that were available, we had about a hundred grand invested before any of us had a light ale, so I wasn't going to let concerns about The Brick spoil it.

The trip was leaving from Heathrow, which didn't suit Danny or me, so we flew from Madrid to Mexico City, where we had a few drinks, a bit of chili con carne and spent the night. The next day we flew to Acapulco where the others joined us and we spent a few days at the Condessa Palace Hotel. I liked Acapulco a lot and we did all the things that tourists are supposed to do there, including seeing the cliff divers. The Mexican peso had been devalued the day before we arrived and we were getting five to the dollar instead of three, and Mexico was cheap in the first place. Most bars were offering three, four or even five drinks for the price of one and seafood was practically free.

There was a great beach bar, Blackbeards, next to the hotel that gave five drinks for the price of one. We discovered this by going in and ordering two Coronitas, which they served us and then gave us an ice bucket with another eight bottles in. Judging by the photos on the walls the place must have been a celebrity hang-out decades earlier. After all, Acapulco was a jet-set resort before there even was a jet-set. There were photos of the likes of Rock Hudson, James Dean, Liz Taylor and Richard Burton and I'd be inclined to think they were all genuine. On the other hand they might have been downloaded the week before and the hirsute chap digitally imposed.

The boat left for the Panama Canal but we stopped for a few drinks in Costa Rica on the way. A trip through the tropical rainforest was one cultural option I gave a miss. The Panama Canal isn't a canal in the sense that Suez, or even the Manchester Ship Canal is. The French company that built Suez was the first to attempt the one in Panama and tens of thousands of Chinese coolies died in the process, mainly from yellow fever. Nobody noticed that Panama isn't quite as flat as Egypt and to follow the French plans would have meant quite literally moving mountains.

The scheme was abandoned for a few years until the Yanks decided to have a go using a system of locks. We passed under the Bridge of the Americas and entered the Miraflores Locks at seven in the morning. I know this because a couple of days later Annie picked up some photos and one showed me, still in the previous night's dinner suit, standing at the stern of the boat with the bridge in the background. Annie assures me it was taken at seven a.m. Once through the locks you sail across an enormous lake then down the other side into the Caribbean Sea.

Our next scheduled port of call was cancelled due to some political unrest and an impromptu stop was made at the San

Blas Islands. I've no doubt these islands all have names but no-one seemed to know them and they were referred to as islands A, B and C. A tender took us to island A from where natives in dugout canoes took us to islands B and C and back to A. All very picturesque but I couldn't shake the feeling that the natives had been flown out from central casting in LA the previous afternoon.

Next stop was Cartagena in Colombia, followed by several islands that were all very nice in their own way. The cuisine and language changed depending on which colonial power had been bossing them about the longest. St Thomas, being American, is a bit more upmarket than most. We played golf there at Mahogany Run but by about the fourteenth I'd run out of balls, cigarettes and enthusiasm and called it a day. St Maarten is half Dutch and half French and both sides are lovely. It's a duty-free island, cigarettes cost half of nothing and booze costs even less. I've been back a couple of times. The trip finished in Puerto Rico where we split up again, Danny and me going to the Dominican Republic while the rest flew back to Heathrow.

We'd met up with a mob of Mexicans on the boat and there was plenty of hugging and kissing and promises to meet up and do it all again when we were heading off. If I remember rightly there were four sisters and their husbands and each couple had four kids plus another few pals. One of the pals had the highly improbable name, for a Mexican, of Norman Sidney. Perhaps he was on a crooked passport. In any case, he was a lovely, big, fun-loving party animal. By the time our group numbered about fifty I dare say we got a bit boisterous, which didn't suit the more temperance-minded Yanks on board, which is to say most of them. I never did meet up with the Mexicans again, though I believe Danny's daughter, being a bit more internet-literate than myself, did stay in touch. Norman wriggled his way as far as the boarding gate at San Juan airport to present me with a particularly expensive bottle of tequila which he'd given me the taste for over the previous fortnight.

The whole trip was a wonderful success, in fact so successful we did it all over again the next year. As is so often the case with these enormously enjoyable experiences, it's impossible to repeat them and while the second one was great it wasn't quite the same as the first.

Over the following few years I was fortunate enough to be in a position financially to indulge my passion for travel. Annie's brother-in-law, Rodrigo, worked for a Panamanian bingo company and his job was to travel around South America and develop sites for bingo halls. We had a fortnight with him in Panama and then went to meet him in Rio de Janeiro. Rio should be on everyone's bucket list: the Sugar Loaf, Christ the Redeemer on Corcovado, the Maracana, once the world's biggest football ground, the beaches at Ipanema and Copacabana. And the bars: Sombre Los Ondes and Plataforma Una, where you can see the Carnival re-enacted three hundred and sixty-five nights a year. I was also lucky enough to visit Cuba and Cancun and I was in The Dominican Republic more times than I can count.

I don't consider all this expenditure squandered, I have memories that will last as long as I live. Maybe, if I ever run into money again, I'll retire to the DR and spend the rest of my life sitting under a palm tree in La Romana, drinking rum and playing poker on the internet.

The Rip-Off

Refreshed from the holiday, it was time to bite the bullet and make a phone call about the result of the other cruise, on The Brick. Thoughts of wreaths and Mass cards came to mind. Phone calls that start off with 'W-e-e-ll' don't usually have a happy ending but this one was an exception.

About a week after The Brick's anticipated arrival, the reception committee had given them up for lost and gone about their festive preparations. It turned out they had run out of food, cigarettes, fuel and the will to live, and were drifting aimlessly around the Irish Sea when they were spotted by a Customs cutter, which pulled alongside.

'What we going to do now?' asked Micky.

'What we going to do now? We're going to get nicked, of course,' replied Clive. 'What did you think we were going to do?'

'Where are you travelling from and where are you bound?' asked the Customs man.

'We're en route from Douglas, Isle of Man, to Fleetwood but we've run out of fuel,' lied Clive.

'Here, catch this,' said the Customs man, throwing them a line, and with that he towed them to Fleetwood, where they tied up at the pier.

The Customs boat recovered the line, gave them a wave and sailed off. They were absolutely stunned that they hadn't been nicked and wandered into town for a drink and to make a few phone calls. The people in Manchester waiting for their gear were no less stunned that they were even alive and set off post haste for Fleetwood with some transport. So it was that the gear was unloaded on the pier on Christmas afternoon. Thank you, Santa.

Getting The Brick home didn't make us feel the luckiest drug smugglers on the planet; it made us feel the best. If we could get The Brick home with its suspect crew, in the middle of winter, the sky would be the limit with a good boat, a crew that knew what they were about and in summer. We went on the hunt for a skipper.

Before long someone came up with two lads who seemed to know their job and we went in search of a boat. I went to see the broker in Portugal who had supplied The Brick and he had something that was perfect. I think that by this time the broker was fully aware of what we were about and he even dropped a few broad hints that he wouldn't mind being in it but we had enough partners at this stage. The boat was quite old, all wood, and very broad in the beam and looked like it could go anywhere. We gave fifty grand for it and Bullets sailed it around to Estepona.

We decided to put Micky on again with the captain and his mate, partly as our lucky mascot and partly to keep his eye on the gear. If anything untoward occurred we wanted an unbiased account. Musa went over and prepared the parcel: 2,350 kilos.

Off they went and the next morning I got a call to say the loading had gone off without a hitch. I wasn't expecting to hear anything for at least ten days, so I was surprised to get a phone call four or five days later from the boat. The story was that they were off the coast of La Coruña and had run out of fuel. Would I be good enough to nip out with a thousand litres of diesel and get them underway? Just to get the task in perspective, I drove down to a supermarket and looked at some five litre cans of cooking oil. So, we were talking something the size and shape of two hundred of these cans and I was supposed to get it to some spot in the Atlantic. Not a fucking earthly. I mean, how? And in what?

He phoned back the next morning and I put him firmly in the picture.

'It's all a bit academic now,' he replied. 'The situation has worsened. We've been buzzed several times by a spotter plane and it's only a matter of time till the odd lot arrive. We're in the process of jettisoning the cargo as I speak.'

They sailed the boat close to a port and abandoned it, going ashore in the dinghy.

I had one brief meeting with the captain and he repeated pretty much what he'd told me on the phone, assuring me the gear had been slung overboard and was now at the bottom of the sea. Micky had gone straight home to London and had been arrested at Heathrow with a crooked passport, so was unavailable for an interview about his version of events, so the whole saga was put to bed. The captain and his mate went off on another bit of graft for someone else.

Six days later, I spotted an item on Sky News. A boat had been captured in a port in North Wales carrying 2,350 kilos of puff. Now, unless I'm supposed to believe there were two independent parcels of 2,350 key, both destined to arrive at the same time on the north-west coast of England, then there's only one conclusion I can come to. My gear was trans-shipped somewhere off Portugal, and the gear captured in Wales was the same gear that was supposed to have been slung in the sea off La Coruña.

The captain and his mate were off busily losing another few million quid's worth of puff. I saw a TV documentary about the escapade. They were lying off the coast of the West Country awaiting the appointed rendezvous when they spotted bright lights approaching. Thinking it was the odd lot, they opened the sea-cocks, jumped into the dinghy and headed for shore. It turned out to be a fishing boat who had seen them lying idle, thought they might be in distress and had come to offer assistance. One fisherman boarded the boat and couldn't help seeing the cargo. He shut off the sea-cocks and they towed the boat into harbour.

During the subsequent Customs search, a receipt was found from a shipyard in Gib with the captain's name on it. They also found fingerprints and an all-ports alert was issued for them both. They managed to get as far as Harwich, where they were given a slight looking-at by Immigration but were allowed to board the ferry for Holland. As the ferry was leaving, the official went to the canteen for a cup of tea and his eyes were drawn to a 'wanted' poster on the noticeboard featuring the two men he had just allowed to board. He phoned his boss, who phoned the harbourmaster, who radioed the boat asking the captain to return but he refused, saying he had a schedule to keep to. So a pilot boat was mustered and several Customs men jumped aboard and set off in a frenzied pursuit of the ferry, desperate to arrest the fugitives before the twelve-mile limit was reached. They found them in the bar when the ferry was still in British waters and they were arrested and charged. The captain got ten years and his mate got eight.

These bits of work aren't put together in a couple of days, they take weeks to organise and you don't organise them without a captain. The only way the captain could know he'd be available for that job was because he knew he wouldn't be halfway across the Bay of Biscay delivering our gear.

The final piece of evidence appeared a few weeks later. I sent a pal up North to recover the boat which had been towed into harbour. He sailed it back to Estepona and when I went to meet him I asked how much I owed him for fuel. He said he hadn't had to buy any, the tanks were half full. If they got from Larache to the northern tip of Spain on half a tank, they had plenty to get them home.

Nowadays, when £4.7 million has a bit more significance than it had at the time, maybe the issue will have to be revisited. Even the £700,000 the job cost to be put together would come in handy.

he had paid to buy any, the cars were half full. If they only [illegible] to one [illegible] on half [illegible], they had nearly [illegible] dead [illegible].

In addition, when £1.7 million [illegible] other [illegible] [illegible] at the [illegible], maybe [illegible] figures from [illegible] the £90,000 the job [illegible] to be put together would [illegible].

Gentleman George

I first met Georgie Stokes in Patsy's Parrot Bar. He stood out a bit, being suited and booted when the normal dress code in Los Boliches was tee-shirts and shorts, and with his steel-grey hair he looked unusually distinguished. The conversation got around to prison sentences, which might seem an unusual topic to anyone who wasn't a Parrot Bar regular.

'I'll never forget the day I was sentenced to twenty years,' said George, joining in the conversation.

'When did you finish that?' I asked.

'Oh, I haven't finished it yet,' he said.

Apparently the prison regime hadn't agreed with him and he'd made his own arrangements about a discharge.

We soon became very pally but Georgie had one major shortcoming. He suffered from what we used to call a grass-hopper mind. During a conversation he could flit, without pause or hesitation, from one scheme to another and it could all prove very confusing. The thing that all his schemes had in common was a means of getting a bit of puff from somewhere to somewhere else. Traditional methods like cars, wagons and boats weren't enough for him. Hot-air balloons and self-propelled rockets were only two of the innovations he came up with. Despite all that, some of his schemes must have worked because he always seemed to have plenty of money.

He came to me one day and when he mentioned the word 'boat' I was hoping he'd quickly flit to another scheme but as he went on I had to admit he might have something.

'I've got a crooked Guardia Civil in charge of a small port who, for a consideration, will allow me to unload a boat with impunity.'

On the face of it this sounds like the Holy Grail of puff smuggling but it has to be remembered that getting a boat unloaded isn't the major concern. I've done it myself countless times without any assistance from the Old Bill. You still had to run the gauntlet from Morocco to the port and put up with all the other trials and tribulations. On the other hand, driving into a port in a transit van and unloading under the watchful eye of a tame local plod did seem a step in the right direction. Another valid point is that very often when a boat is pulled over on the high seas it's because the crew have done something to bring it on themselves, like getting drunk and talking out of school, and the port authorities have had the boat gazetted. That was one less worry here, so I sent Musa over to get a parcel ready.

Amazingly enough everything went like clockwork for the first several trips. Georgie's navigating skills being a little suspect, the Moroccans sent a lad over who knew the loading area and he led them by the hand to the exact spot. The Guardia Civil was as good as his word and the unloading was conducted without a hitch.

Of course, it was only a matter of time until disaster struck. One night the puff was being manhandled aboard on a beach in Morocco and George was stacking it neatly in the stash when he noticed his feet were getting wet. And soon after, his ankles. The puff chain was put into reverse and the parcel was returned to the barge. It seems they had collided with a submerged tree trunk and were holed below the waterline. Abandoning ship was the only option and George and the two crewmen jumped onto the barge and were on the beach in time to see their boat disappear beneath the waves.

They now had a serious problem. They were now three illegal immigrants without passports because, ostensibly, they were only going out a couple miles for a spot of fishing and hadn't brought them with them. Morocco is a difficult place to move about in even if you are a law-abiding Moroccan citizen, of which I'm sure there must be some. I remember one time taking a taxi from Tangiers to Tetuan and the driver had to stop at the police station and produce my passport and tell them where he was taking me. We were stopped four or five times en route and had to produce it again.

I believe George's trip from the beach back to Tetuan was horrendous, scurrying down escarpments to avoid check-points and crawling on hands and knees through date plantations. They were eventually installed in an apartment in Cabo Negro and by all accounts very well looked after but the passports remained a problem. Fortunately enough Musa had a relative that worked in the immigration office in Tangiers port. I got hold of the passports from George's girlfriend and Musa had them sent to his relative, who put backdated entry visas in them. A taxi ride to Cabo Negro and the shipwrecked mariners became perfectly legitimate tourists.

When they got back, George was reluctant to pull up the money for a new boat, since, despite their successes, no vast fortunes had been made. Bringing over a ton at a time probably earned them about two hundred grand, less expenses and less whatever they were paying the Old Bill. In any case George had come up with a new scheme in the Caribbean.

Off he went but sadly things went awry. George spent a couple of years on remand in Trinidad before being extradited back to the UK, where he was sentenced to twelve years. Of course he still owed a few years from the original twenty but they were magnanimous enough to lump it all together and he was released on parole after about seven or eight.

No sooner was he out of the gate than he set about cooking up a bit of graft. One afternoon he was getting a lift in a pal's car and, during the journey, a venture in South America was discussed. Unfortunately the pal was under surveillance and the car was bugged. The conversation was enough to lead to a conspiracy charge. Under British law just discussing a project is sufficient to be charged with conspiracy even if none of the conspirators have ever set foot in England. In fact two people could sit on the moon and talk about sending a bit of gear to England and they're already guilty if the conversation can be proved. Smacks a bit of gamesmanship to me but that's the rule.

Anyway, Georgie was convicted and sentenced to sixteen years, plus whatever parole he still owed on the twenty and the twelve. After a few years away he was diagnosed as needing a heart transplant which he was very unlikely to get, being a pretty low priority on the waiting list. At age sixty-three he died in prison; a sadder end to a genuinely decent character I can't imagine. I hope he is looking down, though I suppose looking up is more likely, from somewhere getting some grim satisfaction out of having cheated the authorities out of his last outlandish sentence.

The Parrot Bar's gone now, too. Laurie and Lorna Nash, the couple who owned it, were murdered in gruesome fashion, both suffering multiple stab wounds. Their lodger, a friend of mine from Manchester called Paul Bains, says he came home to find their log cabin ablaze with one of the bodies inside and the other on the veranda, and went and phoned the police. Shortly afterwards he was arrested and charged with the crimes. He was held on remand for two years, at which point the prosecution can go back to court and ask for a further two-year remand; yes, four years on remand, but there you go. At the same time the defence can go to court and ask that the defendant be released on bail. The fact that he was released on bail would lead me to assume the evidence was a bit thin. Turning up for trial would make me think either that he was innocent or he thought the evidence too weak for a conviction.

The rule in Spain is that when a defendant is on bail, the bail is continued while the judge considers his verdict, which usually takes ten days. I suppose at that point the judge drops you a line asking you to pop down to the local nick with your toothbrush and start the twenty-eight-year sentence the prosecution has asked for. Paul was released but over the weekend the judge had second thoughts and sent the Old Bill around to place him back in custody. A few days later he received the twenty-eight-year sentence.

I have no real opinion about his guilt or innocence. He came to see me when he was on bail and swore on everything that was holy that he knew nothing of the murders and at the time I felt inclined to believe him. The fact that he's now serving his sentence back in the UK probably means he's exhausted all avenues of appeal so, guilty or not, he's stuck with it. Still, he's been away for six or seven years at the time of writing, so maybe he can see some light at the end of the tunnel.

The Irish Rover and Other Bars

The Queen Vic had shut its doors for the last time. Steve and Pauline had split up, Steve going back to England and Pauline doing whatever Pauline was doing. A new watering hole had to found, not that the choice was limited. Most of the hundreds of small bars in Los Boliches are much of a muchness. Quite a few you'd have to go outside and look over the door to know which one you were in, but the Irish Rover was a bit different. To start with, it was a slightly odd shape which allowed for a couple of nooks and crannies. The décor was very much 'Irish theme pub abroad', which is to say pretty unlike most of the pubs left in Ireland. There were Irish road signs and bric-a-brac, a birdcage with two cans of Guinness on the perch with a sign saying 'Irish Toucans' and lots of other stuff in a similar vein. Soon after I started drinking there, they began ordering my favourite tipple, Jameson's whiskey, in my personal five-litre bottle and it didn't take long for a dozen or so of the empties to be added to the décor. All very cosy and reminiscent of how home used to be.

Décor and cosiness aside, the biggest attraction was the barmaid, Lisa. She was one of those amazing girls who probably looked twenty-five when she was fifteen and will probably look twenty-five when she's forty. She certainly doesn't seem to have aged a day in the years I've known her.

Originally there were three partners, Lisa, her pal Grace and Grace's boyfriend, Julio, but after a while Lisa cobbled together a deal and bought out Grace and Julio. Lisa was destined to run the place for ten years, which is an awful long time for one of those little bars not to change hands. It was to become my headquarters for just as long, most of which time I devoted to chasing Lisa, without success. It would be a husband and three kids later before I reluctantly gave up the chase.

Entertainment was provided by Touhy, who was mad as a hatter and had only two ambitions in life: to get stoned and to shag anything with a pulse. He played the guitar and ran the karaoke and now and then would play a few songs he'd written himself. Just recently Christy Moore has recorded two of his songs and he's appeared a couple of times on Irish TV. I wish him every success and hope he'll remember me when he's rich and famous.

Opening hours were pretty flexible. The odd night I'd arrive at midnight and find the place closed and other times I'd find myself leaving at nine in the morning, a bit like the old lock-ins in Dublin. The clientele was a pretty mixed bunch but one thing they all had in common was that no-one seemed to do much in the way of work. Gerry O'Sullivan would take a few bets on the horses, or have a few bets, depending what mood he was in. Irish Wally would do a bit of painting if pushed. There were a few people on the fringes of the timeshare game but other than that I can't think of a genuine worker.

Lisa is the youngest of four sisters, with a younger brother, John, and her mother and father, Derrick and Bernie, and the rest would get over fairly regularly. One night I took Bernie and Lisa's sister Emma, along with a dozen others, to Puerto Banus. I can't remember why Lisa didn't come; she must have been pregnant, she usually was. We dined in Silks, the first time in years I'd been back there, and I was very flattered to spot a photo of myself with Besty and Angie Lynn up in the hall of fame. We did the rounds of the piano bars and finished up in Olivia Valero's until eight in the morning. Bernie became known as Bernie Banus from that day on.

Another time I was in the Dominican Republic for Christmas and Emma was working in St Maarten, just a couple of islands away. I'd arrived on the twentieth and my pal wasn't coming over from Dublin until the twenty-ninth. By the twenty-sixth I was getting a bit bored and thought I'd pop over to St Maarten and visit Emma and her boyfriend, Adam. How hard could it be? I went to make some enquiries and discovered there were only two options: charter a boat or charter a plane. Having had my fill of boats, I took the plane option.

My original thought was to stay for a couple of days but I couldn't come to any sort of a sensible deal with the charter company. In the end we agreed to go first thing in the morning and come back last thing at night for $2,000 and $60 an hour waiting time, a bit dear but what's the point of being an international drug smuggler if you can't be a little extravagant now and again?

Apparently there are three hundred and sixty-five beaches on St Maarten. I wouldn't claim we visited them all but we did do a complete circuit of the island, stopping every ten minutes for a light ale. We ended up in a bar called Sunset Beach at the end of the airport runway. Here they have a little competition every night. People stand at the end of the runway and see who can stay standing longest before getting blown into the sea by the backdraft of the KLM flight taking off for Schiphol.

The flight back was horrendous. Those little light planes aren't suitable transport for a person in the condition I was in.

Bizarre behaviour is pretty much par for the course for all of us when we're drunk. One night, or rather early morning, in the Rover the subject came up of phone numbers and how people nowadays never remember them. I voiced my opinion.

'It's because we don't dial them anymore, we just flick through the menu and press the call button.' I went on to say, 'Thirty years ago I had a girlfriend, Ruth, and I can still remember her phone number because I dialled it so many times.'

A minute or two later, someone mentioned the date, January 19, and I said, 'What a coincidence, that's Ruth's birthday.'

'Why don't you give her a call?' said Lisa.

Looking back on it, I can't even begin to calculate the odds of someone having the same number after thirty years, but we don't always think rationally when we're drunk. I dialled the number.

'Yes?' a man's voice answered. Bear in mind it was about two in the morning by then, though I suppose only one back in Manchester.

'Can I speak to Ruth?' I asked.

'Yes, just a minute,' he said.

As he said it, the battery ran out on my phone. Lisa had a phone with a battery but no credit but, ever resourceful, she set about swapping my chip into her phone, not the easiest of tasks when you're pissed and both know the best way to go about it. It took about ten minutes. I phoned back and Ruth answered.

'Happy birthday,' I wished her.

'Who's that?' she said.

'Maurice.'

'Maurice who?'

'How many Maurices do you know?' I asked her, not very flattered.

The penny must have dropped because she apologised saying, 'Well, maybe, since I haven't heard a word from you in thirty years, that's the reason your name didn't immediately spring to mind.'

We chatted for a few minutes and said goodnight.

The next day she phoned me to say that when she woke up she thought she'd dreamt the previous night's conversation until she saw the Spanish number on her caller ID. It turned out she had a timeshare place in Benalmadena, five miles down the road, and had been coming over to Spain every year for the past twenty years. We now meet up every year and go for a meal.

Without labouring the point about what a great day out the Irish Derby is, one year I was over there and by coincidence Lisa was there visiting the family. I had booked a table and hired a minibus, so I invited her to come along. We were leaving from the Westbury at about eleven and Lisa arrived looking stunning: the dress, the hat, the bag and the shoes. Though she'd probably have looked stunning in a bin-liner and wellies. Among the party were two of Dickie Rock's sons, Jason and Richard. Jason is a very useful person to know in Dublin; hotel rooms, show tickets, restaurant tables are all within his sphere of influence.

Johnny Murtagh came in and did the after-lunch chat, telling us his fancies and then went out and rode the Derby winner. Lisa backed three or four winners and probably won a couple of hundred quid. I can't remember how I finished, which usually means it was nothing dramatic one way or the other. I do remember it was a particularly boozy afternoon followed by a boozy trip home via the Keydean. The bus driver had a Dickie Rock CD and we listened to Dickie tell us all about 'The Candy Store on the Corner' the whole way back to Dublin. I can't even begin to guess what time we all got to bed.

So, though I regretted the passing of the Queen Vic, we had found a pretty good substitute.

Although the Irish Rover was headquarters and I used it daily, there were a number of other places I availed myself of. To try to name all the bars in Los Boliches and Fuengirola would be like painting the Forth Bridge. By the time you'd finished you'd have to start all over, so many would have changed their names. But a few institutions are worth a mention.

I mentioned The Cepa Bar earlier, with its claim to be the first English bar in town. Actually, John was English and his wife Diane was Welsh. Diane's sister, Jill, and her husband, Manolo, who was Spanish, made up the other partners. So, I suppose a more accurate description would be the first English/Welsh/Welsh/Spanish bar in town. Having said that, the vast majority of the punters were English and being in the centre of what was then a small town, it was the main meeting place.

I was having a drink with Neil Robertson in there one day when Freddie Foreman's son Jamie joined us. Today Jamie is a big star in *EastEnders* but back then he would have only been in his early twenties.

After a while Neil said, 'Let's go and have one in the Tall Man.'

Jamie, who is a big believer in fortune telling, tarot cards and that stuff, said, 'Can't, mate. I've got to meet Maria, the fortune teller, here at two o'clock.'

'Well, if she's any fucking good, she'll know you're not going to be here,' said Neil.

With that we headed to the Tall Man.

At the time it was owned by my bullfighting aficionado pal Tony Allan who only worked there under sufferance, his real love in life being music, specifically jazz – he is a very accomplished drummer. Most of the work was carried out by his wife Kathy, assisted by son Steve, known as 'Skinner', and daughter Keely, who was known as Keely. Because of his lack of enthusiasm Tony could get a bit grumpy and his pet hate was being asked stupid questions by tourists.

One day he greeted me with, 'I've got a fucking new one. What do you think someone asked me today? "What day is the Tuesday market held?"'

He walked away, shaking his head and muttering, 'What day is the Tuesday market held?'

The place has changed hands a few times but always kept the name since it's a bit of a landmark.

For a good while it was owned by a lovely Spanish chap called Victor, who had spent most of his working life in Manchester in the hotel trade. For a long time he worked at the Alma Lodge, next door to Jack Trickett's hotel. His wife, Paula, was English and the daughters, Zoe and Karen, were born in England. Sadly, Victor died and the place was sold but the current owner, John, an Irishman, is a friend of mine and I still use it.

The first Irish bar in town was Billy's Bar and it goes back to at least the early Seventies. Billy, from Belfast, had a bit of a look of Santa Claus with his bushy white beard. He had perfected the knack of making Gaelic coffee and could produce a dozen picture-perfect coffees at the drop of a hat. In my heyday, given half an hour and half a dozen attempts, I might produce one. Mind you, I did get to drink the rejects which is probably the incentive for me to keep trying. They tasted pretty much the same as the picture-perfect ones. I think he cheated a bit by slightly whipping the cream to make it more buoyant but whatever his secret, it worked. Those places that make their Irish coffee with that aerosol crap should be nicked for false pretences. Then they stick a straw in it. What for? Don't they know the whole idea is to drink the coffee through the cream?

Harry's Bar was another tradition. Harry was a tall bloke,

over six foot and built with it, an ex-US Marine who'd seen service in Vietnam. Sometimes, around two in the morning, if Harry had had a few drinks, which is to say most two in the mornings, he'd decide it was time for a little bayonet-throwing practice. The bar door was the usual target and it's just as well it was a fairly stout oak affair. When James Michener wrote his book *The Drifters*, he talks of a bar called the Texan. Although in the book the Texan Bar is in Torremolinos, the character of the bar owner was based on Harry. He had a framed letter on the wall from Michener's publishers authorising him to use the name if he ever felt so inclined.

Across the street my pal from Dublin, Andrew, had a place called Harrods. The green and gold sign did look very much like the one from the London store and they took exception to it, claiming it was copyright. He was eventually obliged to change the name to Harpers. Further down the street was the Number Ten, a bar very much for the more genteel expat. I never drank in the place and I'm fairly sure I wouldn't have been served if I'd tried.

One bar I used occasionally, Oscars, might appear a strange choice of watering hole, seeing as how it was a lesbian bar. However, it's amazing how many young lesbians aren't fully decided about their orientation and could be convinced to experiment. My opening gambit would usually be along the lines that I, myself, often felt that I was a lesbian trapped in a man's body. This strategy had a reasonable amount of success and for that reason Bobby, the Scottish girl who owned the place, always referred to me as the Poacher.

There's a street in Fuengirola called Calle de la Cruz (Cross Street), which is known to the locals as Calle Hambre (Hungry Street) and to the expats as Fish Alley. There are probably fifty or sixty restaurants, door to door, fairly evenly divided between meat and fish specialists, all pretty much of a muchness, with the odd Chinese thrown in. One place that does stand out a bit from the others is Aroma, owned by a pal of mine, John Kelly, and his partner Rocky, an Argentinian. John and I were partners, briefly, in the 27 Club, along with his pal Nick and my pal Danny. At Aroma they take a bit more trouble with presentation and the whole place has a more dressy air about it; more a place to dine than just a place to eat. Of course it would be a smidgen dearer than the other places but it's usually the case in life that you only get what you pay for.

A few bars in Fish Alley have survived the ravages of time, notably the Britannia and the Dolphin, which have both been around for years. A couple more, O'Brien's and J.B. Burkes, are more recent additions that look likely to survive. There are several Indian restaurants around town but the best one would be Ronnie Knight's old place, the Mumtaz. It is run these days by Ron's old manager, Ash, and Indians come from all along the coast to eat there, which speaks for itself. I'm not a great lover of Indian food, so I don't use the place a lot, but if someone insisted on going for one that's where I'd take them.

Chinese in Spain is at best mediocre, but it is cheap which I suppose brings us back to getting what you pay for. I was probably spoiled for Chinese when I lived in Manchester, where the best Chinese food in the world is produced. The Yan Sing on Charlotte Street was the first Chinese restaurant ever to get in Egon Ronay's *Good Food Guide*. It costs an arm and a leg but it is wonderful.

Seafood places are everywhere and it's difficult to find a bad one. At the very end of the seafront, at Cavajal, there are two restaurants owned by two brothers, Los Moranos, both top class. They also own some fishing boats, so something that was swimming about at four in the morning can be on your plate by lunchtime.

There are very few places where you can dine and be

entertained at the same time, the only two I know being the Valparaiso and the Mijas Playa. I think it's fair to say the Mijas Playa edges it slightly on the food and the Valparaiso edges it slightly on the views. Being on the beach, the Mijas Playa has a decent view and sitting on the terrace in the summer with the odd fishing boat trawling past is very pleasant. The Val, being halfway up the hill to Mijas, has the same sea view but also all the lights of Fuengirola spread out below. Entertainment I'd make a tie, since Pearse Webb, who has sung twice a week for twenty-odd years at the Val and David Myers, who plays the piano at the Mijas Playa, are both friends of mine. I usually go to whichever I can get a table at and I've never had a bad night at either of them.

Getting a table can often be a problem for me, being a spur-of-the-moment person. I rarely go in for organised dinner parties and usually only start phoning around for a table when I decide to go, not the best policy if you want a good table on a Saturday night at the Val or the Mijas Playa. But I've never been able to understand how people can phone up on a Tuesday afternoon to book a table for Saturday night. How do they know they're going to be hungry at nine o'clock next Saturday night?

One year the Mijas Playa experimented with supper theatres. They had a large banqueting suite on the first floor and the idea was you had a meal whilst watching a play. I've never been much of a theatre-goer but one night I noticed that the following week's offering was a play called *Jeffrey Bernard Is Unwell* and felt I had to see it. I had known Jeff quite well in London in the Seventies and had many a drink with him in the Coach and Horses in Soho. At the time he was writing a weekly column in the *Sporting Life* relating his adventures on the turf.

My favourite Bernard yarn concerned a pal of his called

Lucky, who was the most unlucky man on the planet. One day Lucky ambles down to his local betting shop, penniless, hoping to find someone to put the arm on. He meets a pal who apologises for being unable to help, explaining he had invested every available shilling on a tip running in the last race at Sandown Park. He went on to say that should the horse oblige, he'd be happy to give Lucky a dig-out and told him in which betting shop he'd be listening to the race. Lucky hangs about all afternoon and, come the last race, the tip duly obliges. As it crosses the line, Lucky hails a cab and sets off to pick up his promised bit of assistance. The punchline read, 'It was just as the taxi with its destitute fare was crossing Waterloo Bridge that the objection to the winner was sustained.'

Later, Jeff moved to the *Spectator* and when, as often as not, his article failed to arrive, usually due to over-indulgence, the column was left blank except for an announcement, 'Jeffrey Bernard is unwell', hence the play's title. The gist of the play, written by humorist Keith Waterhouse, himself no stranger to the grape, is that Jeff falls asleep in the toilet of a pub. When he wakes up he finds he's locked in and helps himself to a drink. As the night wears on he gets to thinking over his past and ghosts begin to appear: the Customs and Excise man who arrested him for illegal bookmaking, the steward of the Jockey Club coming to warn him off over unpaid gambling debts, and all the other momentous events of his life. It's a great play and Jeff was a wonderful character. I always admired his ability to go through life doing very little other than drinking and gambling and then get a living writing about the consequences.

I think there's an awful lot of crap talked about food. I don't think I've ever in my life sent a meal back in a restaurant. It makes me cringe when people start making a waiter's life a misery with a 'bit more of this' or 'a bit less of that' while the poor chap is trying to serve a dozen other tables. I tend to eat it or leave it and if I'm really hungry order something else and say I've changed my mind.

If there's crap talked about food, then wine is ten times worse. Twenty-five years is something approaching ten thousand days, so it's fairly likely I've drunk in the region of five thousand bottles of Viña Sol and never had a bad one. Why would I want to go through all that nonsense about sniffing the cork and nosing the wine and sipping it and the rest?

I had one pal, Norman, who wouldn't dream of putting anything near his lips that cost less than three hundred quid a bottle. One day he took Jim Swords out for a meal at the Hungry Monk in Wicklow and ordered a bottle of something in that price range.

'Bring me a bottle of Seven Up,' said Jim to the waiter, which he then poured into the wine.

'You can't do that!' said Norman, appalled.

'Look,' said Jim, 'you drink it how you enjoy it and I'll drink it how I enjoy it. I judge my wine by how much Seven Up I have to put in it. If it's very good, I put a drop and if it's crap, I put a lot.'

Quite right, too. Pour it out, drink it and order another bottle is my policy. Of course, all that's just my opinion and the diligent reader will have already gathered it rarely carries much clout.

The MIAs (Missing In Action)

It is a sad but inevitable fact in the puff job that people go missing in action. More often than not they simply get nicked but sometimes there are more mysterious disappearances. Diver Dave was one example. He left to do a bit of work on a boat and was never seen again. The body of his partner eventually turned up floating in the Bay of Cadiz. The body had some suspicious rope burns which may have come from some entanglement during a shipwreck or they may have had a more sinister significance. Personally I think Dave is dead but who knows?

Billy May was another that left behind doubts. Billy was an ex-pro boxer and had lived on the coast for years. One day he came into the Queen Vic with his face covered in bandages looking like the invisible man looked when he wasn't invisible. The story was that he had disturbed a burglar, who had slashed his face, but the bandaging looked too widespread for that explanation. To me it looked like the after effects of plastic surgery.

A week or two later, he went off on holiday to the Caribbean where, in his early forties and fit as a fiddle, he dropped dead of a heart attack. The sealed coffin was flown to his home town in South Wales and he was cremated. I went to a small service that was held in Spain, coincidentally enough in the Irish Rover before it was the Irish Rover. In all probability that's where the story ends but I'd like to think that he might be sat on an island in the Caribbean happily spending someone else's money.

The fate of Micky Reilly's partner, Neil Robertson, who had made his money in the VAT scam, is a death that will never be explained. He either jumped, fell or was thrown from a multi-storey building in London. Knowing him as well as I did, I would discount jumping. Falling seems unlikely so we're really only left with the third option. But why? Neil was a lovely man and when he had money nobody was skint but the dough from the VAT scam was long gone and he had been obliged to explore other avenues. As I keep saying, there was only one game in town. He was arrested and spent about nine months on remand before getting released on bail. No doubt he spent the entire period in custody plotting his next venture and as soon as he was released it was all hands to the pump. Things didn't go too well and I know for a fact that Neil painted himself into a bit of a corner as regards owing a few bits and pieces of dough. They were not colossal amounts and Neil wasn't a totally skint member; he still owned his villa which at the time was probably worth three hundred grand. Given a bit more time and a bit better luck than he'd been having, I'm sure things would have resolved themselves. He never got the time and I'm forced to believe that someone took a more serious view of his outstanding liabilities than the likes of me had.

Charlie Wilson's murder was another needless death when he was shot at his villa in San Pedro. The episode was described to me by someone who was in a position to know as 'a very strong pull that went wrong'. There had been a disagreement, the basis of which is neither here nor there, and a gunman was sent around to the house to make loud, threatening noises. As we all now know that's not how things worked out. Several other shootings would ensue by way of revenge and retribution.

Eric Flowers was another to leave us in tragic circumstances.

Eric had escaped from Wandsworth prison in 1965 along with his more famous compatriot Ronnie Biggs and had gone to Australia with him. Unlike Biggsy, Eric returned home sooner rather than later and completed his sentence. In the Nineties he came to live in Spain and took a town house in La Cala. We did several bits of work together. One afternoon he was trying to remove some leaves from his gutter but couldn't reach. He tried standing on a table but still couldn't get high enough so he put a chair on the table. As he was stretching up, the chair wobbled and down came Eric. He landed on a pointed ornamental lava-stone and was impaled through the chest. It was tragically ironic that a man who could safely negotiate the wall of Wandsworth nick should die from a fall of something less than six feet off a wobbly chair.

There were others, the West London accountant I have mentioned previously being an example but, as I say, by and large people just get nicked. A lad from Liverpool, Chris, would do a bit of work for me and one day he told me he'd found someone with a parcel of gear for sale. I was looking for two hundred key that four of us wanted to send home but I also had some money belonging to some people from Ireland who were after a hundred and fifty. I told Chris I'd buy three fifty but I was a bit stuck for somewhere to store it. He said he had a rented villa and that he could look after it, so the deal was done. What he hadn't told me was that he was in dispute with the landlady who had refused to return his month's deposit, so he was staying an extra month with little more status than a squatter. The gear had only been there a day or two when the landlady popped in to see if the place had been vacated and could hardly fail to spot it stacked up on the living room floor. Just to make matters worse, the landlady's husband was a Guardia Civil working for the Malaga drug squad.

I decided to move the one fifty belonging to the Irishmen

and sent Chris to hire a car, planning to park it up somewhere sensible until they came to collect it. Chris went around to pick up the gear and was pounced on by Old Bill who had been lurking in the garden for the previous twenty-four hours. I got bored waiting for him to come back and took a walk around to the villa. There was Chris, handcuffed to the railing while the Old Bill were loading my bit of puff into their Land Rover. I left them to it. Chris hadn't told me he hadn't got a driving licence and the car was rented in his girlfriend's mother's name so the Old Bill went around and nicked them. Fortunately enough Chris did the honourable thing and made a statement exonerating them and they were released after twenty-four hours.

The whole saga left me in a very invidious position. Having not informed the Irish lads that I'd acquired their gear, it was a bit late to tell them after I'd lost it. One of those grey areas of responsibility but in all conscience I felt I had to replace it. With my quarter of the two hundred and their one fifty, the escapade cost me a hundred and forty grand. On the other hand it cost Chris three years of his life.

Tommy Two Heads was another casualty. He was involved in the turnout in Algeciras with Flashy and got six years. He was no sooner out than went straight back to work and was dispatched on a mission in Portugal. As is often the case there was delay after delay and Tommy was getting a bit bored. He struck up an acquaintanceship with a couple of kindred spirits down the local boozer and this helped pass the time. One night the new pals said they were off to get their bit of graft done. Tommy, probably with a few drinks in him, said he was doing nothing and would go along for the ride. They were all nicked and Tommy got eight years.

I had one experience with a boat before the episode with Smuggler Ted which was probably the main reason for my reluctance to get involved again. The deal had little to do with me other than an introduction and came about through one of those conversations that were so common at the time. I knew of some people with a boat who had been over several times to Morocco without getting loaded and the people concerned were getting frustrated. By chance someone asked me if I knew of any transport and I told him the story. He said if they failed to get loaded the next trip would they pop twenty miles down the coast and pick up his gear. I introduced them and they made a deal.

Sure enough, the next pick-up was aborted so they sailed down the coast to the second meet and were duly loaded. Unfortunately it cut up a bit rough on the way back and they lost the inflatable so were unable to get the gear to the beach and instead sailed, fully loaded, into port. The boat was a flat-bottomed catamaran and could have easily been run up onto the beach and if it got destroyed it could have been replaced but the crew, two women and a young girl, treated it as their home and wouldn't risk it.

We were now faced with the unloading rigmarole and the boat wasn't moored in the most secluded of berths. My view was to walk it off bit by bit and if it took a couple of weeks, so what, but I was overruled and it was decided to sail it out to a beach. I had spotted an inflatable on a trailer in another marina and we went down with a pair of bolt-cutters and a car with a tow-bar and acquired it. We put one of the workers in it, put him in the water at La Cala and he headed off to the meet. In the meantime the catamaran set to sea.

As it was getting dark they met up and the gear was thrown into the inflatable, which headed for the beach as the others headed back to port. Obviously it hadn't all been as inconspicuous as we thought it had been. The moment the inflatable touched the beach, droves of Old Bill carrying machine guns appeared on the scene. There was even a helicopter flying overhead and a Customs boat steamed out from behind the harbour wall where it had been lurking in wait and intercepted the catamaran. Everyone was nicked and got sentences between three and four years.

Even poor old Musa fell foul. He put together a deal to land nine tons on a beach in Murcia and sent four lads down to do the beach work. How four lads were going to get nine ton off a beach I can't begin to imagine, recalling my own experiences. Anyway, the problem never arose because the whole thing went boss-eyed and the four lads and the people on the boat were all nicked. Musa managed to slip the net and I went to see him before he made his escape to Holland. I asked him if he thought anyone would mention his name and he said he'd already got access to the statements. Mention his name? One of them went into so much detail in his grassing he even told them what music Musa was playing on his CD on the way down. Musa made his excuses and left.

Another saga that led to a host of arrests began in a hotel bar in Blackpool. Eric Mason, a London villain who had lived in Manchester for years, was staying at Dennis Crolla's Blackpool hotel for the weekend and got talking to two blokes over a drink. As the night wore on, one of those you-show-me-yours-and-I'll-show-you-mine situations developed. The two blokes claimed to be Northern Irish money launderers with connections to the IRA. Taking them at face value, Eric told them of his frequent trips to Malaga and all his acquaintances in the puff job. This would turn out to be a major lapse of judgement from someone as experienced in the world of villainy as Eric. The two blokes would turn out to be MI6 agents on secondment to the organised crime and anti-drugs mob. With the end of the Cold War, a number of underemployed security force personnel were sent on loan to assist in the war on crime. Finishing their drinking session in the early hours, they exchanged phone numbers and agreed to get in touch should anything of mutual interest come along.

All this was no chance encounter but rather an orchestrated plot. Mason had written a book, in fact several books. One, *The Black Knight*, was a joint autobiography with Ronnie Knight but the one that brought the heat on him was his own autobiography. In it he told of his career with the Krays in the Sixties and all the underworld figures he knew in London and Manchester. He was invited to appear, representing the criminal fraternity, on one of those talk radio shows that have become so popular where criminals recount their exploits. Representing the forces of law and order was Tony Blair's 'drugs czar', Keith Hellawell. After the show they bumped into each other in the car park and Mason signed a copy of his book and gave it to Hellawell. Reading it, Hellawell soon realised that Mason knew, or at least claimed to know, an awful lot of people and decided it might be worth his while to devote a bit of time and attention to him. Hence the engineered meeting in the Blackpool hotel.

Before long, the two MI6 men were on the phone, wining and dining Eric, taking him to race meetings and allowing him to con them out of a few quid with mythical tips. Anything to give him the impression he was dealing with a couple of rich mugs. Time passed, Eric found himself in Malaga and he got into conversation with a pal, who told him a tale of woe. He had a parcel of puff stranded in Morocco for want of thirty grand in exes. Eric said he might be able to help him and gave his pals in MI6 a call. They flew over and pulled up the thirty grand. They would subsequently first deny giving the money then later admit they had but when they gave it they stipulated that it must not be used for drug trafficking. What two Northern Ireland money-launderers would be doing giving thirty grand to some Costa del Sol drug dealers other than drug trafficking remains a mystery. Anyway, nothing came of the deal, not one gram of puff arrived and the thirty grand got ate.

Several more meets occurred; I attended one myself in Dublin. We were all over for a race meeting at Leopardstown on the Saturday and on the Sunday afternoon we went for a drink in the Hole in the Wall on Blackhorse Avenue. By this stage there were about twenty in the party, some from London, some from Spain, a couple from Holland and a few local pals. All in all, enough for MI6 to think they'd stumbled on a nest of international rogues but most of the group were totally innocent bystanders.

The Hole in the Wall was originally little more than a cottage but over the years they've bought next door and next door and next door and today it has to be one of the longest pubs in the world. Walking through it is a bit like walking through a series of railway carriages. On a Sunday the live music is in the first bar, which is where we gathered. Eric's pal and his partner went for a chat a couple of carriages down and when they came back, an hour or more later, I was introduced to the MI6 men. By this time I was too drunk to hold a coherent conversation and that's why I got my second get-out-of-jail-free card. I think there are only two, aren't there? All I needed to do was open my big, stupid mouth and say something like 'If you know anyone looking for a bit of puff, here's my number' and I'd have been in the net with the rest of them. Micky Reilly, who was between ten-year stretches at the time, agreed how lucky we were. One of our gang, known as Tantrum because of his lack of patience, was the only one to say he didn't fancy them one bit. Then again, Tantrum never fancied anyone so he had to be right some of the time.

Eventually a deal was put together whereby MI6 would pull

up another two hundred grand and a recovery and profit-sharing mission would be undertaken, but things never got that far. By now MI6 had enough recorded gossip to bring a charge of conspiracy, once again without a gram of gear changing hands, and arrests were made. People were lifted in Manchester, London and Leeds and some were extradited from Spain. Sentences ranging from a couple of fours through a seven and an eight up to a couple in double figures were imposed.

What's that they say: loose lips sink ships?

I've known a few very tough people over the years but, with the possible exception of Jim Swords, I'd struggle to think of a tougher one than Pikey Mike. The Pikey was from the Sligo travelling community and had done his share of bare-fist fighting. He was far from being a bully but after a few drinks he could have a fairly short fuse. I was having a drink with him one night when a dispute developed. Something of a scuffle broke out and during the ensuing huffing and puffing a bloke lost half his ear. Mike totally denied knowing anything about it but the missing half ear did turn up, in the breast pocket of my jacket, a couple of days later. The victim was known from that day forth as Eighteen Months because he only had an ear and a half. No charges were ever brought over the incident but the Pikey was later arrested and extradited to the UK on another matter. He was sentenced to six years and should be home any minute.

Another pal, Fritz, was remarkably adept at getting hold of the artificial stimulant of choice of any particular person. The quality was generally indifferent to piss-poor and he soon became known as Dr Mengele, having probably done in so many people with his scientific experiments. One night Fritz was having a drink in a bar in Fuengirola where the girlfriend of another pal was working when a fight broke out involving a bunch of young locals. They were slung out but came back with a couple of dozen pals. Fritz phoned Rory's bar, our regular hangout, for some reinforcements of his own, and myself, the Pikey and half a dozen others jumped in a couple of cars and went off to relieve the siege.

To this day the scene that greeted me always conjures up two visions. Fritz is quite a big bloke but, well, I think it's fair to say, a little bit weird. He had snatched up a pool cue and broken it in half but unfortunately he threw away the wrong half. Instead of keeping the weighted handle he kept the skinny pointed bit, which he was brandishing to keep the hordes at bay. I thought he looked like Sir Malcolm Sargent conducting the Royal Philharmonic. That is, if Sir Malc had spikey hair, wore black leather chaps and had several conspicuous body piercings. The other vision I get is the bit from Rorke's Drift in the film *Zulu*, where the beleaguered Welsh engineering battalion are striving to hold back the waves of Zulus. I often find myself breaking into a chorus of 'Men Of Harlech' when I bump into Fritz.

Given his line of work, it's not surprising that Fritz eventually got himself nicked. A pal was released on bail and told me that during his interviews he'd seen Fritz's name mentioned in dispatches and the Old Bill were on the point of nicking him. By coincidence the following day I was going to Fritz and Tracy's wedding, which hardly seemed the time or place to be breaking such depressing news but he had to be told. He took it pretty philosophically and you'd think he'd have had the sense to go home and do a spot of house-clearing. But no, a couple of days later his door was kicked in and a trunk containing a whole cocktail of bits and pieces was found. He spent his honeymoon in Malaga nick.

Geoff 'The Poodle' Lapidus was another casualty. It didn't take him long to go through whatever few quid he brought over and he got a bit of work driving some gear up to Madrid. He was captured in Malaga city centre and got three years. When he came out, he went back to Manchester and was arrested at Ringway airport on a warrant over the cheque from earlier on and got another four years. He died not long after getting out.

The jockey Graham Bradley got himself in a bit of bother. There was a drugs trial in London and a quite damning part of the evidence was the amounts of money the defendants had access to. Brad stood up and testified that he had been giving them information and the money was profits from horse racing. It didn't do much good because they were found guilty anyway and got twenty-five years. Brad was brought up before the disciplinary board and charged with disclosing privileged information. He'd just retired from racing and had got off to a flying start as a bloodstock agent but the charge led to him being warned off for eight years. The sentence was reduced to five years on appeal but, unable to set foot on a racecourse or training establishment, his new career was in ruins. I can't for the life of me see the difference between Brad giving a pal a tip and, say, Tony McCoy going on the Racing Channel and telling the world what he fancies. I'm not suggesting they go out and nick Tony, just questioning why they nicked Brad. In any case jockeys are the worst tipsters in the world. I've met quite a number since my time in Ireland and if there are ten horses in a race you'd get ten opinions in the weighing-room.

Trainers are not much better. One time Jim Swords was going to Haydock Park with his wife Lynne and the trainer Micky Hammond. When they got to the turnstile, Micky told Lynne to say she owned a horse called Pink Gin. The owner wasn't coming and her badge would get Lynne into the owners' bar and the paddock and all the other places that are hard to get into. Come the time for the race and Lynne said she was off to back Pink Gin and Micky told her to keep her money in her pocket, the horse had more chance of being struck by lightning than winning. Having had a few drinks, and gin being her tipple, she took no notice and went off to make her investment. I think she had twenty quid on it, which is about what it should have cost her to get in anyway. The horse won at a very handsome price, admittedly probably only because most of the others fell but it does just go to show you. Lynne's dead now, dying in her early fifties, yet another victim of the dreaded cancer. Such a crying shame; she was a lovely girl and nearly as close a pal as Jimmy is. I got drunk with her on countless occasions.

I came close to becoming an MIA myself. When Ronnie Knight sold the Mumtaz he opened a bar, calling it R. Knights. One night there was a bit of a tear-up, nothing terribly dramatic but someone got a small cut on the lip. The next day's *Sun* reported it as a man taken to hospital with an axe impaled in his skull but that's the *Sun* for you. There was some talk that a gun was produced, though I didn't see it myself. Anyway, the man with the cut lip went away and returned with two Old Bill, who were soon joined by another couple of carloads. They began a search for the suspected firearm and, being the only Spanish speaker, it was left to me to go out and talk to the head man and his pal. The other alleged participant in the row, Johnny Morrissey, walked out behind me and I heard one cop tell the other that he looked like the man they were looking for. I marked his card and suggested that now might be a good time to do a bunk, which he did. Now Johnny is over six feet and about sixteen stone and his nickname, 'Nightmare', gives a clue as to how intimidating he could appear. Plus for all the Old Bill knew, he was carrying a gun, so I can understand their reluctance to give chase but what happened next was a diabolical liberty.

One of the Old Bill, who was a large enough chap himself, threw himself on the floor and told his pal to arrest me for police assault. They later added a charge of aiding the escape of a fugitive as a sort of makeweight. All this happened on a Wednesday night and they held on to me until I appeared in court on the Saturday, when I was released on bail.

I have a pal, Conche, who works as a flower-seller. She came to see me and said there wasn't a bar in town that she didn't visit during the course of her night's work and she would say she was in Knighty's place and saw the incident and I did nothing wrong. It was very nice of her but she gets her living under sufferance of the local Old Bill and if she puts their backs up they could make her life a misery. In any case the charges were such a farce I was convinced that I'd be found not guilty. I did make a mental note to bear Conche's offer in mind should the need ever arise for an impartial, independent witness in a more serious occurrence.

The trial was an even bigger farce than the charges had been. My barrister cross-examined the copper and got him to describe his time at police officer school. He went into detail of all his classes on self-defence and crowd control and all that stuff, and then she asked if he was seriously trying to maintain that a man my size – I am not the biggest or heaviest, by any means – had wrestled him to the floor and held him down while the fugitive escaped. He said he was but looked a trifle shamefaced.

I went away for ten days to await the verdict, extremely confident about the outcome. I was stunned to be informed I'd been found guilty and sentenced to twelve months. Fortunately enough in those days, and probably still today, any sentence of twelve months or less on a first offence has to be suspended. This was my first offence in Spain so at least I wouldn't have to serve the time. I thought about appealing but my faith in the Spanish judicial system was at a pretty low ebb. A few years later the ebb would get lower still but that was yet to come.

Horses, Cards and Other Ways to Burn Money

After numerous delays and false starts, the long-awaited Costa del Sol racecourse, the Hipodromo, opened just down the road from Fuengirola in Mijas. As racecourses go it was nothing special, being an all-weather track, but it was handy having one on my doorstep. Before long a pal of mine, Eddie Creighton, became the kingpin and leading trainer. A few years later, in partnership with some friends, Eddie took over the place lock, stock and barrel. His principal owners were two girls who went by the name of 'the Vixens' and one year Eddie was champion trainer and the Vixens champion owners, Eddie's son, young Edward, was champion jockey, his younger son Alan was champion amateur and Irish Wally's daughter, Carla, was champion lady amateur.

All this didn't give me a lot of help in the quest for winners. To tell the truth, Mijas must be the only racecourse I've ever been to and not had much of a bet. They'd get a crowd of five or six thousand but a large part of it would be families with kids, which meant the betting market, which was tote only, was very weak. If you got in trouble for five or six hundred quid it was nearly impossible to get out of it. Having a couple of hundred quid on a three-to-one chance would make it an even-money chance and it still had to win. I soon decided to just enjoy the day out and only have tenner and score interest bets.

Enjoying the day out was no difficult task. The weather was nearly always roasting and one of Eddie's interests was an Irish bar where Lisa's husband-to-be, Simon, played in the band. The booze was only Fuengirola prices and there were half a dozen fast-food places, so the whole day out only came to a tripe supper.

One year Eddie and his wife Kathleen, the Vixens, myself and a few others went off to Paris for the Prix de L'Arc de Triomphe at Longchamp. On the Saturday before the big race, they hold a horse auction at St Cloud and we went along to do a bit of window shopping. I really don't think they should have bars in auction rooms. Before I knew where I was, I'd bid thirty grand for a horse on Eddie's Tattersalls account. Thankfully the Vixens took over the horse and Eddie brought it back to Mijas where it did win a few races. All's well that ends well.

It's not the first time I've got myself in trouble mixing booze and auctions. Years earlier, Jack Trickett had been chairman of the footballer Lou Macari's testimonial committee and had arranged a big dinner at the Piccadilly Hotel, which was to include a fund-raising auction. Hassan had bought a table for ten but when he saw it was black tie had refused to go and had given me the tickets. He also gave me strict instructions not to bid for anything at the auction. The headline of the back page of the *Sun* read 'A Silver Lining For Lou' and went on to say that the star item at the auction would be a silver fox jacket donated by furrier Micky Edelson, a director of United.

After the meal and a fair amount of booze, the auction started. A pair of Besty's football boots went for £400 and a ball signed by the United team went for £600. By the time the coat came up I was convinced it would go for a couple of grand at least. The girl I'd brought with me, Elaine, was a bit special and I was keen to impress her and thought I'd have a few bids early on just to show willing. The bidding opened at £500. I said six. Someone said a grand. I said twelve hundred. Silence. Going once. Going twice. Sold to the representative of Brambles Discotheque for twelve hundred pounds. Hassan wasn't a bit pleased and Elaine never did get the coat, Hassan's wife did. Elaine gave me the elbow shortly after.

Anyway, back to Longchamp. Eddie got us VIP passes for the enclosure to which I was refused admission until I went and bought a tie. Between races, I spotted Lester Piggott, without doubt the greatest ever flat-racing jockey, talking to three very important-looking blokes in top hats and tails. I pointed him out to Eddie who gave him a wave and he immediately excused himself from the nobility and came over to join us. I couldn't really say we had a chat because Lester isn't what you would call a chatty person but we shook hands and had a short conversation. The story went that Lester had once ridden a horse in Istanbul and when it got beat, the locals weren't too impressed with the ride he'd given it. Eddie got him out of the stadium in the boot of his car and they'd been firm friends ever since.

I met him again a few weeks later when he came to Mijas doing a book signing and he was polite enough to pretend he remembered me and autographed a programme for me. I should have bought a copy of his book really.

Another new course was opening at Dos Hermanas in Seville and off we all went again, taking five horses with us. We stayed at a nice hotel on the Rio Guadalquivir but checking in was a slight embarrassment. One of Eddie's stable lads, Eugene O'Brien, was staying at a hostel a few miles out of town and rather than drive all the way out and back, Eddie asked if he could shower and change in my room. I'd booked a double in case I got lucky and with the Vixens being a gay couple I'm sure the receptionist had me down as a middle-aged pickle-stabber off for an hour of passion with my toyboy. I don't know who was more embarrassed, me or Eugene. The poor kid was dead a year later from a heart attack at the age of twenty. It must have been a bolt from the blue for his parents.

One of Eddie's horses, Noel's Ganador, won the first ever race on the course, which is a little bit of history. We took the trophy out with us for a drink that night and finished up in a flamenco bar. Before we left we were drinking some weird cocktail from the cup and had the flamenco band playing Irish rebel songs. Another night to remember.

The highlight of the racing calendar at Mijas is the Spanish Derby. There had been a race in Madrid for years referred to as the Derby but Eddie discovered that the name had never been officially registered, so he went and registered it. Next thing there was a sign in six foot high letters outside the track welcoming people to the home of the Spanish Derby.

One year Johnny Murtagh came over to ride a horse for Eddie in the Derby and I took him and his wife and several others out for a meal the night before the race. A few years later, when Kieren Fallon hung up his saddle, Johnny would land the best job in racing, riding the best horses in the world for Aidan O'Brien and winning more classics than I could count. I think at that time he was still riding for John Oxx. With hindsight I probably took the wrong jockey out for a meal since Johnny got left in the stalls and finished last. Warren O'Connor, who had come down from Germany to ride one for another trainer, won the race but we had a good drink with him afterwards.

The racetrack got even better when it was used as the venue for a string of pop concerts. UB40 played there and I went to see Rod Stewart's gig which was probably the best live concert I've seen. I could have jimmied my way into a good seat down the front but the good seats were an awful long way from the bar so I watched the whole show from the terrace of Eddie's bar. Then all of a sudden the last few concerts were cancelled. Apparently one of the organisers went through the slips with the readies, about par for the course on the Costa.

Of course the horse racing hierarchy in Madrid took a dim view of Eddie's hijacking of the Derby and began to make his life a misery. I think at one point they even suspended his licence to train. In the end he salvaged whatever was salvageable, packed his bags and went and opened a yard in Newmarket, where he had a fair degree of success. The two sons got good jobs riding for Mick Channon, though I believe they're both riding in Australia now.

One of the Vixens died and Eddie came over for the funeral. At the end of the service as we were leaving the church, the Old Bill arrived and arrested Eddie. It was some sort of contretemps over a missing horse-box. They only held him for an hour or two and the matter was resolved. Eddie returned to England and I've never seen him since but I'm sure I'll bump into him some day at a race meeting somewhere.

After a few years' abstinence, I fell back in love with Texas Hold'em and decided to take a year off and play on the European Poker Tour. I had the time of my life, though not an awful lot of success. The old-timers on the poker scene are very much like the characters I'd meet at the races. In fact a lot were characters I'd met at the races. Unfortunately, nowadays an awful lot are young people who have learned to play online and a good few are quite good players, but what they haven't learned is manners. They neither know nor care anything for the good, old-fashioned etiquette of the game. There's even some sort of award for 'Trash-talker of the Year'. Very nice, a prize for the most abusive player. I think it's a fucking disgrace, but then that's just my opinion. Again.

An EPT event usually lasts from four or five days to a week and there will be various games in various formats, with the main event being the highlight and played over the last two days. Entry fees will be from fifty to five hundred quid for the minor events and a grand or two for the main event. If you want to play in all the events – and what's the point of going if you don't? – you're talking about three grand in entry fees plus flight, hotel and a light ale. Call it five grand. If you go to twenty venues you have to win a hundred grand to finish level, a fairly daunting prospect for someone of my limited ability. I did have some minor successes. I finished fourteenth in Barcelona, where the entry fee was a grand and got £3,500 for my efforts. I finished fifth in, amazingly enough, an Omaha tournament in Dublin. All I can say is the hundred and nineteen people who finished behind me must have been piss-poor Omaha players.

Dublin was a lucky venue for me. I won a small satellite that got me into the main event for £200 instead of two grand but finished out of the money. Along with a few other early casualties, I started a cash game and looking around the table I didn't fancy my chances too much. Julian Gardner, whose father Dave is a pal of mine, had been to the final table a couple of times in Vegas and is reckoned to be in the top few dozen players in the world. Howard Plant from Blackpool is at least a semi-pro. Tony Cascarino, the ex-Irish soccer international and now a sportswriter for the *Racing Post*, is a highly respected player, as is his pal Teddy Sheringham, the ex-United and West Ham player, who was also on the table. There were two or three more I didn't know personally but they looked as if they knew what they were doing.

I played my normal game, trusting a bit more to luck than skill and it was one of those rare nights when everything went right. In next to no time I'd turned a few hundred quid into five or six grand. I got involved in a couple of what, even by my standards, could be considered bad-beats for fairly small money and was on the point of turning it in when I got involved in a monster hand. I'd risen with ace-king of spades and been re-raised by what turned out to be a pair of queens. Someone called the re-raise with something and I went all-in. The queens called and the other player passed. The third queen appeared on the flop and I was just thinking, same old story, when the jack and ten arrived, winning me the pot with a straight. I cashed in nearly ten grand and walked away feeling very proud of myself.

The following day was Easter Monday and I set off for the Irish Grand National at Fairyhouse. On the way the cab driver got a text advising him to back a horse called Number Six Valverde, apparently the address of the owner's holiday home in Portugal. I made a mental note to look at the horse that would turn out to be the bane of my life. As I usually do, I invested a few hundred quid in the tote jackpot which had a guaranteed prize pool of thirty grand. I made Tony McCoy my banker in the first leg, might as well know your fate early, made fifteen selections in the National, eight of the twelve in the third leg and all the runners in the last leg. When Tony obliged in the first leg I was in with a very live chance. On the final circuit of the big race, Dave Maloney was up on one of Denis's boxes giving me a commentary. Every horse he mentioned I confirmed was one of my selections. Three or four fences out he mentioned that horse number fifteen was going well and I checked my coupon, which doesn't have the horses' names, just their race card numbers. I said no, I hadn't included number fifteen. He looked at me as if I'd lost my mind and asked how the fuck I could leave the favourite out. I looked through the race-card to find the name of horse number fifteen and lo and behold it was Valverde, which I knew I had included. In fact it was the very first horse I'd marked off and for that reason the X in the box was a bit fainter than the others. When they put the coupon through the scanner at the tote window it had failed to show up. Needless to say Valverde won and I'd covered the winners of the last two legs. There were five lucky winners who shared the jackpot, receiving six grand apiece, whereas there should have been six winners getting five grand apiece, myself being the sixth. To make matters worse, Valverde went on to win at Aintree the following year and cost me another fortune when I was making a book at Rory's bar (see Chapter 31).

I screamed the place down but I knew I was pissing against the wind and would get nowhere. In frustration I had a few bets a bit bigger than I normally would and my luck took a turn for the better. I finished the day winning a few grand and returned to Spain about twelve grand to the good, or nearly enough to cover my next two-and-a-half expeditions.

A few weeks later I found myself back in Dublin. My pal Gerard was sponsoring a charity dinner to raise money for the Corinthians entitled 'An Evening With Marvin Hagler'. The do was held at the Red Cow, which sounds more like the back room of a pub but is a much more upmarket venue than the name suggests. It was a black-tie affair and I had a table for ten, bringing some pals over from Spain and Salford. Micky Martin, a friend of mine from Manchester who'd been in the event-promoting game for donkey's years, came over to make the arrangements. He made a fantastic job of it and put on a fabulous night for anyone with an interest in boxing. As well as Marvin Hagler, unquestionably one of the greatest middleweights ever, heavyweight Earnie Shavers was on the top table. Earnie won sixty-nine of his seventy-five victories by knockout and was one of the hardest punchers ever. John Conteh, who won the world light-heavyweight title back in the days when world titles were still difficult to win, was another guest. Jim Rock, a very popular Dublin boxer, made up the table with John H. Stracey, a world champion at welterweight, as compère. After the dinner, videos of their fights were shown and the diners invited to ask questions. Micky introduced me to Marvin after the show and it turned out he'd lived in Seville for a time. We chatted for ten or fifteen minutes and I found him a true gentleman. It was another great night to remember.

Over the next twelve months I played in Paris, Deauville, Vienna, Amsterdam, Brussels, Monte Carlo and probably a few more I've forgotten about. Monte Carlo was the most disappointing place I visited; the marina isn't a patch on Puerto Banus as regards bars, restaurants or even the boats. The place is full of cheap pizza gaffs that aren't even cheap. Casino Square, with the Casino and the Hotel de Paris, is lovely but that's about it. I stayed at a place called the Balmoral which I'd been told was next to L'Hermitage but a fraction of the price. I should have spent the other few quid.

The entry fee in Monte Carlo was ten grand, which I had no intention of paying. Very few people do. The vast majority have won a seat online for something small, while others have won a tournament elsewhere where a seat in the final was part of the prize. Most of the remainder are people sponsored by the big online sites or invited celebrities like current and past World Series winners. Not falling into any of these categories, my only option for sensible money was to try to win a satellite, where ten people put in a grand each and the winner gets a seat. I had three attempts without success and accepted I wouldn't be playing in the grand final.

It just shows the kind of money in the game these days. When the World Series first started, it was ten people putting in ten grand, winner takes all. Last year there were something like two and a half thousand entries at ten grand, making a prize pool of £25 million. I'll say that again just to make sure I've got my sums right: twenty-five million fucking dollars. In a poker game. Okay, the winner only gets about twenty per cent – only five million! – and finishing about four hundredth would get you some small amount but still, a tidy old game.

I resolved to restrict my poker playing to online, where it could take me three months to lose five grand instead of a long weekend.

The Slippery Slope

By the turn of the millennium I had moved from El Castillo, via an apartment in El Coto, to a villa in Mijas. It was on a third of an acre with electric gates, a long tree-lined driveway and a couple of Rottweilers to deter the local scallywags. It had four bedrooms, a pool and gardens and was altogether a much more comfortable abode than I'd ever anticipated.

I'd bought two apartments in Los Boliches off-plan, paying thirty per cent of the £150,000 total. They were now finished and worth nearly £150,000 each. I still had the studio in Las Chapas. I had a quarter share in the best disco in town – though, admittedly that didn't last long – and I had a Merc convertible worth £25,000. My own and Annie's stock of jewellery had increased and I wasn't short of readies. Adding it all up, I had a conservative net worth of around £750,000 and I wasn't thinking of retirement. Perhaps I should have been.

It's hard to say where it all started going wrong but if I had to put my finger on one particular event I'd have to say it was when Annie left me. I'd never had big money prior to meeting Annie, I was never really short of money all the time we were together and things went downhill from the time she left. I can't help thinking that when I let her go my luck went with her.

I had a bit of work on with three pals and it was going very well. It had started off small enough but with a few innovations and a bit of ingenuity we were getting a decent parcel home every six weeks or so. The packaging had to be a bit elaborate and we went to a lot of trouble. We also bought a vehicle to get the parcel up the road to the yard where it was being picked up. This meant we were fully in control of the gear from the minute we bought it until it was delivered home. Nothing was going to go missing and it wasn't going to get stumbled over and a tracking device implanted to get everyone nicked when it arrived. Without us being consulted, the plan was modified by the people taking it up the road and instead of using the vehicle we bought they employed a local transport company. When we were told, nobody voiced any major concerns, we were all just happy that the gear was getting where it had to go by whatever means.

In the meantime another deal came up in Holland and the four of us agreed to put two hundred on a new bit of transport. The advantage of working from Holland is that you know your fate in hours rather than a week or more. The disadvantage is that the gear is dearer so the profit margin is less but the increased turnover compensates. Speed is essential to make the job viable. This deal went on and on and everyone was getting a bit grumpy about the dough lying about for weeks on end. In the end, not wanting to fall out with either my pal in Holland or the people I was working with in Spain, I said I would take over responsibility for the whole parcel and replace the two hundred key in Spain. At the time I didn't have £140,000 around me and had to go to my supplier and negotiate a bit of credit.

The load went home a couple of times more and I chipped a few quid of the owe each time. Then my father died, which entailed a lot of expense. What with flying people over from England and Ireland, the funeral itself and the after-funeral booze-up, it probably ran to fifteen grand but at least I was able to give my dad a decent Irish send-off. This all meant the supplier got nothing off the owe that trip and he was beginning to get a bit grumpy. I promised to level him up after the next trip.

Of course the next trip was the one that fell and to make matters worse it fell in the hands of the local transport. This gave everyone the opportunity to bitch, saying it was my fault for changing the original plan. I could only remind them that there had been no complaints when it was getting to where it was supposed to go. I do have to admit that had we stuck to the original plan the parcel might still be going home today. On the other hand it could have fallen the next trip anyway, we'll never know. Sometimes things are just fated.

After several fruitless trips to Holland and several even more fruitless arguments, still nothing had transpired with the deal up there. I decided to sell the villa and move into one of the apartments in Los Boliches. The main reason was to get my supplier levelled up but it wasn't the only one. Being on my own, I didn't need a four-bedroom villa with all the expense of a gardener, pool cleaner and colossal electric bills. Besides all that, it was a long drive home from town full of booze. I put it up for a quarter of a million euros and quite quickly got a bid of £190,000, which is much the same thing. I took it and moved to Los Boliches. The second apartment I sold to my cousin Colm, in whose name it already was and who was renting it from me. After paying the supplier I was still well in funds and the deal in Holland was still on the backburner. So, nothing to worry about.

The apartment was very nice but a bit on the small side after the villa and with nothing much in the way of a terrace. It was only after I moved in that I realised it had no bath, only a shower. How are you supposed to smoke a cigarette in a shower? A pal of mine had bought an apartment off plan that had just been completed and he wanted to sell it. It was nice enough, two-bed, two-bath, a decent sized terrace, a pool and private parking. It was in Miramar, which was a bit further away from Los Boliches than I wanted to be but you can't have everything your own way. I gave him twenty grand profit and took over the mortgage. Lisa's sister, Emma, came back from St Maarten and rented the bathless one.

Eventually I found a bit of transport of my own from Amsterdam and went up to make the arrangements. The gear was passed over on the Thursday afternoon and Friday lunchtime I get the call to say it's home safe and sound. That's more like it. Not a vast amount of profit, but at least my £140,000 was liquid again. It was Monday before the screams started. The gear was total crap. I phoned Amsterdam and did a bit of screaming of my own. The supplier agreed to go to London, inspect the parcel and if need be have it slung in the Thames and replaced. That's all very well but in the meantime the transport people still wanted their thirty grand and they didn't care whether the gear was crap or not. Had they been nicked with it, then it would miraculously have become top-of-the-range gear and people would have gone to prison.

This is where the story diverges and it makes little difference to me who was telling the truth. It was one of those arguments that are difficult to resolve without someone getting shot, which wouldn't get me any money. The supplier claimed he went to London twice and never saw a bar of gear. The sales people claimed he went once and at that time they were still trying to make something of it and it was still out on the streets. From that day to this I've never been able to get the two parties together and never seen a penny of the money. Maybe that's another issue that needs revisiting.

All very frustrating but all part and parcel of the game I chose to be in. Speaking of frustration, I was finding the trip from the Rover to Miramar every day more than I wanted to put up with and started looking for something in Los Boliches.

With a bath. I found the perfect place and short of moving in the Rover I couldn't have got much closer, since they backed onto each other. Lisa's partner, Simon, drilled a hole through the wall and connected me to the bar's cable system. Another hole and I had access to the ADSL phone line. Nice to keep the exes down.

I sold the place in Miramar, thankfully earning about forty grand, and Emma went back to Dublin so I sold the other one as well. All in all I had a net worth of around £200,000, so things could have been worse. I invested a few quid in a project in South America, about which the less said the better, and sat back to wait. And waited. And waited.

Jimmy the Weed's two sons, Tony and Dominic, and their partner Andy had, for reasons best known to themselves, decided to open a bar. They had found the place they wanted but thought the rent was a bit steep. I was doing nothing at the time and said I'd come in with them and do the bookmaking, paying a quarter of the rent for the privilege. With the arrival of the Racing Channel and At The Races, there was televised horse-racing coverage seven days a week, football most nights and golf every weekend. Most sports bars soon had a resident bookmaker and that was as much as I ever thought my involvement would be.

The lads had a sort of major-domo called John the Parrot and the original plan was to put everything in his name: lease, licence and all the rest of it. There were two problems with getting anything done with The Parrot. The first was getting him out of bed in the morning and the second was keeping him sober once he was out of bed. On top of that, he wasn't in Spain permanently so wouldn't be always about when bits of paperwork needed accumulating.

Obtaining a licence in Spain is a very long and tedious exercise and people are always moaning about the system. I often have myself. On the other hand, should a Spaniard open a pub on Deansgate in Manchester and all he had in the way of paperwork was a note from his accountant saying he was thinking of applying for a licence, I don't imagine it would carry a lot of clout. That's basically all you need to get the doors open in Spain.

However, you do have to be available to meet the droves of inspectors that are going to arrive over the next year or two, if you last that long. I think it's all some sort of job creation programme. There's health and safety, hygiene, fire prevention and more. You need a pest control certificate and a food handler's licence, even if you don't sell food. Noise abatement became a particular bone of contention. A mob comes around with a thing like a sputnik which gives off a tone and they stick it in the centre of the room. They then gain access to several adjacent apartments and sit with meters to decide the maximum decibel level. Some sort of limiting device is then installed which trips the power if the noise level is exceeded.

It soon became apparent that all this was going to be a bit beyond The Parrot and I found myself promoted from part-time bookmaker to CEO in a single bound. Fortunately enough I had very little to do with the expense of getting the place open, which must have come to something colossal. The place, called Rory's Sports Lounge, was one hundred and thirty-five square metres, which is enormous as these bars go. Ironically, prior to being a bar the building had been part of a police station, the lost property office I think. The floor was stone and the walls were wood-panelled up to chest height, the ceiling was wood-panelled with sunken lights and the bar and all the fittings were of mahogany brought over from Ireland. All we needed was a bit of furniture.

I'm afraid we went a bit over the top with the furniture. We bought twelve leather bar stools at £400 apiece. We bought a dozen leather chairs at £500 apiece and another dozen upholstered chairs for not much less. Two leather armchairs at £700 apiece and a few wrought iron and glass coffee tables brought the bill to close to twenty grand. Then of course we needed a TV or two. Or four. Or twelve, as it turned out. We bought a ninety-inch projection screen and three forty-two-inch plasmas. Then I needed eight small screens for the teletext with the race betting and results. Oh, and a computer to keep in touch with Betfair. It was no good having all those TVs without a good satellite system so we got three: English, Spanish and cable. I think if E.T. had dropped in we could probably have got a home game on for him.

No point spoiling the ship for a ha'porth of tar, a state of the art sound system was required. This allowed for the speakers to be diverted to different parts of the room so that commentaries from more than one football match could be played at the same time. Just a bit of stock and we were ready to roll. With six draught beers and needing at least two barrels of each, that was a grand, wines and spirits a bit more. Then the bottled beers and mixers, call it three grand.

We covered the walls with framed photos, fifty or sixty of them, at ten or fifteen quid apiece for framing. Add on the incidentals like glasses, ashtrays and monogrammed tee-shirts, oh, and the £46,000 we gave for the lease, we were well over a hundred grand behind the clock before we got the doors open. Actually, I keep saying 'we' but the truth is not one penny piece of all this expenditure came out of my pocket so I was reasonably satisfied with progress up to this point.

You need to do something special on opening night if you want to get yourself on the map. A celebrity personal appearance is just the ticket. At the time Ricky Hatton had just won the IBF World Light-Welterweight title and was probably the most popular British boxer since Henry Cooper. He agreed to come over and do the opening. We needed a fair amount of staff for the opening and Eddie Creighton's brother-in-law, Phil Connelly, who ran the bar at the racecourse, had the numbers of a lot of girls that worked casually for him. He fixed us up with a couple of barmaids and three or four waitresses.

The opening night, which was a Saturday, went very well, though Ricky Hatton didn't arrive until the Monday. I don't know about fighting him but I wouldn't want to be in a drinking competition with him. He came in every night for the four nights he was over and he told me if he had to choose between giving up drinking or boxing it was the boxing that would have to go. He said he couldn't imagine how boring life would be if all he did was trained and boxed and boxed and trained. He needed to blow out for a few weeks after a fight.

We were going to need some permanent staff and one of the girls Phil brought, Mary from Bulgaria, I'd known for years although she was only nineteen at the time. She could only have been fifteen when I knew her first at O'Brien's Bar and later at the racecourse. She came to work the evening shift. Mary was a little stunner who spoke half a dozen languages and stood for no bollocks from anyone. One day my cousin's wife Sandy came in and started chatting to her, speaking very slowly so the foreigner would understand. During the conversation Sandy said '…and I have a grandson who is four,' and held up four fingers so there'd be no mistake.

'Why are you talking to me like I'm a fucking retard?' asked Mary.

Sandy put her drink down, walked away and asked her pal if she'd heard what the cheeky bitch had said.

'And I'm not fucking deaf, either,' shouted over Mary.

Pretty typical Mary. She once told me I was the best boss she ever had because I knew absolutely fuck all about anything.

We needed another barmaid for the day shift and Jimmy the Weed sequestrated Kelly from Moo-Moos Bar around the corner. Kelly was great too and took on a lot of the responsibilities I should have had myself. Like ordering the stock and paying the bills. And opening up at lunchtime when I was still in bed.

We needed a third barmaid to cover the four shifts when Mary and Kelly were off but, for the life of me, I can't remember her name. I always referred to her as the Porn Star. You know how in a porn films there's often a girl playing a secretary or a librarian or a nurse, sometimes even a policewoman. They're always very attractive but have their long hair tied up in a bun and wear horn-rimmed glasses. Two or three minutes into the film the hair comes down and the glasses come off and she's giving someone a blowjob. Not that I ever caught her giving anyone a blowjob, it's just the vision she conjured up. Perhaps it's just me and my imagination again.

All in all, the bar got off to a flyer and for a while I thought I might join the very small and select group of people who had made a bar pay. There were a number of quite big players on the horses and a lot of them weren't bad drinkers either. The evenings were a lot quieter than the days but we had built a stage and I organised live music three nights a week. Pearse Webb, who had appeared on the opening night, agreed to do the Friday nights. He would appear every Friday for the next two-and-a-bit years. He had a big following locally so we were guaranteed one busy night a week and with a bit of luck the people he attracted would come back during the week.

The one problem with the place was location. We were a bit isolated. If we could have picked up the bar and moved it two or three hundred yards south we'd have had the best bar in town. There is no doubt that crowds attract crowds and if there's a street full of bars they'll all get some sort of a spin. At the time I thought it was a good thing being far enough away from the Rover not to cause Lisa any damage but with hindsight I'd probably have done her less harm if I'd opened up next door. At least that way people could pop in and out of both places. As it turned out we finished up with two pubs dead as doornails.

At least I had the racing to keep our heads above water. It got to the stage many a night, when there were only the last few diehards in our place, that I suggested closing and going for one in the Rover. On quieter nights when there weren't even the diehards, I'd go around to the Rover on my own. Then we got problems with the racing. The Old Bill got it into their heads to have a purge and went around nicking people for illegal gambling. It had all been a bit blatant with pubs all over the place having signs outside inviting people to come in and have a bet but even so I don't think we were doing anyone much harm.

Then a solution arrived. A company called Global Tote was set up, based at the racecourse, that apparently had a licence to install computer terminals in bars linked directly to European and South African racecourse tote pools. Phil Connelly was one of the principals and he arranged to have one installed in Rory's, along with a couple of dozen other locations along the coast. The deal was that we would have no liabilities and would be paid a commission of between four and nine per cent depending on the type of bet. Before long we were turning over twenty to thirty grand a week and everything in the garden was rosy.

Then the bubble burst and it was the only time being isolated worked in our favour. By the time the Old Bill had kicked the doors down in about fifteen other outlets, I'd had a few phone calls marking my card. Although I had a licence on the wall issued by the Junta of Andalucía in Seville, with all the fancy stamps they like so much, as presumably did the other places, it had been decided by someone that what we were doing was illegal. I watched the raids on local TV that night. One pal of mine, Kendal O'Brien, had a place in Fuengirola that was literally a betting shop with a bar in it as opposed to a bar that took a few bets. He'd spent fortunes opening this place and had a sign the size of the building advertising Malaga's longest serving bookmaker. He'd done all this on the basis that what he was doing was perfectly legal but it didn't stop him getting nicked. Fines of thirty and forty grand and the confiscation of audio-visual equipment were the order of the day.

I never did get nicked. Having had the word, we had time to remove the terminal and take down the publicity but without the racing the place was a white elephant. The bills began to mount up and it wasn't long before we had to shut the doors. After a month or two we decided – there I go with the 'we' again – to throw a few quid in and give it another go but we were pissing against the wind. Within a few months we accepted defeat and shut the doors for the last time, salvaging little other than the satellite dishes and TVs.

With Rory's closed, my things-to-do-today list consisted solely of breathe in, breathe out, but Lisa's sister Andrea was getting married in Dublin and I was invited over for the wedding. It was a great day, Andrea looked stunning, as brides always do and the bash was done with a lot of style, down to a Roller for the bridal car. Lisa, Emma and the eldest sister Nicola were the bridesmaids and younger brother John was a groomsman. I say younger, as opposed to little, because he's well over six foot. The whole day was something to remember. By this time Mary from Bulgaria was working in a pub in

Bray and came along for a drink after work. I found it amazing that after such a short time in Ireland she was talking like she'd been born and bred in O'Connell Street. On a sadder note this was to be the last time I would ever see Bernie Banus. The following January, Lisa's mother lost a long battle with cancer. She's sadly missed but I'll always remember her how she looked that day, having gone to so much trouble to look her best despite how she must have been feeling.

In the September there was another wedding, one that I had mixed feelings about. Lisa was marrying Simon, her long-time boyfriend and father of her two, soon to be three, sons. On the one hand I was delighted to see her happy but on the other I had to accept that it was time to hang up my running shoes and give up the chase. Well, almost. I suspect Gerry O'Sullivan felt much the same way.

It was another spectacular day. There can't be many locations more perfect for a wedding than southern Spain. A horse and carriage instead of a Roller took the couple to the reception at a hotel on Mijas golfcourse with a guest-list running to more than a hundred. During the speech, Derrick spoke of Bernie and said it was me that named her Bernie Banus. Actually, it wasn't, it was a pal of mine, Peter, but I don't suppose it makes much difference now. Such a shame she wasn't there to see it. I don't know what sort of stock the hotel carried but a place that size must carry a fair bit. Even so, they managed to run out of vodka and I think Lisa might know something about that.

That just leaves Emma to get married off now, but I hear that's well underway.

Last Throw of the Dice

With the demise of Rory's, things were looking a bit grim. The bar had been losing something small, a hundred or two a week, and not having made any contribution in the first place it was difficult for me to keep going back to the lads asking for more dough. In any case, I saw very little of them. Dominic came over for the opening and maybe a couple of times later. Tony came over about once a month for a few days and always found the place busy, mainly because we were our own best customers. Andy was there a bit more often and we kept the place going as long as we could.

It wasn't the bar that was the main cause of my difficulties anyway. It was the sitting about for two-and-a-half years doing nothing that did the damage. The problem was it had been so long since I'd been stuck for money that I had forgotten the correct procedure, namely go out and earn some. Instead of that I began borrowing a few quid here and there. After all, a couple of million quid would be dropping through the letter box any minute from South America, wouldn't it? Well, actually, no, that was another saga that went tits up.

I borrowed ten grand, which I invested in a share of a container load of cigarettes from China. My corner would be worth a hundred grand and they'd be home in six weeks, so everything would be fine. The cigs did get home, five months later, by which time they were only good for lighting the fire with. Apparently cigs have a combination of about four hundred chemicals in them and if the formula isn't exactly right they have a very limited shelf-life. That's the story I got anyway. I don't know if they were any good to start with. I did salvage a few quid with the fly-pitchers at the races selling the odd few sleeves but it came in dribs and drabs and I was never in a position to put the ten grand back.

I took out a pen and paper and started jotting out a balance sheet. It made pretty dismal reading. Assets: nil. Liabilities: I owed the ten grand for the snout, another ten grand sterling to one pal, a seven grand and a five grand to two others, and numerous bits and pieces. On top of that, the debts from Rory's were in my name. In two-and-a-half years I hadn't paid one penny piece in social security for myself or the staff. Likewise the VAT and income tax. Somehow I'd managed to turn a net worth of three-quarters of a million into a negative equity situation of about a hundred grand in six short years. I wasn't losing any sleep over the government bills. I can't imagine how much money I'd have to have before I'd sit down and write a cheque to the Hacienda for seventy or eighty grand. The only pressure from the other debts was coming from myself and I was rapidly coming to the conclusion that if anything was going to get done, I was the one who was going to have to do it.

It seems life is always a feast or a famine and when things start to go wrong everything goes wrong. Let me give you a for-instance. One Saturday night I was lying on the sofa minding my own business when the phone rang. It was a pal of mine, Barry Carrington, asking if I was going to the poker tournament in Marbella. I hadn't even known there was one on but when he said there was a prize pool of eighty grand and the entry fee was five hundred, I was sorely tempted. I told him to pick me up. Barry phoned and booked the seats using his credit card, which was just as well because I'm not sure I had a monkey at that particular time. When we got there and went through all the palaver of signing in and registering, the tournament was well underway. Only a hundred and twenty-odd players had turned up and by the time I was seated over twenty had already been eliminated.

My first hand I got pocket kings, made a decent raise and got two callers. The third king arrived on the flop and I bet something small, hoping to get paid. Both called and when nothing happened on the turn, I bet the pot. One called. On the river I went all in and he passed but I'd nearly doubled my stack. The second hand I got pocket sixes. The blinds were thirty and sixty and I raised to three hundred. The man next to me raised to twelve hundred and everyone passed around to me. I seriously considered passing and had he bet more I almost certainly would have but having put three hundred in I decided to pay the other nine and see the flop, which came three, six, jack. There were a very limited number of hands he could possibly have had to have made the re-raise. He either had a pocket pair, tens or bigger or he had some combination of ace, king, queen, possibly jack and probably suited. A pair smaller than tens and he'd have been in exactly the same situation as I'd been in myself, faced with flat-calling or passing. The rest don't bear thinking about. One thing I knew for certain was that if I checked he would be obliged to make a continuation bet whatever he was holding. I checked and he bet the same twelve hundred. Probably, and not with hindsight because it wouldn't have made any difference, I should have raised there and then. The only hand I could be losing to was pocket jacks but the flop had produced two spades so it was conceivable he was on a flush draw. I just called and the turn came a three, making me a full house and making his possible flush draw academic. In fact I was hoping he was on a flush draw and made it. Now, besides the jacks I could be losing to pocket threes but I'd already discounted a small pocket pair.

If he's got the jacks, good luck to him. I checked and he bet as I fully expected him to do. I went all in and he called immediately and turned over a pair of aces.

As he turned the aces, someone muttered that he'd passed an ace. Assuming the mutterer was telling the truth, and I've no reason to doubt him, that leaves exactly one card in the pack for me to lose to and makes me a 98.08 per cent favourite. Or to put it the other way round, he had a 1.92 per cent chance. About the same odds of getting pregnant if you're on the pill. That is, assuming you're a woman; men obviously have a smaller chance.

Anyway, over it came, the big, fat, ugly ace of spades. How big a favourite do you have to be? Of course, a purist might say that he had aces when I had sixes and he won which is exactly what's supposed to happen, so what am I bitching about, but that discounts all the drama between the deal and the river. I'd managed to go from scraping into the event by the skin of my teeth to almost certain chip-leader to being out, all in the course of four short minutes. Sometimes poker is enough to make a man want to eat his children. I know I could have run into a monster the very next hand and been out anyway but that's hardly the point and we'll never know. What I do know is, had I won the hand I would have been chip-leader in a tournament with fewer than a hundred players that was paying down to thirtieth place. I don't think I would be unduly optimistic to think I'd have made the money list and maybe things would have turned out differently.

Still, that's just a gambler's way of looking at things, we do tend to be a fairly optimistic bunch. It's rarely you'll everget one to admit he's losing. After a bad day someone might say, 'Yeah, but I'm about level on the week.' After a bad week, 'Yeah, but I'm about level on the month.' I had one pal who, when he was absolutely penniless, would describe himself as being exactly level on the lifetime.

So, dreams shattered, I had to get a bit of work done. Bullets had served a nine-year sentence in Finland and during his time there had met a few kindred spirits in the puff job. He convinced me that if I could get a bit of gear to Finland, where it was making two-and-a-half grand a key, he could get it sold for me. I bustled about and with a little bumping and boring got my hands on thirty-four key of quite good quality pollen, a slightly more expensive version of puff which was what the Finns were after. It's ironic really, bearing in mind the tons and tons of puff that had been through my hands over the years, that I had to do any bumping and boring. But still.

Having acquired the gear the next problem was a vehicle. I wasn't in a position to buy anything presentable and I didn't want to be setting off in an old banger. The trip was perilous enough without having to worry about breakdowns, so that just left a hire car. I didn't want to be driving through France and Germany in a Spanish-plated car and I certainly didn't want to be arriving in Finland in one either. Irish plates would have been okay but in the end I decided on Swiss plates. Swiss plates just reek of respectability, I always thought.

The next item was a legend, a cover story that would get me past any cursory Customs interviews. I must say I put as much time, effort and ingenuity into this legend as is humanly possible. It wasn't just because I was juggling with other people's dough, with which you have to be more careful than your own, but the fact that if anyone's arse was going to prison it would be mine that led to my more than normal professionalism. The story went that I was an Irish property developer, based in Zurich, who was planning a complex of holiday log cabins in Killarney. I created an email account in this mythical company name and emailed log cabin manufacturers in Finland. They sent me brochures and price lists and the address of an agent in Dublin. This led to more emails and more brochures and price lists. In a short time I had quite a collection of very convincing folders documenting my business dealings.

I opened a bank account at a bank that would allow me to use my Dublin address as the billing address for a credit card, making my passport, driving licence and credit card all match up with no mention of Spain. Hertz would have no reason to suspect their car had ever been anywhere near Spain. I downloaded maps from Google Earth and traced a route from Lisbon to Zurich for use on the first half of the trip. Midway through France these could be discarded and a new map showing my route from Zurich to Helsinki would take their place.

Things started to go wrong right from the outset. A pal had told me of a particular model of Merc that had a ready-made stash in it. According to their website, Hertz in Zurich had the very model and when I booked it I wrote in the special notes column that I was contemplating buying such a car and wanted to give it a couple of weeks' trial run. When I got to Zurich they had a Toyota SUV waiting for me. No matter how much I screamed, the best they could offer was to try and get me the Merc in a few days. I was now on a tight schedule and didn't have a few days so I took a look at the Toyota. It certainly looked big enough to have room to conceal my humble parcel so I took it. I got back to the Rover in twenty-two hours only to find Bullets had been nicked on an outstanding warrant and was in serving a two-year sentence. It was looking like all my planning and expense would come to nothing.

The next day something extraordinary happened. A pal came to me and said the previous night two Finns had been in his bar asking after Bullets. Not wanting to disclose Bullets' current predicament, he simply told them he wasn't about but if they came back the next day he'd arrange for Bullets' partner, me, to come and speak to them. Off I went.

They seemed genuine enough and after they tried a smoke they said it was fine and if I got it to Finland they'd give me the two-and-a-half grand a key for it. They even drew me a map of where to deliver it, which entailed leaving the motorway and driving to a clearing in a forest somewhere in Lapland. This was now approaching the realms of a high-risk operation. I was to go and meet two Finnish Hells Angels in a forest clearing in Lapland, give them thirty-four key of puff and hope they gave me eighty-five grand. On the other hand, giving thirty-four key to Bullets to do the same thing was only less risky from a personal safety viewpoint. I told them they had a deal.

That only left the vacuum-packing as my last chore by way of preparation. I'm not a great believer in vacuum-packing. I think once, in the dim and distant past, someone got a parcel home that had been vacuum-packed and became convinced it got home because it was vacuum-packed. Ever since then it's become part of the puff smuggler's folklore that it's an essential part of the job. I see it as little more than a mere superstition, not far removed from crossing your fingers or touching wood. On the other hand, I've never heard of anyone getting nicked because the gear was vacuum-packed, so I crossed my fingers, touched wood and went home to do the vacuum-packing.

When I got home the electricity had been cut off, quite a common occurrence in Spain. Getting it reconnected was a nightmare and to get it done in one day needed a very early start and a lot of luck. It was too late to do anything that day and so I went down to the Rover for a drink and to bring the lads up to date on the latest delay. Gerry O'Sullivan said he had a calor gas lamp I could borrow. I said that was very helpful but did he have a calor gas vacuum packer I could borrow. He hadn't. I don't think they make them. In fact I'm sure they don't.

The procedure for reconnection is you go to the local electricity board, which in this case was eight miles away in Arroyo, queue up to get a copy of your bill, queue up at the post office to pay it, return to the electricity board and queue up to produce the receipt. You're then put on the list for reconnection which will be done in their own sweet time. The post office has been in the same place in Arroyo since post offices were first thought of. I know this because I've been through this rigmarole numerous times. I pulled up at the spot and all I found was an empty croft. I did eventually find the new post office and very nice it is too. I'm sure the population of Arroyo are very proud of it but I could have done without the delay. I could also have done without the mile-long queue as well but I did manage to get back to the electricity board before the one o'clock deadline for having any chance of getting the lights back on that day. I went home to wait.

You might well think, given all these hiccups, I should have seriously considered aborting the mission but there's two ways of looking at the situation. You can think these are all signs that the whole project is doomed to failure or you can think well, it's better to have all the things go wrong before you leave than when you are in the middle of the job. Having always been a glass-half-full person I took the more optimistic view. I may have mentioned that I'm often wrong. The lights did finally come on and I set to work with the vacuum-packing which is a very irksome job and if it's not done exactly right is a total waste of time. That's if it's any use in the first place. You need three rooms: one to store the unwrapped gear, one to do the wrapping in and one to store the wrapped gear so it's not contaminated by the unwrapped gear. I did all that and then went a stage further.

A new, hybrid version of puff had come on to the market which was known as skunk because of its unbelievably noxious smell. A pal had told me that to hide the smell during transportation they submerged the vacuum-packed bundles in molten candle wax, which left them with a few millimetres' coating that sealed the smell in perfectly. I did that as well. Sort of belt and braces if you like.

So, with the gear wrapped and packed and installed in the car I set off, a little behind schedule but I thought I should be okay. It was Saturday morning and I had to be in Travemunde on the German Baltic coast by midnight on Monday to catch the ferry for Turku in Finland. I hadn't realised how bad my eyesight was getting – I was in need of an operation for cataracts. As darkness was falling I had only got as far as Benidorm but I knew if I didn't stop for the night I wouldn't be going anywhere. I found a hotel, had a few drinks and an early night, and set the alarm for seven-thirty.

One o'clock Sunday afternoon found me in the last service station in Spain, about two or three miles from the border crossing at La Jonquera. I stopped for a cup of coffee and took a couple of diazepam just in case any signs of nervousness were to give the game away, not that I was very concerned about the Spanish–French border. Five days earlier on my way back from Zurich I had come through without changing gears and you couldn't have found a Customs man with heat-seeking radar. It was a different story today.

It would turn out that a high-ranking member of ETA, the Basque terrorist group, or Basque freedom-fighters, depending on your point of view, had been captured at that crossing that morning. There was more Old Bill than I've ever seen in any one place at any one time. The capture had been made in the early hours and no doubt the Old Bill were enjoying a lucrative bit of overtime. They had little else to do but spin every car that came through. I didn't even have a chance to get into my log-cabin fanny before they told me to drive my car onto a ramp and wait in one of the Customs booths. Two or three of them started tapping and probing and they'd have had to be remarkably incompetent Customs men not to have found the gear.

Unfortunately they weren't.

So, what does the future hold? Well, difficult to say, isn't it? Having very little to offer in the way of a defence it's a certainty I'll be spending some time in prison but that's all part of the game I chose to play. In any case, in the circles I move in, staying out of prison for twenty-seven years would be looked on as something of a success story.

Would I change anything? My first inclination would be to say I'd like to leave out the bits where I went to prison but that's not possible and still be the same person that I am. All in all I'm quite happy with the person I am and it's the bad times as well as the good times that made me what I am. Without the time in prison I wouldn't know the people I know or have the respect in the circles I have. There's no doubt that there's a sort of camaraderie, strangely enough a sort of trust, amongst people who have spent time away. When you've seen with your own eyes how a person performs under the day in, day out pressure of a lengthy prison sentence that only a person who's been there can begin to understand, you know if you've got a person you can depend on and a person you can vouch for. Very often being vouched for is the only way to get things done. In a nutshell, I guess you've got to take the rough with the smooth.

I think back to my school days and wonder how many of my old school chums have led the life I have. How many have swum with dolphins in Cuba and Mexico, how many have climbed the Corcovado in Rio or sailed the Panama Canal? How many have got drunk on most of the islands in the Caribbean? How many can walk into a bar in Paris, Brussels, Amsterdam or Dublin and not be surprised to bump into someone they know? In fact, be surprised not to?

How many have helped, albeit in a small way, to promote a world title fight? Or a bullfight? How many have given a five hundred euro note to a crippled news vendor and when he said he had no change told him, 'I didn't ask you for any change'? Whilst the smile on his face was worth every cent, there have been times since when I've been tempted to go back and ask him if he's got my change yet.

How many have had a twenty-five grand, uninsured Merc stolen from outside their front door and said, 'Fuck it. I suppose everyone has to get a living. Even the car thieves'? I guess that's easier to say coming from someone who's spent half his life driving around in stolen cars.

I think the answer to all that would be not many.

Yes, yes, I know. How many have spent a cumulative fourteen years behind bars? About the same amount, but if the alternative was spending fifty years working in Massey Ferguson's tractor factory and having a fortnight in Rhyl every twelve months, I'll take what I've had every time. I suppose another relevant point is that if a jailed drug trafficker is the nearest we've got to a success story it doesn't say a lot for the Secondary Modern education system. Still, it's not for me to tell people how to run a school and I certainly don't expect to be invited back to give a speech on careers day.

Anyway, the game's not over yet. There are still things I want to do. I haven't seen Cape Town or Phuket yet and I plan to see both. I've been to Paris dozens of times and never eaten in Maxim's but I plan to put that right. Over the years, at one time or another, I've owned most of the world's best automobiles: a Bentley Turbo, two Rollers, a Porsche, numerous Mercs, a few Jags and BMWs and an Alfa Romeo Spyder. I've also driven a Polski Fiat and something called a Nissan Pulsar when times weren't so good but I've never owned an Aston Martin, specifically the DB6 in midnight blue for preference. I plan to own one. In fact, one day I intend to pull up in my midnight blue DB6 outside Maxim's where I'll have a stunning lunch and pass a couple of pleasant hours awaiting my flight to Cape Town. Or Phuket, as the case may be.

Where's the money going to come from? Well, short of winning the lottery or a major poker tournament, two events of roughly similar remoteness, I can only think of one way. Guess we'll just have to wait and see how the dice fall next time. I suppose there is one other possibility, probably at the outer reaches of the remoteness scale, that this book becomes a major seller and the likes of MGM and Twentieth Century Fox start outbidding each other for the film rights. Maybe they could get Leonardo DiCaprio to play me. I remember him making a pretty good fist of playing a diamond smuggler in *Blood Diamond* and I seem to recall some Irish connection in *Titanic* – remember the dancing? I know for a fact Jim Swords would settle for no-one less than Robert De Niro playing him and as for The Weed, look no further than Danny DeVito. Jack Trickett? Well, John Cleese in his Basil Fawlty persona would be perfect.

Hmm, this is starting to show promise. Perhaps if anyone is passing a major film studio and happens to have a copy of the book upon their person they might be kind enough to drop it off with whoever does the bidding.

Endnote: Maurice was eventually sentenced to three years and fined 91,000 euros. Contrary to his more optimistic expectations he was obliged to serve every day, plus a bit more for the fine which he was unable to pay. He used his time to write this book. His current whereabouts are unknown but he was last seen in a very dubious bar in Cartagena.